INTERPLAY

INTERPLAY

Jerome L. Jacobs, M.D.

READER'S DIGEST PRESS

McGraw-Hill Book Company

New York   St. Louis   San Francisco
Mexico   Toronto   Düsseldorf

616.8914
J17

1234567890BPBP7832109

LIBRARY OF CONGRESS CATALOGING IN PUBLICATION DATA
Jacobs, Jerome L
   Interplay.
    1. Psychotherapy—Cases, clinical reports, statis-
tics. I. Title. [DNLM: 1. Psychotherapy—Case
studies. 2. Physician-patient relations—Case studies.
WM420.3 J17i]
RC465.J3   616.8'914   78-13347
ISBN 0-07-032146-9

Book design by Joan O'Connor

To my wife, Francine,
for sharing in this and
in everything, with love

A man burdened with a secret should especially avoid the intimacy of his physician. If the latter possess native sagacity, and a nameless something more,—let us call it intuition; if he show no intrusive egotism, nor disagreeably prominent characteristics of his own; if he have the power, which must be born with him, to bring his mind into such affinity with his patient's, that this last shall unawares have spoken what he imagines himself only to have thought; if such revelations be received without tumult, and acknowledged not so often by an uttered sympathy as by silence, an inarticulate breath, and here and there a word, to indicate that all is understood; if to these qualifications of a confidant be joined the advantages afforded by his recognized character as a physician,—then, at some inevitable moment, will the soul of the sufferer be dissolved, and flow forth in a dark, but transparent stream, bringing all its mysteries into the daylight. . . .

—NATHANIEL HAWTHORNE, *The Scarlet Letter*

CONTENTS

FOREWORD

At a time in the history of Western medicine when the concepts of "holistic health" appear to be at the brink of receiving long-overdue recognition, *Interplay* stands out as a unique blend of the timely and the timeless. It is timely in that psychiatry truly is moving into the mainstream of medical practice and health care; it is timeless in that it illustrates the power of the mature, nonjudgmental physician to help those who seek help. In this volume the psychiatrist comes alive. He reveals feelings, reactions and ambivalences as well as intellect. He is a real person rather than skilled technocrat. Describing episodes in the lives of five persons, the narrator does not obscure the human drama with undefined technical words; these are accounts of human interaction in a medical context.

Attempts to deal with disorders of emotion, thought and behavior are steeped in a history of occultism, fear and the unknown. For the past three-quarters of a century, psychiatrists have struggled to make their profession a respectable and respected branch of medicine. But why this historical schism? Why is the world of psychiatry so often misunderstood, even resisted, by those outside the world?

Progress in reconciling soma and psyche, psychiatry and medicine has been hampered in large part by a continued mystification of the field and by the often convoluted jargon of psychiatry. It is in these areas particularly that *Interplay* goes a long way in dispelling the intrigue.

With respect to the demands of both modernity and tradition, the volume promises to be a core nutrient in the enrichment of skills and competencies required of nonpsychiatric physicians and others who deal with the mentally ill and emotionally disturbed.

It is a particular pleasure for me to write this foreword. Dr. Jacobs and I were fellow medical students. Both of us have pursued careers in psychiatry. My work as a national administrator, specifically as Director of the National Institute of Mental Health, was in the service of those who treat and help troubled people. Dr. Jacobs has performed an even broader service in sharing his hard-earned wisdom in this absorbing book. Read it, and you will cry, laugh and learn.

Bertram S. Brown, M.D.
Assistant Surgeon General
U.S. Public Health Service

INTRODUCTION

I n the summer between my third and fourth years as a medical student, having yet to determine the direction of my future career, I chose for my elective program to pursue an externship at a large, well-known psychiatric hospital. There I was assigned minimal duties, but permitted unlimited access to certain patients, the inactive cases—voluble old syphilitics, brain-damaged and demented alcoholics, and chronic, unresponsive psychotics. I had little instruction; I was to learn what I could from the patients.

Hall G was one of the male back wards, a locked unit, a museum stocked with well-maintained living relics and a few carefully watched younger specimens. It stank with the rank, fetid odor of stale, wasting humankind. The attendants were kind, patient, largely self-educated men who saw to their responsibilities with pride and reserve. One had to approach them tactfully, with sincere professional interest, before they would volunteer information from the fund of knowledge they had acquired about their patients. This information, obtained from infrequent visitors, gossip, and years of personal observations, was material not to be found in charts or textbooks.

One day I inquired about a tall, pale blond young man about my own age, whose ceaseless activity and peculiar habit of reaching upward to touch invisible objects had attracted my attention. I was amazed to discover that he had been in residence on Hall G for three years and that in that time, he had never been visited. "I wouldn't be wasting your time with the likes of him, Doctor," I was warned. "You won't learn much from young Robert; he hasn't spoken a word to anyone but himself since he's been here." Why I persisted I cannot say, but I was to participate with this strange individual in a brief, enigmatic experience that helped alter the course of my professional life.

Robert was agoraphobic; he dreaded open spaces and avoided the outdoors. I learned that each afternoon, when the other patients went out to meander in the wide, grassy, fenced-in yard adjacent to Hall G, Robert remained indoors in the dayroom. I found him there pacing back and forth between opposite walls, touching them as if to be certain of his boundaries. He took no notice of my friendly greeting. When I sat down, he glanced my way disdainfully, then went about his peculiar business. Now and then I saw him stop and stretch as if to touch an imaginary butterfly or windblown thistle. I remained, uninvited, for half an hour, ignored each time I attempted to communicate.

Robert, I was informed by the medical director, was hebephrenic; he suffered from a severe, chronic form of schizophrenia and was beyond salvage—a mental shipwreck. Nevertheless, I was intrigued and challenged by him. Every day I returned at the same time to sit in the same chair and smoke a cigarette and be with him. Occasionally, when his back was to me, I thought I heard him speaking softly under his breath; never did he acknowledge or speak to me. One day, to my astonishment, he suddenly approached and demanded, "Give me a light, will you?" As luck would have had it, I had forgotten my cigarettes and matches that afternoon. I simply apologized, and he marched off again.

The following day I brought both. Robert took one of my cigarettes and a light and began to smoke and cough furiously as he paced. Nothing more was said. But each day for a week this behavior was repeated. The attendants were incredulous; Robert had never smoked before to anyone's knowledge.

One day I brought along a roll of Life Savers and offered him one, without arousing his interest. When I opened the roll and began sucking on the candy, however, he gladly took one. "You tick!" he announced. From his friendly smile I deduced that he was not calling me an insect, but was complimenting me in some strange way.

I wrestled with his phrase all day, unable to decipher it. When I entered the dayroom the next afternoon, Robert smiled at me like an old friend, and suddenly his meaning struck me. I produced the Life Savers again and said, "I don't really know how I tick or what makes any of us tick, Robert, but I am glad to share some time and a few simple things with you." He nodded, accepting me, and began a long, disjointed monologue, most of which I found incomprehensible. I have rarely felt so excited, so impotent, and so frustrated in my life. I never succeeded in understanding poor Robert, but I learned what I must do.

*   *   *   *   *

Much later, when I first came to the community where I now practice, I applied to the local general hospital for membership on the staff with privileges like those of other physicians to admit and to attend patients there. My application was summarily rejected. The medical board informed me that patients with psychiatric problems were not admitted to the hospital.

I might have protested the absurdity of such a position and argued that all persons ill enough to require hospitalization were anxious and potentially psychiatric patients, but it did not seem prudent to dispute the matter. I was, after all, a newcomer. Instead, I accepted the disappointment and contented myself with "coffee privileges"—taking lunch with the other physicians in the hospital cafeteria. Day after day I sat with my medical colleagues, listening to their informal consultations and discussions; occasionally they sought my opinions and views. Thus, I was gradually initiated into the medical community. After several months of this "probation," the medical board reviewed my application, and I was admitted to the staff as an attending physician with equal privileges—the first psychiatrist to be so received.

This experience taught me something valuable. If I was to be a help to other physicians with their patients, I had to speak plainly and avoid the jargon of psychiatry. In order to make a contribution, it was necessary to translate psychiatric concepts into layman's language. Even complex formulations can be expressed simply by the use of analogies and case histories to illustrate them. I relied on practical knowledge gained from my own clinical experience to provide material for this purpose. These anecdotal stories provided the impetus for this book.

Each case you encounter in these pages is a composite put together from clinical experiences that span over twenty years in psychiatry. In every instance, details have been changed to protect the identities of the persons involved, and to avoid any breach of confidence.

I define certain frequently used psychiatric terms in the text so that the reader may understand these words if he encounters them elsewhere. An in-depth presentation of the theory and practice of psychotherapy, however, is not my goal; that is beyond the scope and purpose of this book.

It is my purpose to use the stories here not only to share some of the challenge of psychiatric practice with my medical colleagues but also to enlighten the lay reader. I wish to show how a psychiatrist functions in attempting to treat troubled persons, to reveal what the therapist thinks about in his work, how he develops his plans for treatment, what he says, and why at times he remains silent. In each of the stories many separate decisions are made. Leads are pursued in certain directions while other paths are forsaken. So it is in actual practice. There are many useful and different ways of approaching and dealing with problems such as those I describe. If the reader, on his own, considers alternatives to the solutions I reached, then certainly I shall have succeeded in my aims for this book.

SILENT DIALOGUE

Cathy Erno

I t was a cold, gray Thursday afternoon early in February when I first met Cathy Erno. The director of West Hill, a residential school for troubled youngsters from the city just beyond county limits, had referred the fourteen-year-old girl to me. Cathy was a recent arrival, whose difficulties in adjusting and relating to others at the school were causing concern. For the past two weeks, since she had come to West Hill, she had spoken to no one.

I opened the door to my waiting room at two o'clock to find a slender adolescent girl about five feet tall standing near the window, gazing out into the gloom. Hearing me, she turned, but she avoided my eyes. She had a small, round face and short brown hair cut and trimmed like that of a Dutch lad. Indeed, she could have been a boy, dressed as she was in a simple man-tailored shirt, jeans, and moccasins, for her figure had not yet matured.

1

"Please come in, Miss Erno," I urged, trying to welcome her in a friendly voice. She hesitated momentarily, as if to summon up her courage, then marched past me into my office. I closed the door behind her. "Please sit down," I said, gesturing and taking my place behind the desk. Cathy continued to stand immobile in the center of the room, staring down at the carpet, looking frightened. Now her shoulders began to pivot toward the door behind her. Slowly, cautiously, she turned her head and furtively lifted her eyes to examine the door. She appeared ill-at-ease and undecided about staying.

"The door isn't locked, Miss Erno, but won't you sit down?" I spoke gently, hoping to reassure her. She stiffened and twisted back to face me; still avoiding my glance, she peeked at the chairs in the office.

There are two identical easy chairs in my consultation room; there is no couch. The chair closest to my own is a few feet away, directly to my left. Patients seeking reassurance frequently prefer to sit there. When they feel especially anxious, they often perch at the edge of the cushion and lean forward to get even nearer. I have set this chair at an angle pointing away from mine so that the patient need not face me. There are moments when people find it easier to speak of sensitive matters not looking into someone else's eyes.

Cathy Erno chose the other chair, farther away to the left of my desk. Though this chair faces me, the end of the desk intrudes like a barrier between the patient and me. I have observed that persons who are guarded and tend to fear dependency seem to prefer this chair. Cathy shrank deep into the seat almost as if she deliberately were intending to emphasize the distance between us. She even shunned the armrests, drawing back, her elbows close at her sides, her fists clenched in her lap. The chair is neither tall nor massive, but it seemed to engulf her.

"I am Dr. Jacobs," I said. But she sat as still and silent as a statue before me, staring at the foot of the desk. Her face revealed no clue to her mood or attitude. When it became clear she did not intend to respond, I went on. "Mr. Cooke, the director at West Hill, arranged this appointment so that you might have a private consultation with me. I want to assure you that anything you wish to discuss here will remain entirely between us and will be held in the strictest confidence. You may regard me as your personal psychiatrist if you wish. I have no responsibility to your school other than to advise them in a general way, if you consent, how better to meet your needs and wishes."

Cathy watched me impassively as I spoke, her face revealing nothing. As soon as I finished, she immediately dropped her gaze once more. Apart from this movement of her eyes, she remained like a life-size doll, one of those whose eyes roll down when their chins are tilted.

Long silent moments passed. Cathy's blank face held no hint of the traumatic events that had so recently and tragically altered her life and led to her coming to West Hill. I had been informed that two months earlier Cathy had been an apparently well-adjusted teenager living at home with her mother, her grandmother, and her retarded younger brother; her parents had separated years before.

In the past two months Cathy's grandmother had suffered a sudden, fatal heart attack. Mrs. Erno, who worked, could not stay at home to care for her son, who was placed in an institution. Thus, in one swift blow, Cathy lost both her grandmother and her brother. Her life was abruptly overturned; all at once she was alone. Each day after school she returned to a now-silent, empty apartment to wait until evening, when her mother came home from work. She lost interest in her previous activities and avoided her friends; she withdrew and became seclusive. Her studies deteriorated. For the first time she failed to complete and hand in assignments; she left school early without authorization: she played truant. Mrs. Erno remonstrated and lectured her to no avail. She began to find Cathy sitting alone in the dark when she got home at night. At first, Cathy offered feeble excuses, but then she just sulked at her mother's reproaches. She communicated less and less until finally, shortly before she was sent to West Hill, she stopped speaking altogether.

Cathy sat there as motionless as a mannequin. Minutes

went by; the stillness was unbroken. She may need more time than others to accept help, I thought, and settled down to wait. The faint high-pitched whistle of a dental drill filled the room from the office next door. Cathy did not appear to hear the sound. Now and then she moistened her lips or shifted her gaze somewhat; otherwise, she remained still.

I considered how to proceed. Other physicians can treat a patient who is unable to cooperate. Surgeons, neurologists, or internists frequently minister to persons in coma. But how can a psychiatrist help someone who is uncommunicative and resistive? Could I accomplish anything without Cathy's participation?

The silence endured, creating subtle tensions as it lengthened. Cathy sat rigidly fixed for spells which were interrupted by gasps and quick breaths. She had taken to holding her breath to pass time. When she became aware that I noticed, she colored slightly and stopped. Once more her shoulders shifted toward the door. I was concerned that at any moment she would get up and leave. I had to say something to continue seeking a rapport.

It is unusual for adult patients visiting a psychiatrist's office to behave in such an uncommunicative fashion, especially in an initial interview, except perhaps when they have been coerced into appearing by concerned or desperate relatives. Even then a psychiatrist is usually able to break through and dissipate their recalcitrance to an extent by discussing their misapprehensions. As impenetrable as a severely depressed or suspicious person may at first seem, one is almost always able to succeed by tact and patience in establishing at least some verbal contact.

Significant silences, often laden with tension, also occur later in therapy, after a relationship between psychiatrist and patient is relatively well established. They take place at points in the course of treatment when it may become particularly painful for the patient to recall or to reveal a critical or crushing experience. Sometimes the silences signal that the patient's feelings involve the therapist.

Adolescents taking their first shaky steps toward autonomy are hard pressed to expose their weaknesses and problems to adults, especially to psychiatrists. They see their struggle to establish their independence imperiled by disclosure of their doubts. Lacking more sophisticated defenses, they frequently employ silence as a screen to keep their uncertainties from being revealed. Using silence, they will discourage inquiry and shield themselves from anticipated criticism and advice. They dread judgment which may find them too childlike and almost equally resent appraisal according to adult standards. Having recently emerged from childhood, they lack sufficient experience to rely on for decisions, yet they will deny themselves access to mature judgment until they are assured of being adequate to cope in an appropriate way. For this reason, I continued, for the present, to address Cathy as Miss Erno to emphasize that I respected her and did not regard her as a mere child.

"Mr. Cooke said that you came to West Hill two weeks ago, Miss Erno," I said, breaking the quiet. "He is quite concerned about you and thinks you may be very unhappy."

Cathy looked up at me. Her eyes were two large brown buttons, but they had no gleam. The scowl which crossed her face seemed to say, "I know all that," and to dismiss me. I knew I was getting nowhere.

The silence resumed. It settled in again as if it were an ether filling the room. Cathy, like a blind person used to darkness and able to use it confidently to confront a sighted adversary, rejoiced in the renewal of the quiet. The advantage seemed to be hers; she permitted herself a slight, but triumphant, smirk. It seemed as if she were goading me into becoming a reluctant participant in an unwonted, absurd duel, a contest of strange skills and stratagems in which she obviously felt practiced and certain. She mocked me wordlessly, scoffing at my awkward position. When I shifted in my chair and it squeaked, Cathy exulted.

The heat came on with a thud and a soft blowing murmur from the ceiling vent overhead. A little startled, Cathy lifted her eyes to it, then lowered them once more to stare at the wall next to me. I noticed some weakness in her right eye, which tired easily and strayed when she fixed her gaze too long on one spot.

"She certainly isn't mute," Phil Cooke had said. "We have

heard her talking alone in her room at night. None of us here, however, has been able to get through to Cathy. We can't seem to find any means of developing a relationship with her. She is absolutely uninterested in our efforts, turned off completely. Yet sometimes she seems pathetic, scared stiff, frozen, as if she'd done something terribly wrong and expected to be found out at any moment. You can't approach her at all when she gets that way; she will walk away and withdraw completely if you try. Other times she is more playful; she holds back in a more teasing way as if it's a game.

"When we have our group meetings, which everyone at West Hill must attend, someone always has to go find Cathy. She will hide in her room, behind the door, or in the toilet. At the meetings she usually sits somewhere as inconspicuous as possible and never contributes to the discussion. While the other teenagers demand privileges or gripe and complain, Cathy looks as if she would like to disappear. Still, she seems to take it all in; if changes in the rules are announced, she conforms. The other kids aren't sure how to take her. She ignores their friendly overtures and keeps to herself."

I decided to try again, to say something about her silence that might end the game. "You don't speak, Miss Erno." I drew an impatient sigh. "I can't help wondering why." She sneered. "What reason compels you to be silent?"

Cathy clenched her teeth and swallowed. Her lips remained sealed, perhaps even more firmly now than before. She glowered, furious at my words, at the challenge to her mastery of the silence.

Seconds dragged into minutes; time crawled past. The atmosphere in my office was defused and subtly transformed, as if the girl before me had disengaged herself and drifted off to some distant place. Her facial expression suggested intense concentration that seemed oddly inappropriate to the circumstances. She also looked wary. I wondered if she were deep in thought or listening to voices she alone could hear.

Should I disturb her? At the risk of further antagonizing her and of sounding foolish if I were mistaken, I decided to comment on her disposition. If she is hearing voices, she may be relieved to know I am familiar with that phenomenon, I reasoned. On the other hand, if she isn't hallucinating, there is little risk in her finding out how misleading her stillness is.

"You look as if you were listening to something I can't hear, Miss Erno. When that happens to patients, I always feel a little left out."

A sly, enigmatic grin appeared on Cathy's face. Just then there was a muffled bang. It caused her to duck and hunch her shoulders abruptly. It was the kind of exaggerated reflex one observes in persons who are very tense and hyperalert.

"That's the damper in the heating system shutting down. I'm sorry you were startled. It sounds especially loud because it is so quiet in here."

Cathy caught herself nodding and froze. She made no comment but stared at the side of my desk. She seemed to be tracing the lines of graining in the wood with her eyes. The hush resumed. A faint whirring sound I had been unaware of before came to my notice now. I traced it to the digital clock sitting on my desk. The time was only two-twenty-five. It seemed later to me, and that made me realize I was stymied. Our silent dialogue was at an impasse. If I continued unilaterally to create conversation, then I would be accepting exclusive responsibility for the session. The focus would be on my efforts, on my words. There would be no pressure on her to participate or to assume any active role.

I debated what to do. Maybe I should ask her direct questions. I preferred to avoid that, if possible, because her refusal to respond would tend to aggravate our deadlock and make our situation even more untenable. I had to find some opportunity to interpret her silence, to deny her its use. Until then she would continue to divert herself from her internal conflicts by playing verbal hide-and-seek with me. It was a game she must not be allowed to win; victory would deprive her of help that I suspected she urgently needed.

The thought that I might keep quiet also occurred to me. Would she accept my silence as a concession and end her battle of wills? Or would my silence worsen matters because she wouldn't know what I was thinking and feel threatened? She might even suspect that I was retaliating by imitating her. I didn't want to give Cathy the impression that I was angry or vindictive, so I decided to continue to speak intermittently, as I had been doing. In that way I could maintain at least a limited contact while preventing the silences from taking over.

A plant on the corner of my desk had attracted Cathy's interest. There was a small pink bud on one of the stems. "It's called *impatiens*," I said. "Over the summer I grow them in my garden, and each fall I pot the hardiest ones for houseplants. This one may flower in a day or two. But sometimes a bud such as this merely falls off without ever opening. I am trying to understand why that occurs. It's a shame when a bud fails to open and become a lovely flower."

Cathy stared at me searchingly. She seemed to sense that my words had more than one meaning. I slowly shifted my gaze from her to the window and the bare treetops bending in the winter wind. I had deliberately revealed a bit of myself to her. Perhaps she needed time to study me unobserved to satisfy herself.

This is going to take considerable time, I thought. It may be necessary to develop the relationship unhurriedly over an extended period. Brief, frequent sessions, I decided, would be less stressful and provide opportunities for her to get used to me. Repetition, without great urgency and pressure, could help her achieve sufficient confidence to speak and benefit from coming.

At two-thirty I announced, "This is enough for today, Miss Erno. You may come again tomorrow at the same time, if you wish." I walked beside her to the door, opened it, and said good-bye; she went into the waiting room without a word and sat down to await her transportation. I wondered if she would return. Cathy's silence, a formidable obstacle to treatment, was a desperate defense. Could it be overcome without her being overwhelmed with anxiety and without her personality being further devastated? Would I have the opportunity to try?

I telephoned Phil Cooke and told him what I planned. We

arranged for Cathy to see me for half-hour sessions four times a week. I asked for more details on her background.

The casework information on Cathy was based on interviews with her mother. Stella Erno was described as a determined, intelligent woman, no longer given to the headstrong impulses that had apparently characterized her younger years. She worked as an office assistant–bookkeeper for a group of dentists. Before her marriage she had held a more remunerative and prestigious position as office manager for a moderately large and successful company that sold and leased industrial equipment. Dominick Erno was a salesman there. Despite reservations about his easygoing nature, and though it meant giving up her job, Stella married him just before her thirtieth birthday.

Catherine Elizabeth was born a year later, following a normal pregnancy and delivery. Mrs. Erno remained at home with Cathy for ten months despite her husband's uneven and often inadequate earnings. Then, over Dominick's objections, her mother, Mrs. Cutrone, joined the household to care for the baby while Stella returned to work, taking her present job. Dominick resented his mother-in-law's presence and made little effort to conceal it. He began to travel more and to stay away on business trips for longer periods.

When Cathy was five, her brother, Vincent, was born, the result of an ill-fated pregnancy intended to produce a son and preserve a teetering marriage. This child was eventually discovered to be retarded. Dominick Erno seemed unable to reconcile himself to this disappointment. He openly expressed doubts about his paternity and ultimately precipitated a final conflict with his wife and mother-in-law by insisting that Vincent be institutionalized. When Stella, at the urging of her mother, refused to give her consent for this, Dominick Erno left home for good.

The household managed on Stella's salary and sporadic support from her estranged husband. Then Mrs. Cutrone died and Vincent was sent to a state facility.

Friday. Cathy was punctual and slipped past me into my office when I opened the door for her. She wore what she had on the day before. This time, without hesitation, she went directly to her chair and slid into it. I hoped this presaged a favorable change in her attitude and she would be more cooperative.

"Good afternoon, Miss Erno."

Cathy made no response. Instead, she studied my diplomas on the wall. There was no hint that anything was to be different today. Water boiled in the electric urn I keep on my file cabinet in the corner behind me. "I wonder if you would like some hot tea to warm you up a bit after being outside in the cold," I said.

She didn't answer, so I prepared two cups of tea and placed one near her on the desk. She stared at it but did not touch her cup.

I waited and sipped my tea. "Time seems to pass slowly when someone isn't speaking to you," I commented. Cathy scowled and passed her eyes over me to read the titles on my bookshelves. I felt I was once again being tested.

Time did pass slowly. I decided to inform her that I had received information on her background from West Hill. I feel that it is generally unwise to withhold from patients information one has been given about them. I am certain it tends to affect one's style and responses within the treatment relationship to keep such foreknowledge secret. Sooner or later the patient will sense the therapist's advantage, and rapport will be damaged. I told Cathy, in summary, what I had learned. She listened intently to my synopsis but did not react outwardly.

We lapsed into a long silence. Cathy examined my desk plant. Her eyes searched for the flower bud; it had apparently fallen off without opening and been removed. Her jaw dropped disappointedly.

"Miss Erno—may I call you Cathy? It sounds sort of formal and stuffy saying Miss Erno all the time. I hope you won't mind my using your first name now that we know each other a little better." Cathy turned away to hide a grin. I quickly took advantage of it as if she had responded directly. "Good! Then it will be Cathy from now on." She regained control almost immediately and faced me expressionlessly once more. But her effort disintegrated, and she was forced to turn aside once more to conceal her smiles. I was getting her to react but was concerned lest the session deteriorate into an unproductive game. I tried a more sober tack.

"Cathy, since we met yesterday, I've been thinking a great deal about your silence. Psychiatrists, you know, are trained to listen carefully, to analyze and grasp what people who are troubled tell us. But you've helped me realize how little we understand about silence and what it may communicate. You have created this obstacle between us for a purpose. While it must seem to protect you in some way, I suspect it also is more of a clue to what is really bothering you than you realize."

Cathy stared at me uneasily. "At first," I continued, "like most busy people, I thought of silence as nothing, a void between words at most, perhaps a mild gesture of disrespect, poor manners. But you're teaching me lots more about it. I'm learning that there are different kinds of silences that communicate all sorts of feelings and messages. There are those of fear and timidity and others that are determined, grudging, don't-give-an-inch struggles. Silences can be simple and peaceful or full of meaning, hope, and trust. Sometimes, with you, I sense that the quiet may be an expression of loneliness so heavy and painful that it is difficult to overcome."

She lowered her eyes; her face masked her feelings. Unconsciously Cathy began to stroke her right arm. "I am trying to understand and to share the silence with you, Cathy." She squirmed in her chair and fidgeted nervously. Her discomfort was mounting. Perhaps I was intruding too far into her territory, closing in too quickly. She had withdrawn behind silence in desperation; it was her last stronghold, and I was rattling the gates. I had to be cautious now not to panic her, to communicate that I would not attempt to storm her refuge but stood ready to lead her out of it. I retreated, allowing the silence to protect her once more.

We sat there across from one another, each in his own private thoughts. From a distance I heard a siren approaching, growing louder, then abruptly stopping outside; an ambulance was turning into the hospital drive across the street. I checked my desk clock. Our time was over. I rose and escorted Cathy to the door, explaining that I had arranged my schedule to see her each weekday except Wednesday, when I don't come in. Cathy made no comment and gave no indication that it mattered.

For the next two weeks I saw Cathy as planned. My "lessons" in silence continued while I tried to find ways to relate to her more effectively without apparent success. The same curious highs and lows continued to occur during each tiring session, moments when I sensed we were in relatively close contact and other times when Cathy was withdrawn, as if in a separate universe. She never spoke or uttered a sound. The silence endured, unbroken. Once, however, I happened to sneeze loudly, and reflexively she opened her mouth to say something, then caught herself and grinned triumphantly, proud of her control. On another occasion I scalded my lip with hot tea, and she appeared concerned.

It was disheartening and frustrating. Finally, I was ready to give up the effort and admit I had failed. Though I imagined at times that an odd bond had developed between us, there was little to substantiate this. I called Phil Cooke at West Hill to report my lack of progress and to discuss terminating the project.

"I am sorry, Phil, but I am not able to help Cathy Erno. I hate to let you down; however, after ten sessions and a lot of effort, she is still uncommunicative. We have a tenuous sort of relationship at best. I have failed, and I am sorry; but I just cannot justify continuing with her."

"Jerry," he replied, "we think you are getting somewhere. No one here is forcing her to see you. She knows she doesn't have to go. She certainly knows how to avoid things she doesn't want to do around school. Maybe it doesn't show in her visits, but we've noticed a change since she's been seeing you. For one thing, Cathy's come out of her shell a bit more. She's begun to talk to a few of the kids, and she seems to like her counselor,

Nell Penser. She's confided little things to her. In fact, Nell has seen some cartoonlike drawings of you taped to Cathy's walls. Don't be surprised if Nell drops by to see what you really look like one of these days."

"Can you describe the drawings to me, Phil?"

"No, I haven't seen them myself. I gather that they are not particularly flattering works of art; nevertheless, it seems clear that seeing you is important to Cathy. We'd like you to continue."

Phil's news was encouraging. I was heartened and agreed to go on. Despite some mutual concern to preserve the privacy of Cathy's sessions, Phil and I agreed that more contact between us was desirable. I needed feedback.

It began snowing heavily early Monday morning, but I made it to my office. Schools in the area remained closed, and several patients called to cancel their appointments because of the weather. There was no message about Cathy, but by two-eight she had not appeared. I stood at the window watching the snow come down in thick white clots. Suddenly I heard stomping, followed by a giggle, in my waiting room. I opened the door. Cathy was just hanging a sodden peacoat on the coatrack. A rosy-cheeked young woman stood nearby. She smiled in a friendly, apologetic way.

"I am sorry, Doctor. It is my fault Cathy is late. My windshield wipers weren't working well, and I stopped at a service station to see if they could help. I was going to phone from there to tell you we couldn't make it, but Cathy dragged me through the snow to get here. I'm Nell Penser, Cathy's counselor at West Hill."

I introduced myself to Ms. Penser and turned to Cathy, but she looked away. "Listen, Cathy," Ms. Penser said, "if I am not downstairs at two-thirty, meet me over at the gas station, okay?" With that, she said good-bye and hurried off.

Cathy took her usual seat, rubbing her hands. "The blizzard outside looks awful. I'm pleased you made such an effort to come, Cathy." She lowered her eyes; her cheeks, already scarlet, glowed even more. I went on. "I hope you like snow. We get quite a lot of it up here compared to the city."

She said nothing and stared at her boots. Here we go again, I thought, disappointed that her obvious effort to come seemed to change nothing between us. The stalemate persisted. Though Cathy demonstrated her eagerness to continue, she was unable or unwilling to show it. How could I gain her cooperation? I searched for a means. This would be a good time to have extrasensory perception. I decided it would be best to let her know that I was aware of her progress at West Hill.

"Cathy, I called Mr. Cooke the other day. He told me you had made some friends at school. He also mentioned something about certain pictures he's heard about that he thought would interest me."

Her crimson cheeks grew even redder. Cathy's face expressed a mixture of embarrassment and rage. I pushed my pen and pad across the desk in front of her. It was a mock challenge, a gentle, humorous dare. To my surprise and delight, she responded and took them onto her lap. Leaning forward, she placed her left forearm and hand on her knees as a screen and began to work. Two or three times she raised her head to study me like a portraitist. I controlled my excitement. This was the first overt interaction of any consequence between us.

After several minutes, Cathy seemed satisfied. I raised my eyebrows to show my curiosity. Abruptly she bent forward to add some further touches. Then, with elaborate secrecy, she printed something in large letters at the bottom of the page. Finally, she was done. Cathy carefully tore the sheet from the pad and shoved the pen and the pad back toward me. She neatly folded her work, dropped it in her lap, and sprawled back in her chair, grinning mischievously. I was eager to see what she had produced but suspected she would not show it if I asked. If she intended me to see her work, I would have to wait until she made up her mind to reveal it to me. Moments passed. Finally, curiosity won out over discretion. "I was hoping you would show me what you've done, Cathy."

A half smile appeared on her face; she had won a skirmish.

My entreaty was ignored. Cathy stared at a lithograph on the wall. Two steps forward and two steps back; we were marching in place, going nowhere. She had come so close to an open exchange, however, that I couldn't give up that easily and just let the moment slip away.

"You make it terribly difficult for me to know what you really feel, Cathy." Her grin broadened. Was she gloating? "Yes, you frustrate every effort I make to understand," I complained. My tone sounded stronger than I had intended. Cathy's smile vanished. She seemed surprised at my accidental severity. The game was done. Was she frightened or merely bored? I could not tell.

"Like everyone else, even psychiatrists get frustrated, though usually we try not to show it. If you think that I don't get impatient from time to time, it's not true. The only reason I try not to express it normally is that I don't want to transmit my tensions to the person I am trying to help. It is not that I am embarrassed about my feelings or feel weak because I experience them. In fact, being able to discuss them with you is helpful and relieves me. I often sense that you are toying with me here, playing a game whose rules I can't seem to learn. So, Cathy, I've decided to turn my cards face upward, hoping you'll finally feel confident enough to do the same. Both of us can see what is happening between us that way. I would like to understand more about you, so I can help with your troubles."

I had spoken deliberately, being careful to sound warm and sincere. I also wished to be direct without backing her too far into a corner. Now I wondered how effective my tactic was. Cathy sat perfectly still, as motionless for a moment as on the day she first came. Then she sighed deeply; sadly, I thought, her shoulders seemed to droop.

Doubts assailed me. Was I responding too much to my own stress, putting too much pressure on her? What was I asking of her? I had no idea what she would experience if she surrendered her silence to face and communicate her problems. I wasn't struggling to avoid the anguish and pain that she had perhaps known. Yet there comes a time in certain cases where treatment is stalled, when there must be some push to press ahead, despite risks, or the forces of inertia and resistance will doom the effort, and therapy will abort.

Our thirty minutes were almost up. I rose and walked to the window. In nonverbal language I wanted to signal a change from the normal, a departure from routine. I wished to be able to show her that I could be flexible and was not some rigid authority. I hoped she might realize that if she also bent a little, our relationship would benefit and therapy could become unstuck.

One must be pliant with adolescent patients. It takes a certain ingenuity to defeat their tendencies to stereotype psychiatrists, along with other adults, as parental figures, obstacles to their freedom and maturation. It is not easy to bring them to the insight that their own fears and illusions are the only real impediments keeping them back from assuming the grown-up responsibilities they regard with so much ambivalence. One must work around their compulsions to assert their adequacy or prove their sophistication.

It is a milestone in their treatment when these tendencies come under their self-control and can be put aside. Still, there is a final barrier to be overcome: their need to defend their autonomy, their airs of self-sovereignty. Adolescents will conceal their thoughts and untried ideas. They will keep secrets and deny or rationalize the impulses and drives they have yet to master and tame.

I peered outside; the snow was deeper. Plows were clearing the streets. I described the scene to Cathy, hoping she would join me. I heard her leave her chair, but I didn't turn. She never came. "By tomorrow," I said, "the roads will be fine. There shouldn't be any difficulty traveling." I looked back. Cathy was standing in front of her chair, looking toward the door. I noticed the paper she had been holding was missing.

"Our time is up now," I said quietly, and led her to the door. After I was certain she had left, I hurried back to my desk, expecting to find her sketch, hoping that it would provide some clues to her attitude. Did she find me sympathetic? Foolish?

Frightening? The sheet was nowhere in sight. What had she done with it? I bent down and sifted through the wastebasket. Hidden among some advertisements and discarded mail, I found it. I flattened the paper on my desk and was confronted by a crude likeness, complete with eyeglasses and balding head. Beneath the picture was a one-word caption: "SHITHEAD!"

Phil Cooke called to discuss a change in plans. Because of the snowfall, classes at West Hill had been canceled for the following day, Tuesday, so that the youngsters could take part in special activities. Cathy's group was scheduled for a snowshoe trek through a nearby wildlife sanctuary with a naturalist. It conflicted with her appointment to see me.

"She was quite excited and enthusiastic about going until I called her in and reminded her that she had a session with you at that time. Then she froze. I could see she was uncertain what to do. I wanted her to make the decision to keep her appointment or to cancel it, but after a few moments I didn't think she could. The kids have been waiting for a good snow like this for weeks to hunt for animal tracks. Cathy is closer to the group now, and I know she is eager to go with them. I finally told her she could."

I didn't have to remind Phil that ordinarily I prefer to be consulted before, not after, such decisions. He was an able and intuitive professional; I could rely on his judgment. We discussed how to handle this interruption to avoid the misimpression of any rivalry between us. It was decided that I would mention his call and take the matter up with Cathy in her next session.

"Hello, Cathy," I said, letting her in. She went directly to her chair without acknowledging my greeting. I started to pass her on my way to my desk and paused; then I sat down next to her in the other easy chair. I was still innovating, trying not to encroach too far and threaten her, but trying, rather, to alter our set pattern. Cathy glanced over at me warily, but then a faint grin appeared on her lips. I noticed that she was wearing a green tartan skirt. It was the first time I had seen her in anything but pants, but I decided not to comment on this.

"Mr. Cooke called late on Monday, after you had left. He told me about the class trip so I would understand. . . ." Cathy looked annoyed. "You seem to resent it when he and I talk," I said.

Cathy scowled and sighed loudly in a gesture of impatience. I kept on, wishing to keep her feelings on the surface even if they were hostile. She seemed increasingly confident of expressing her negative feelings toward me, and though I did not wish to be excessively provocative, I was eager to encourage their exposure. Positive emotions are revealed at greater risk; if she harbored those also, they apparently still made her feel far too vulnerable to hazard their disclosure.

"Last time when I mentioned that I had called him previously and I said that Mr. Cooke told me about your drawings, you seemed furious. . . . In fact, I know you were."

Cathy's eyes dropped automatically to the wastepaper basket. Her cheeks flushed; an embarrassed grin appeared. She tried to suppress it.

"I'll tell you whenever he and I speak about you, Cathy. I told you I would try to help the school to meet your needs better if I could; that is, if you have no objection. But it is difficult to be very helpful when you don't express yourself adequately." At that moment, my telephone began its peculiar ticking sound: *Ti-Ti-Ti-Ti-Ti. . . . Ti-Ti-Ti-Ti-Ti. . . .* I ignored it and remained seated with Cathy. She looked over at the phone on the far side of my desk, then turned to me, puzzled.

"It is an odd noise for a telephone, Cathy. You see, I put bubble gum on the ringer to soften the sound."

Ti-Ti-Ti-Ti-Ti. . . . The ticking resumed. It seemed to trouble Cathy. She frowned worriedly and shifted about in her chair. With each series of sounds, she glanced at the phone and then back at me expectantly. It was ironic, in a way, for her to become so agitated thinking that I might be indifferent to someone else, while she would not avail herself of my services.

Ti-Ti-Ti-Ti-Ti. . . . Ti!

"There, my answering service has it, at last. They are supposed to take all of my calls when I am seeing patients. It leaves me free to concentrate and give whomever I am with my complete attention." I explained that I returned calls when I got my messages between patients and that people who want to speak to me directly are told to call in the ten minutes before each hour, when I am ordinarily free.

Cathy seemed relieved. She sat back, less tense now. "I can see you were concerned that I was not answering someone who needed to speak to me, Cathy. It must have struck you as something very wrong and unfair. That's the trouble when people don't respond. It can be misleading. Your silence is like that. How is it possible to understand what you mean by it? Does it accomplish what you wish?"

She stared at me uneasily. I went on. "Your silence sometimes seems to indicate that you wish to be left alone. At other times I wonder if it isn't your way of calling attention to yourself. It could also be that you're just shy and scared or that you are struggling to keep a secret. I guess, on occasion, it might also suggest that you are very angry and acting hateful."

It was the first time I had openly confronted Cathy's hostility. She looked anxious. She moistened her lips and swallowed. She squeezed her hands and looked about nervously, almost desperately; her eyes darted toward the door several times. She rocked forward, as if to rise, but lacked the strength or the will to stand. Finally, her lips parted, she drew breath, but no words came.

Now I was still. I withheld reassurance. The silence was mine. Cathy scanned my face for some sign of support and found none. I allowed her to think our rapport and whatever it meant to her were endangered. I let the silence endure and the pressure of her doubts build. Suddenly the relationship I alone had nurtured seemed up to her to preserve. The balance had abruptly shifted; the silence she felt she had commanded had risen against her. I saw her begin to quiver and sensed that the final barrier had been breached.

For weeks I had waited, frustrated, for her resistance to

yield, for her to speak. Now, witnessing her distress as she fought back tears, I felt a rending sense of relief. Instead of speaking, I rose and walked over to her. I gently placed my hand on her shoulder. She stiffened, then bent forward and began to cry. I stood beside her for a moment, then brought her some tissues.

The time was almost up. I considered extending the session, now that she was openly expressing feelings, but, weighing the possible gain against the risk that Cathy would resent my exploiting her distress, decided against it. There is more benefit to patients who accept their responsibility to themselves and willingly cooperate than to those whose secrets are wrenched from them. And while I wished to be flexible, it seemed wise to be regular about time. A balance must be struck between the resiliency the therapist demonstrates and the effort the patient is willing to expend in treatment. The therapist must be consistent and reliable to encourage trust, but he cannot help anyone unwilling to invest himself in the effort.

Cathy's whimpers subsided. She rose and discarded her crumpled tissues. "All right now?" I inquired softly. She nodded. I led her to the door. "You care a good deal about what happens in here, Cathy." She looked up at me with her large, sad eyes. I let her out.

I did not return directly to my desk but went, instead, over to the window. Ordinarily I use the minutes after a patient departs to make notes. I try to capture, in the patient's own words as much as possible, the salient ideas expressed in the session along with his or her related feelings while they all are still fresh in my mind. Interpretations offered later tend to have more meaning and impact when the patient recognizes his own phrasings. Other notes I may make are questions to be pursued in subsequent sessions. Sometimes I jot down my speculations. But often, when a particularly critical or pivotal session has occurred, I like to ruminate a bit before I write.

The sky outside was heavy and leaden. I reviewed the developments in Cathy's course. Prior to Phil Cooke's revelation that she was improving in her adjustment at West Hill and had taken to making caricatures of me to exhibit on her walls, I had been disheartened about Cathy's treatment. His disclosure had given me the hope that despite her reticence in our sessions, Cathy was responding to my interest and developing ties to me. While it was true that she had come freely all along, her loyalty became apparent when she struggled to keep her appointment despite the snowstorm. Even her pique at my knowledge of her drawings and the message on the sketch she deposited in my wastebasket gave me confidence in our rapport. Hostile feelings are evidence of a relationship; only indifference is not.

When the telephone incident occurred, I saw an opportunity to exploit it, to mobilize her feelings and draw her out. I manipulated, letting her first think I was callous and unkind, frustrating her image of me, confusing her defenses. As a result, anxiety welled up within her, enabling me, by withholding my support, to turn her silence against her. I hoped to defeat Cathy's resistance by confronting her with the burden of her own behavior.

The intensity of her reaction surprised me. I had underestimated just how important I had become to her. It is easy for the therapist to misjudge his significance to the patient. The psychiatrist sees many individuals and has a personal life apart from his professional one, but the patient often has only the psychiatrist to understand him. One must comprehend how isolated and alone the patient may feel to know how important the therapist can become to him. Cathy's silence had misled me. But she too had miscalculated; her reticence had provided her with an unwieldly shield. It was a weapon that could backfire, an uncertain defense she could not always control.

In the long run it usually does not prove helpful to attack a patient's resistance to treatment until one is confident the relationship is adequate to withstand such a confrontation. This is a point generally missed by the numberless jokes and cartoons which depict a patient fiddling while the analyst takes notes. The patient appears to be making a mockery of the treatment and a fool of the psychiatrist. But what is really happening? The patient is resisting a treatment he may desperately need and desire. He finds himself, nevertheless, unable to discard his defenses. These defenses are not mere garments impeding examination, coverings to be stripped away to get at the patient within. Resistance is much more like the skin, an organic part of the person without which he is neither completely intact nor whole.

A patient needs time to adjust to the therapist. He must develop confidence in him to permit more than the most superficial examination; even then he permits the psychiatrist only to observe and gently to probe, like other physicians, through his skin. This trust, cooperative respect, and understanding that develop between the patient and therapist constitute the therapeutic relationship. Resistance yields slowly, in stages, as the therapeutic relationship becomes stronger. It is the principal reason that the treatment process is so time-consuming.

The patient is in a struggle to cope with an onslaught of unwonted, unconscious impulses. He fears his self-control may disintegrate, that he may not be able to manage these internal forces and continue, at the same time, to meet the demands of the real world. This fear is especially strong in adolescents who already feel apprehensive about the new responsibilities of adult life which confront them.

Extraordinary defenses are sometimes employed to help the adolescent cope with his discomfort. Some, like Cathy, withdraw, to reduce the external demands upon them. Others may seek relief in a religious cult, promiscuity, drugs or alcohol. This defensive behavior may further impair the individual's capacity to function in a normally productive way; it may also alienate him from his family. Feeling alone and misunderstood, the adolescent frequently becomes sullen and moody. Actually, it is he who does not understand himself and projects this onto others.

The therapist who seeks to help such a youngster must be patient while he strives to foster the therapeutic relationship. The pace of treatment is slow and measured, in order not to threaten the patient's autonomy. Repetitions permit insight to filter through the patient's layer of resistance, to penetrate his "skin" and become absorbed. The therapeutic alliance between the individual and his psychiatrist helps the patient to feel less alone and insecure; his resistance eases. He can better tolerate anxiety and admit to consciousness previously inadmissible fears and other feelings. As these are discussed and clarified their intensity abates. The patient's self-confidence increases. He alters his defenses and becomes free to pursue more acceptable and realistic ways to express himself. Psychological growth is a tedious process. Like digestion, it is begun by much chewing on small bites.

It was Friday, and we were to meet for the thirteenth time. I hoped that did not bode ill for our session. Cathy wore a light-blue corduroy jumper and a white turtleneck sweater. Her attire was becoming more varied; clothes now seemed to interest her. I watched her take her chair and sit there, silently waiting. But I had decided to attempt a technique that I had found useful years before, when, during my residency, I worked for a time with younger children. I withdrew a set of checkers from a drawer in my desk and opened the board. Cathy watched me, curious and mildly amused. I piled the red and black checkers on the board, separated them, and chose the black pieces. Suddenly I realized that I had forgotten how to arrange them. Cathy quickly recognized my lapse and chuckled.

"Would you show me?" I asked.

She rose and dragged her chair up to the desk. Without looking at me, she leaned forward and arranged the red checkers at her end. I copied her with the black; then I moved a piece forward.

"Red goes first!" Cathy uttered.

I made an effort not to show my excitement and retrieved the checker. She had spoken at last. It was as if a siege had been lifted. I found it a task to play and was in difficulty very quickly. Cathy won readily. She set up the game again. "You take red and go first now," she said confidently.

I was delighted. We played three games. By the end I had

learned the perils of advancing my pieces without backing them up to avoid being trapped and double-jumped. "One mistake and the game is yours each time," I lamented. "How did you learn to play checkers so well?"

"My grandmother and I used to play a lot," Cathy answered.

"You must have been pals then."

"Uh-huh, when I was little," she said a little wistfully.

"You mean you haven't played since you were small?"

"No, my grandmother got too old and nervous for games."

"And how about your mother? Did she do things with you too, Cathy?"

"No, she works all week and half a day on Saturdays. She is tired all the time from standing on her feet. My mother works for a bunch of dentists."

"What about weekends?" I asked, encouraging her, hoping to learn more how her family had functioned.

Cathy made a face. "Well, Saturdays, after work, Mom goes to get her hair done. Saturday night is her night out; she and her friends go places together. Sometimes she has a date with Dr. Poletto, one of the dentists. He takes her out on Sundays, too, once in a while. But usually Sunday is when she and my grandmother used to cook for the whole week. They made pots of soup and other things that we could heat up quickly for supper because she got home late every night."

"It doesn't sound as if there was much time for you," I observed.

Cathy let that pass. Apparently she wasn't ready to discuss her feelings yet. I contented myself with her willingness to describe the household and how it operated. For as long as she could recall, her grandmother, Nonna, had run the home. Until a few months before her death it was Nonna who had bargained furiously in the fish store and humiliated the butcher until Cathy's embarrassment was unbearable. Nonna had seemed indefatigable. She did the laundry, the ironing, the cleaning and straightening and took care of Vincent. With it all, she was a perky, spirited woman who could enjoy a good story and delight in repeating a joke.

"My mother complained all the time, about almost everything; nothing ever seemed to make her happy. But Nonna really did all the work. The neighbors all knew it. They would say things especially after my mother'd find something to make a stink about. Everybody in the building knew about it when my mother was angry."

"Did your Nonna quarrel with her?"

"No, that wasn't her way. Nonna would just clam up. My mother couldn't stand it; especially after a day or two, when Nonna wouldn't talk."

"I see. . . . You learned more than just how to win at checkers from her, didn't you?"

Cathy looked surprised, as though the thought had not occurred to her. She smiled self-consciously, then went on to tell more about how hard it was to please her mother and how quick-tempered she was. "Even Vinnie, my brother, kept out of her way. She made him so nervous sometimes he had 'accidents' in his pants when she was around. That would really set her off. 'One day I won't come home at all. I'll take off like Dominick and live a little for a change,' she'd yell. I used to hope she meant it."

Despite vilification and damning of him by both her grandmother and mother, I learned that Cathy did not harbor any bitterness toward her father. Dominick Erno sent his daughter little gifts and sums of money from time to time, characteristically after her birthdays and at Christmas. Cathy knew he still thought of her.

When our time was up, I opened the door and said goodbye as usual. But this time Cathy turned and responded, adding, "The checkers . . . it was fun, thank you."

"I'm glad you enjoyed it, Cathy."

"You don't play very well," she answered. "My Nonna would've beaten you easily."

Monday morning I heard again from Phil Cooke. He reported that Cathy was participating much more in school activities and was becoming much more sociable. Phil was already aware that she had finally spoken to me and was pleased. I asked him if Dominick Erno knew that Cathy was at West Hill and was told that letters informing him of her admission and requesting information had gone unanswered. I suggested that further efforts to contact Mr. Erno be undertaken. I wanted to learn more about his attitude toward Cathy.

Shortly before two o'clock, after releasing my previous patient, I took out the checkers set and placed it on my desk. It would provide a reminder to Cathy of our new relationship. When I opened my door, the young woman I had met on the day of the snowstorm stood beside her.

"This is Nell, Dr. Jacobs. She's my counselor at West Hill," Cathy blurted, her cheeks burning.

"Yes, I remember Ms. Penser. It's a pleasure to see you again," I said.

Cathy turned to her and whispered, "Go ahead, you promised!" and gave the young woman a playful shove.

"Hello again, Doctor. . . . I understand that you are a whiz at checkers."

Cathy giggled and fled into my office to her seat.

I chuckled. "Reports of my splendid form and expertise may well have been exaggerated, Nell. I am still perfecting my game." I added a wink and closed the door. Cathy noticed the checkers, and we bantered lightly about it before more serious discussion resumed. I recalled for her that she had been telling me about her family. She continued without further prompting.

"My brother, Vinnie, is in a special school, too, now, but it's not like mine. He is retarded. Vinnie's nine years old, but he's really more like a baby; he can't do very much for himself. He can't even tie his shoes right. Unless I watched him, he'd pull out the laces and lose them. I spent a whole afternoon in Wilson Park once looking for his left shoe. I didn't find it either, and did I get it from Mom!"

"You were responsible for watching Vinnie?"

"Nonna used to. Then she got angina, pain in her heart, and she couldn't keep up with him anymore after that. I had to take him out and chase after him from then on. My mother even complained about that." Cathy's face reddened; her eyes became puffy. "She—" The words seemed to catch in Cathy's throat. She was suddenly upset and on the verge of tears. She turned away and regained control. "I don't want to talk about it anymore—okay?" she said, facing me once more.

"All right," I agreed.

"Can we play checkers again?" she asked.

"Sure." I opened the set and we played. Cathy was not quite as cutthroat an adversary this time, and I made fewer blunders. Our games were easier, and we chatted as we played. Cathy told of her frustration with Vincent. He got into her things and ruined her games; he crayoned on her homework and tore pages from her books. Because of him, she could not bring friends home to the apartment to play.

"He must have made your life difficult," I observed. She nodded and became taciturn.

At the end of our second game, when my king was hopelessly outnumbered and trapped in the double corner, Cathy pushed her chair back and looked at me speculatively.

"Are you married, Doctor?"

"Yes, Cathy, I've been married many years. Why do you ask?"

Personal questions from patients pose a problem in therapy. They test the quality of the therapeutic relationship. I usually try to respond to these questions in a way that will not offend, but I am not eager to permit the patient to divert our attention from his problems to satisfy his curiosity about me. Beyond observing the simple amenities necessary to assure the patient that he is respected as an equal, socialization of the therapeutic relationship does not usually serve the aims of the treatment process. My object is to keep the focus of the interview where it should be: on the patient. When I deliberately make an exception, it is because the patient is too anxious and his stability is in jeopardy. When I judge that a patient's adjustment is precarious, I modify my technique and later my goals.

I find that providing patients' questions with immediate and direct answers almost always makes it more difficult afterward to get at the reason behind the question. For as soon as the patient's interest is relieved, he tends to forget quickly what motivated him to ask. Nevertheless, one must accept certain hindrances in working with adolescents. They are so very easily affronted by any tactic they may misinterpret as condescension that it is necessary to bend more at times in handling their queries. In Cathy Erno's case, I was prone to be especially careful. After struggling so long to promote our dialogue, I was not about to place it in danger. It was not difficult to anticipate her answer or her next question.

"I don't know why I asked." She shrugged. "Do you have any children?"

"I have a daughter and a son. But you were telling me about Vinnie," I reminded her, directing her back to her own family. I probed to see if I could elicit what had caused her to become upset earlier. "I gather that your brother sometimes made trouble for you."

"Well, for Nonna and me. Sometimes, when I forgot to do something for Vinnie, Nonna got the blame," Cathy admitted. "My mother would raise the roof and scream at her, 'When you die, you're not going to stick me with him! You're the only reason he's still here! When you go, I'm taking the girl and moving to Florida! Let the state or his father look after him!' " Cathy was excited and bitter.

"I can see how that upset you. It was even hard to tell," I said.

"I'd never go with her!" Cathy vowed.

During the next several sessions, which brought us to the middle of March, Cathy and I continued to discuss her family. She angrily recounted how her mother blamed much of her misfortune and unhappiness on Nonna and abused her. It seemed that as the aged woman's health deteriorated and she faltered, unable to manage the household chores and look after Vincent effectively any longer, Stella Erno's calumny and vituperation increased. When she observed that Cathy was assisting her grandmother more, Stella complained that her mother was ruining Cathy's life, too.

"It got so that Nonna and I wouldn't tell her anything," Cathy confided. "I was doing all the shopping and taking Vinnie out to play, too, but we made believe it was a secret."

"What do you mean?" I asked.

"Well, anyone could see Nonna couldn't do it. Everyone in the building was doing favors for her; they all liked her. My mother really knew what was going on; she just pretended not to know. Except, if anything happened that she didn't like, she'd wait till I was there, and then she'd holler at Nonna and blame her."

"I can see it must have been a very unhappy situation, Cathy. You seem to have been very close to Nonna. Tell me about her death."

"It was on a Friday," Cathy said, tensing. "I got in a fight after school. If I hadn't, it would never have happened!" Her poise disintegrated; she began to whimper. "It was all my fault . . . I was to blame . . . if I'd only come straight home. . . ." She bent forward and rocked from side to side in anguish. Her voice became inaudible. I brought her a cup of water and a tissue.

"There was this little pest at school who was always bugging me, giving me the elbow in the halls or pulling my books down so they would fall and my notes would go flying. I had had it with him! So I waited to get him after school that day, and I punched him out good. It made me feel terrific; he had it coming!"

Cathy paused and finished her water. "I knew I had to get Vinnie where the special bus let him off, so I went straight there instead of going home first, like I usually did." Again she paused, then broke down.

"I was too late," she said, sobbing. "Vinnie wasn't there . . . I was scared . . . I couldn't find him. . . . All the way home, I thought he was lost. When I got there and opened the door, though, there he was, playing on the floor. I was so happy I hugged him. . . . I thanked God. Then I found Nonna in the bathroom. . . . She was dead!"

I watched Cathy cry, hoping the tears would drain away some of her pain. Then I spoke to her quietly. "To lose someone so dear is terrible in itself, Cathy. But you feel responsible for Nonna's death, though I don't see why."

"Because I should have come right home after school like I was supposed to do. They called from the school," she cried. "They let Vinnie out early. It was my job to get him . . . there would have been time. Nonna went out and got him instead. He was too hard for her to handle outside—Vinnie could be a big pain, sometimes—he must have run off and worn her out."

Cathy reached for some more tissues and rubbed her eyes. "My mother doesn't know it was my fault Nonna died. Nonna was always so afraid Mom would send Vinnie away that we kept it a secret that I used to bring him home. Are you going to tell her now?"

"No, Cathy, whatever you tell me is a secret, too."

"It doesn't matter anymore anyway. What can she do to us now? She put Vinnie in that place, and I'm here."

"You must have been very frightened that your mother would find out. Is that why you stopped talking?"

"I don't know. . . . At first I couldn't say anything because I was too scared. Then, after she sent Vinnie away, I just didn't feel like talking to her or to anyone. After a while I liked it that way. I guess I was angry at Mom and the whole world. I clammed up."

Cathy and I talked at length about her feelings of responsibility, guilt, and rage. It took several additional sessions before she began to accept the realities of her grandmother's coronary artery disease and her death. Only then, as her guilt subsided, was she able to admit to ambivalent feelings toward her Nonna. As she conceded this, she was able to view her mother's attitudes and difficult life in a more understanding way. The impact of circumstances and the collision of interests that had surrounded her and shaped her perspectives became clearer to Cathy.

It was not long after his birth that Vincent Erno began to reshape the destiny of his family. As I listened to Cathy's account, Vincent emerged as a hapless octopus whose clumsy tentacles entangled those about him, creating problems and conflicts. I probed for feelings of resentment and guilt—because of it—unsuccessfully. As destructive as he was, Cathy could admit only to frustration and pity for her brother.

She had few memories of her father but was pleased to have been told she resembled him. Nonna, the source of much of her information about her father, little of it pleasant, had revealed the resemblance to her more as a warning than a compliment. To Nonna, Dominick Erno had been a handsome but unsubstantial charmer, a smooth man not to be trusted. She disapproved of his friends, his love of sports, and his free-spending ways. She hinted that he had not always been a faithful husband.

Both of Cathy's parents openly accused Nonna of meddling and destroying their marriage. Nonna herself told her granddaughter this in an effort to vindicate herself. Cathy, however, had always remained skeptical, especially about her father's vices. She was aware that long before her mother came of age to marry, her grandfather had deserted Nonna, leaving her to bring up her child alone, dependent on relatives. She came to distrust men.

I became more aware of Cathy's feelings about her father in April. On the eleventh of the month, nine days late, there arrived at West Hill a package containing a gold locket with a photograph of a husky man nearing fifty. It was a birthday present for Cathy from her dad. Dominick Erno had dark hair with a streak of gray to the right of his part and a broad, friendly smile.

Stirred by the gift, Cathy filled several sessions with speculations and fantasies about her father. She had a highly romantic image of him. In her daydreams he would return one day, perhaps soon, to reward her faithful love of him. She imagined him taking her to the shore or on a trip west to the Rocky Mountains, to California. They would laugh and have adventures. . . .

Cathy's fantasies made me uneasy. I feared for her disillusionment. Tactfully I pointed out the fairy-tale quality of her illusions. She was not Sleeping Beauty, nor was her father likely to be Prince Charming.

I cautioned her that pinning too many hopes and ambitions all on someone else to fulfill was unrealistic. Cathy's response surprised me.

"I know," she said. "I found that out already. When Nonna died, I was sure my father would come. I waited for him to show up, to telephone, or to send me a letter; he never did. He knew about it, too. He had to sign for Vincent to be sent away and for me to come here. But I never heard from him. You know, when I first came to West Hill, I was sure he would come any day to take me out to live with him. I used to pretend he was around and talk to him at night in my room. Then, when I started seeing you, I stopped that."

"More and more you may discover, Cathy, that making your wishes come true is entirely up to you. Waiting for your father or someone like him to come into your life and change it for you isn't really too wise."

Cathy grinned. "You better believe it! That's why I stopped play-talking to him and began playing checkers with you."

Cathy continued to do well at West Hill. Nell Penser called to report that Cathy had begun to menstruate and had handled it well. They had discussed it, and Nell had answered her questions. I commented to her on Cathy's increased interest in her appearance and was warned to be certain that I noticed her pierced ears and commented on them. Cathy's appointments were also discussed. Cathy and I had already agreed that she needed to come only twice weekly, and now Nell and I planned to reduce the frequency of her visits to once a week as soon as I could discuss it with Cathy. We agreed to aim at a termination by the end of the school year, in June, when those youngsters, like Cathy, who were not graduating or leaving usually went to summer camp.

Mr. Erno was heard from in May. He had reluctantly met with a social worker from the agency that operated West Hill. The social worker's report was not encouraging. Dominick Erno, though interested in his daughter, was reluctant to assume any responsibility for her. His principal concern was that he not be burdened with any expense for her. "I manage to send the kid a few bucks for Christmas and a present for her birthday, but don't get the idea I have any extra money. I just get by," he was quoted as saying. He also revealed that Mrs. Erno was planning to obtain a divorce. He was nervous lest he become obligated to support his children.

Cathy received a brief letter from her father telling her he wished to visit her. She was excited and apprehensive about meeting him. We discussed it, and I asked Cathy if her mother had informed her of plans for her divorce.

"Yes, I know about that. She always said that the only thing that stopped her before was Vinnie. Now that he is where he is, I guess she will get it. Nonna always said there was something between Mom and Dr. Poletto; she and Mom would fight about it. Nonna said my mother was a fool, that Dr. Poletto was just taking advantage of her. But Mom insisted he would ask her to marry him if it weren't for Nonna and Vinnie."

"What does your mother say now?"

"She doesn't say anything definite. She might marry him or move to Florida. I don't really care; I won't live with her again either way. Not ever! I mean it!"

Dominick Erno came alone on a Sunday. Nell Penser told me that Cathy was reserved and awkward while her father, garrulous and convivial, strove to entertain her with effusive, funny chatter. By the time she had shown him around the school, however, Cathy and her father seemed well acquainted and on easy, familiar terms. Mr. Erno also won over Cathy's classmates with his hearty, friendly manner and generosity; he topped off his visit with a flourish by driving Cathy and her closest friends to town for sundaes.

"My father's not at all how I imagined him. He's more like Nonna described him. But that's all right. I'm going to see him again next month. Loretta, the woman he lives with, is coming also so I can meet her. I saw her picture; she's a little fat like him, but she has a pretty face. He promises we'll get along. . . . Boy, was he nervous with me; he never stopped talking, and all about himself. I think he is really a nice person, but he wanted me to like him so much that I felt sorry for him. I think he must find it hard to express his feelings the way we do."

"You sound like a psychiatrist, Cathy."

"Oh, that reminds me, I've been saving this joke to tell you: A man went to see a psychiatrist, but once he laid down on the couch, he couldn't think of anything to tell him. After a while he asked the psychiatrist what would happen if he didn't say anything that day. 'Oh, that happens to people all the time,' said the doctor. 'Just be patient, and something will occur to you.'

"When the time was up, the man got up, thanked the doctor, and started to leave. But the nurse said: 'That will be fifty dollars, please!' So the man paid her and went on his way. The next time he saw the psychiatrist, the same thing happened. He didn't say a word and was assured that it occurred to lots of patients. So he paid his fifty dollars again and left.

"For six weeks it went on like this. Each time the man said nothing and paid the fifty dollars, until one day, he had an idea. 'Doctor,' he announced, 'today, I have something to say.'

" 'What is it?' the psychiatrist asked eagerly.

" 'Doctor,' the man said, 'do you need a partner?' "

Phil Cooke, Nell Penser, Cathy, and I held a conference in mid-June to discuss termination of the treatment and to plan. Mrs. Erno was in the process of obtaining her divorce and intended to remarry as soon as it became final. Cathy preferred to remain at West Hill. It was agreed that she would stay on through her last three years of high school. She would see both her parents regularly, and separately, on visits. I would remain available to her, but most of her problems would be managed by Cathy with Nell Penser's help.

Psychotherapy cases don't conclude, like fairy tales, with happily-ever-after endings. But often I feel a certain satisfaction when treatment terminates. I did when I last saw Cathy Erno, the day before she was to leave for summer camp.

THE UNSEEN FRONTIER

Douglas Welborn

H er identification pin read: "J. Nieder, R.N." She lifted her
uncapped blond head and asked, "Yes?" I introduced
myself and explained. "He's in three-eleven," she announced,
rising from her charts. I was to be escorted. Ms. Nieder was a
husky woman in her mid-thirties who had been attractive. In a
uniform too tight now to be comfortable, she apparently reigned
here on three north, her ward.

"I hope I can help," I offered as we walked along the dull
green corridor past an intravenous apparatus and an electrocar-
diograph machine. My tone was warm and deliberately tentative
to dispel the alien image of the omniscient psychiatrist. She
softened, turned toward me, and paused.

"I can't tell you much more than Dr. Knapp did; I was there
when he called you. Mr. Welborn—Mr. Douglas Welborn,
we're sure that's his name—came up about nine-forty-five this
morning from the emergency room. He hasn't been any trouble
. . . just very quiet . . . hasn't asked for anything," she said,

shrugging. "He does what you ask of him, but"—she made a face—"he seems kind of lost, mixed up, you might say."

"In what way?" I asked, interested. "Are there specific matters he is confused about?" Ms. Nieder considered for a moment, then shook her head uncertainly. What she meant, she explained, was that Welborn had not responded normally to questions. In fact, he hardly answered at all but stared intently, grimacing, as if it took great effort for him to concentrate and keep his mind on their queries. His few replies had been almost inaudible. For a time his answers confounded his examiners even more, until it was realized that his responses were tardy replies to earlier, unanswered questions.

"Has Mr. Welborn said anything strange, anything inappropriate?" I asked.

"No, nothing peculiar if that's what you mean. It's more like his mind is off somewhere else and he isn't able to pay attention. You get the feeling that everything inside his head is working in slow motion," she answered.

"In slow motion . . ." I echoed. "You are a perceptive observer."

Ms. Nieder smiled. "I'll tell you something. I've been a nurse fourteen years now. I haven't had much experience with psychiatric patients, but I've seen a lot of people come and go. You develop a sense about them after a while, you know what I mean? Whoever this Welborn turns out to be, and I have a feeling that he is a fine person, a gentleman, I think he has had it!" She shook her head gravely. We resumed walking. "I hope you can do something for him," she said dubiously.

"I'll certainly try," I said, pleased that Welborn had her sympathy and her regard. It was a clue which made it likely that whatever the reasons for his reticence, Welborn was probably not paranoid. Ms. Nieder would have detected the suspiciousness and distrust that characterize the uncommunicativeness of a paranoidal personality; she would have reacted differently, perhaps hostilely to him, had it been present. No, I decided, she likes him too well for that. She will help with him if I need to ask it

"You may see him with me for a little while if you wish," I offered at the door to 311. Her eyes widened, surprised, a hint of concern in them. "On the other hand," I added quickly, "if you have a lot to do . . . ?"

"The others are all down to lunch just now. I'd better stay at the station," she answered, more at ease.

"I'll talk to you later then, when you have a moment," I said.

The room was undisturbed except for the man who was sitting, motionless, at the edge of the bed, his back to the door. It was almost 1:00 P.M. He has probably been sitting there three hours now, I estimated, and by the neatness of the bed sheets, hasn't moved. I walked around in front of him. He did not stir. Finally, he lifted his eyes to meet mine.

Mr. Welborn appeared to be in his early forties. He had dark brown hair, short and graying at the sides, which were well clipped, almost military. His face was clean-shaven and handsome. He was trim, looked physically well and out of place, almost comical, sitting there with the short hospital gown reaching only to his mid-thighs.

I held his glance for a moment. I did not smile, nod, extend my hand, or make any natural gesture; then I sat down. I chose the armchair whose location placed me a little farther away from him and somewhat lower than he. As I sank back into it, I casually crossed my leg. I wanted to appear relaxed and nonthreatening.

The moment of meeting a patient one knows little about is always important. How one acts, what one says or neglects to say will affect and influence whether or not the patient will choose to cooperate and enter the therapeutic process. The encounter abounds with pitfalls. A friendly smile, for example, may be misinterpreted as a sneer, mistaken for a sign that the interviewer has foreknowledge or is omniscient. An offered hand may seem presumptuous, intimidating, or coercive.

In this initial contact the psychiatrist tries to be careful, constrained, and sensitive. For the patient, often frightened and feeling vulnerable, can be readily alienated or aroused. Yet, as crucial as is this moment of encounter, it is never the same with different patients. Each time the psychiatrist must decide how to act, relying on his observations, his intuition, and his experience. His manner and behavior will be the outcome of choice, the first of countless discriminations he will make. These decisions, of which the patient will be unaware, will create a basis for the rapport the psychiatrist hopes to develop. This relationship will form the core of the therapeutic process.

"Hello, I am Dr. Jacobs. Dr. Knapp, who examined you in the emergency room, asked me to see you; I am a psychiatrist."

Slowly, deliberately, Welborn turned his head toward me, shifting his glance from where I had previously stood until it rested once more upon me. "I . . ." His voice faded. He stared, heavy-lidded, his lips still. I searched for some sign of his mood. Was he depressed? His face was without expression.

"I . . ." he began, and faltered again. Now he turned away and sighed wearily. I had the impression of a man struggling within himself, fighting, perhaps, to remain aloof and apart, yet knowing already that his efforts must fail. I waited. The outlines of a mental status examination formed in my mind: appearance, behavior, attitude, level of consciousness, affect, mood, thought processes and content, memory, knowledge, insight, and judgment.

"I'm sorry," he managed at last, turning to face me again, accepting that I would not leave.

"I understand that you were at the railroad station here this morning," I said. "Do you know what town this is?" Slowly he shook his head, uninterested. "This is Brentwood," I explained. "What is your name?" Again he hesitated, but remained silent. "Do you know where you are right now?" I gestured at our surroundings.

"This is a hospital," he answered resignedly, sighing once more.

"Do you recall the police bringing you here earlier, this morning?"

"Yes, I remember."

"That was about nine-twenty-five, I was told. Do you know what time it is now?" I asked.

He started to shake his head incuriously, paused, then raised his left wrist and read, "One-o-five," from his wristwatch. He was right-handed. His responses, though delayed somewhat, were better than I had been led to expect. Perhaps he was brightening.

"Can you tell me, if you arrived at nine-twenty or thereabouts, how long you have been here?"

"About three and a half hours," he answered. His eyes now scanned my face as if judging, appraising me. Was there a plea to be left alone and unaccountable in his glance? I had no choice but to persist.

"You must have seemed ill for the police to have brought you here to the hospital. Yet Dr. Knapp reports that you appear to be well. He found nothing to suggest that you had been injured in an accident, struck your head, or had a seizure."

It was as if my words were traveling across a great distance to reach him. He continued to gaze at me; then, slowly, as if he found my persistence wearing, he shook his head. "I am not ill," he murmured.

"What is your name? Where are you from?" I asked. He lowered his eyes and said nothing.

"Your identification indicates that you are Douglas Welborn of North Hill Drive in Millway," I volunteered.

Upon hearing his name, Welborn seemed to wince. He closed his eyes. When they opened once more, he stared straight ahead of him at the blank wall as though he were peering through and beyond it into infinity. He is trying to shut me out, to escape again, I thought. I'd learned at least that he was oriented to time and his immediate circumstances. I also had reason, from his reaction to his identification, to believe that he knew full well who he was but did not wish to acknowledge his name for some reason. Perhaps he does not want to resume being Douglas Welborn, I speculated. Maybe he is trying to abandon that identity. Why? I wondered uneasily.

Though my contact with him had become even more tenuous than before, I felt urgently that I must continue to prevent Welborn from withdrawing or he might become lost. I sensed that he was at some unseen frontier, wavering, trying not to look back. I was determined to arrest his flight, to stop him if I could. Whatever he was fleeing from, exile into mindlessness would afford him no asylum. It would have its own terrors.

I glanced past Welborn, across the room. A dark-gray fall suit, blue shirt, and striped rep tie hung inside the open locker behind him. "Please get dressed, Mr. Welborn," I urged, deciding to restore him to his normal attire and dignity.

He did not appear to have heard me at first. I reached out deliberately and gripped his shoulder gently to make contact. "Please get dressed," I repeated. Welborn turned to follow my gaze, then stared at me unbelievingly. I rose to stand before him, waiting. Slowly, heavily, he stood. Then he shuffled in his paper slippers around the bed to the locker. I left him laying his clothes out on the bed and went out into the corridor. Getting him up and into his own clothes once more would be a step back from the abyss that seemed to confront him, I hoped. I walked down the hall to the nurses' station.

"Is it amnesia?" Ms. Nieder asked.

"I'm not certain what is wrong," I confessed. "I have the impression, however, that Mr. Welborn hasn't really lost his memory. If his problem is entirely psychological, it may be that he is trying to lose it. In any event, something very wrong is disturbing him." I picked up Welborn's chart and reviewed the admission note and summary of his examination. "There was no evidence of drugs or an alcoholic hangover, was there? No hint of a seizure? Tongue bitten, trousers wet?" I asked.

Ms. Nieder shook her head. "No, there wasn't a hair out of place. He just seemed sort of fuzzy up here." She pointed to her temple. "They found an attaché case that belonged to him on the platform. He is an investment broker with the firm of Kahlbrunn and Macefield." She flipped through her cardex. "He is forty-three and married. We called his wife, but so far no one has been home. Do you think we should call his office?"

"No, no, I don't think that would help right now. His wife can handle that later. Please give her my name and my office number when you do reach her," I said.

"He's really out of it, isn't he?" she asked sympathetically. "I mean, he doesn't answer when you ask him simple things, especially about himself. Trying to lose his memory, huh? You think he could be running away from something he's done? Faking?" I shook my head. "But we did have to look in his wallet to find out who he was," she said worriedly.

I reassured her and rechecked the report of Welborn's neurological examination. It was thorough. Except for his mental state, Welborn had no neurological impairment. A preliminary reading of his skull films was also negative. Urinalysis and blood tests were under way. I guessed that they too would be normal. "Is the conference room free? I want to take Mr. Welborn in there to talk," I said. Ms. Nieder nodded, curious. "It is less hospitallike," I explained, and started back to 311.

Along the way I tried to organize an impression of the problem. A middle-aged man in apparent good health, appropriately dressed for work, is found standing idly on a railroad station platform after the commuter rush has subsided. When questioned, he seems to be abnormally dull and unresponsive. He appears to be unable to furnish any information about his identity, looks bewildered, and is brought here to the hospital. Initial examinations fail to reveal illness, evidence of intoxication or head injury. There are no signs of brain dysfunction except for his clouded mental state.

Despite my suspicions of a psychological disturbance, a host of organic, or physical, causes had to be ruled out. These ranged from relatively common conditions to unusual ones. Among them were abnormalities in blood sugar levels, to which the brain is extremely sensitive, and irregularities in the vital circulation of the brain, such as occur transiently in various forms of migraine disorders or in cases of circulatory insufficiency because of low blood pressure or an obstructed vessel. Increased fluid pressure within the brain, tumors, and viruses with a special affinity for the cells of the brain could affect an individual this way. Certain inherited diseases may first appear in middle life, and there are types of epilepsy that produce no apparent convulsion but leave their victim dazed, temporarily disorganized, and unable to remember. Various poisons, psychedelic chemicals, and even common medications, to which a particular individual may react atypically, can have similar effects. The list of possible causes was long.

A clinical puzzle like this could take considerable time to solve. Repeated examinations, extensive laboratory studies, and special tests might be required: electroencephalography to detect abnormalities in the brain's electrical pattern; brain scan, with radioactive isotopes, or an echogram, using ultrasound waves, to reveal unusual densities or masses; spinal fluid analysis and culture; and special computer-assisted X-ray techniques to produce series of films resembling cross sections or slices of the brain.

All this might be unnecessary, however, if I could establish that Welborn's problem was psychological, not physical, in nature. The absence of pathological evidence pointing elsewhere, while suggestive, was anything but conclusive. The burden of investigating the riddle of Douglas Welborn, at this point, rested with me.

I opened the door to 311 to find Welborn dressed and seated. He rose stiffly as soon as I entered to summon him. His reaction, I noted, was fairly brisk. I explained that we would go to another room to talk. "You'll want to take that with you," I said, pointing to the scuffed brown leather case on the broad windowsill.

He turned to stare at the attache case, then took it up and followed me down the hall past a watchful Ms. Nieder. The conference room was a large, square, windowless chamber with a long table and chairs in its center, a gray metal desk strewn with notes and journals to one side, and vinyl-covered sofas and lounge chairs around its walls. I chose a corner, and we sat down.

Before me now was a neat, conservatively well-dressed man who looked quite ordinary except for the somewhat preoccupied expression on his face. When I had observed him earlier, sitting immobile in his room, inelegant with his long, thin legs protruding from the coarse, wrinkled hospital gown, he had seemed unique and out of his element. Dressed in his own tailored clothes, however, he looked anonymous in an entirely different way. He bore the almost uniform appearance characteristic of many aging alumni of Exeter, Choate, Dartmouth, Yale, or Princeton. I wondered whether my tactic of having had him dress would succeed in jogging his associations and restoring some link to his accustomed role or merely impel him to retreat even further.

We sat in silence. I would not hurry him now. Welborn stared at the floor. I have seen other men sit this way, eyes unblinking, barely breathing, in wooden postures like human statues. They line the halls of mental hospitals, languishing there for years, for lifetimes. As a medical student I had performed physical examinations on these wasted souls. I remember wondering who these people were or had been, what they thought, and whether thinking, as I understood it, had long ago ceased behind their empty faces. Welborn reminded me of them. He too was a mystery, a cipher, unknown. He lacked merely the burned-out, vacant look that comes only with time. I resolved to prevent that.

What could account for his desire to erase from memory his own identity? I thought about the various psychological syndromes that could afflict Welborn. There are many ways for an individual who has become undone to manifest this. One usually finds features of his breakdown commingled with elements of attempted repair and restitution.

In hysterical amnesias, the victim's dramatic and obvious disability floats like a buoy marking the site over his real concern, which has sunk beneath his awareness. The patient has repressed his problem; as a result, he is restored to ease and is unperturbed. The hysteric may display little impairment apart from his symptom. He tends to be alert and responsive. He may even enjoy a measure of gratification from the attention he receives and show it. Welborn did not appear to be suffering from hysteria. I sensed in him something different, a more profound retreat, a more intense striving to withdraw, to escape somewhere deep within himself.

Welborn pursed his brow. His gaze shifted. I wondered what his thoughts were and where they led. Was he one of those people who find themselves in unbearable situations without hope, who become estranged from their persons and environments? By disassociating himself psychologically from whatever has been so intolerable, such an individual endeavors to achieve peace. While this process of detachment is purposeful, however, it is not practiced deliberately or consciously as a form of meditation or self-hypnosis; it is unconscious. The resultant state may superficially resemble amnesia, but the victim has not really lost his memory. He has instead withdrawn his attention and his emotional attachment from the untoward circumstances of his life. His existence itself may seem remote and unreal to him.

The sufferer of such a dissociative reaction is usually frightened by the strange alienation that is occurring to him. He fears he is losing his mind and may be reticent about revealing this. Indeed, he is often a borderline case, sharing in his depersonalized and alienated condition symptoms common to schizophrenia. Here the break away from reality is more severe; memory may be denied or so distorted as to be inaccessible. Though the onset of schizophrenia generally occurs before middle age and is usually more insidious than seemed to be the case here, in the absence of a history, I could not exclude it. It was possible that Welborn's difficulty was a recurrence of a preexisting problem.

As it does in other branches of medicine, diagnosis affects the techniques of treatment in psychiatry. Here, however, the nature of the rapport developed between patient and physician is paramount; it will determine success or failure in psychotherapy. I had to find a means of inducing Welborn to relate.

He lifted his somber grayish eyes and discovered me. "You seem very unhappy," I began, and regretted it immediately. It was a slip. Now, having taken a cue from my remark, he looked downcast. Inwardly I cursed my blunder; it was an expression of empathy, a natural enough effort to relate, but presumptuous and unpsychiatric. It denied him the chance to tell me.

Welborn said nothing. I waited, allowing time and the silence to dilute my error. The muted sounds of the public address system echoed in the corridor outside: "Dr. Redding . . . Dr. Redding, to the O-R. . . ."

I began once more. "Do you remember getting off the train this morning, Mr. Welborn?" There was no response. "Did you have business here in Brentwood? Were you to meet someone?" His lips remained still. Now, however, he scrutinized my face. Very deliberately I repeated my questions. Perhaps his thought processes were sluggish.

"No," he answered in a low voice. "No, I just wanted to get off. . . . I don't know anyone in Brentwood."

"Were you feeling ill?" I asked, encouraged. Welborn slowly shook his head. "Did you believe you were in any danger?"

"No," he murmured.

"Were you upset about something then? Did you feel that you couldn't go on any farther, was that it?"

Welborn hesitated enigmatically. He arched his brows; his face drained of color and seemed strained and desperate. His breath came in quick, deep, audible drafts. He was becoming agitated. After some moments a rasping sound emerged from his throat, but words didn't come. He tilted his head back and shook it as if to say, "Enough! I don't wish to hear any more!"

I considered what to do. Should I heed his warning and subside, or continue in spite of it? My natural impulse was to respect his wishes and withdraw. It seemed insensitive to pursue and harass someone who presumably was tormented already. It was also dangerous. Persons who are distraught and feel they are being oppressed can become violent. They are not to be harried without peril. One must carefully weigh the risk of arousing them.

I peered at Welborn, trying to read the expression in his

eyes. He gazed back, unflinching, revealing nothing. As we looked at one another, a slight quiver passed through his cheeks; his lips remained sealed. It seemed to me that he was straining to maintain his outside composure, while something gnawed cruelly at his innards. I decided to press ahead. The chance to ease his ordeal and abort his flight from life was worth the risk of antagonizing him. Alienation is a great price to pay for peace. It can mean a long and treacherous exile.

"So you decided to stop here in Brentwood—anywhere. You could not continue. You would not endure even one more day as things were, is that it?" I probed.

Welborn gave me a sharp, fierce look. He seemed to find my temerity incredible. Then his control disintegrated. All at once, with an abruptness that startled me, he heaved himself up out of his chair. He stood over me panting, seething, his fists raised menacingly.

I tried to keep my voice even and calm in spite of the constriction I felt in my throat. "There is no solution in what you are doing. Running away or retreating into yourself won't help you. Even if you were to succeed in hibernating for a time, it would likely only create a new set of problems. You know I am trying to help you. Why don't you sit down again and tell me what is wrong? There may be other answers."

Welborn stood there glowering down at me. I made no effort to move. Then his tense, grim face eased. He moaned and threw his hands up over his face and kneaded his forehead. After a moment he twisted around and collapsed into his seat once more. I looked at his crumpled form, bent forward, leaning on his knees. His large frame rocked slowly back and forth, then was still. Color flowed back into his face. He straightened. "I'm sorry. . . . I wasn't thinking. . . . I—I'm sorry," he said, his voice catching. He began to sob softly.

I let myself breathe more easily. My neck ached dully. I settled back in my seat and tried to relax. There was no triumph in seeing Welborn crumble, nor was there comfort in my relief.

I had intruded upon his sanctuary and evicted him. Now I had to watch while he wept, perhaps remembering things, feeling pain.

It is difficult to witness another person suffer, worse to know that he is aware you are watching. Yet I made no gesture to console him. I sat there silently, observing, waiting. Until the reasons for his reaction were clear, sympathy would be out of keeping. If guilt were part of his problem, any demonstration of compassion before he confessed might well persuade him that I was incapable of understanding the depths of his remorse. If shame were his undoing, pity, in effect, would only intensify his sense of failure and inadequacy.

"You're right," he said, sobbing, his face tracked with tears he made no effort to wipe away. "I couldn't go in again. . . . I've thought about getting off that train and disappearing many times. Then today . . . I couldn't go in. I had to get off!" Welborn drew out a handkerchief, mopped his face, and blew his nose. "What happens now?" he asked, as if his fate were suddenly my responsibility.

"That rather depends on what is wrong and what can be done about it," I answered.

"No . . . no." He shook his head. "There's nothing wrong. It's not that kind of problem. What's wrong is me! Do you understand, it's me! I'm what's wrong. Oh, God, there is no answer, is there, Doctor?"

"We'll see, Mr. Welborn, we'll see. You seem to feel that you are in some terrible difficulty which I know nothing about yet. Explain it to me."

"I can't," he replied. "It's too much. It would take too long."

I made no comment. Troubled as he was, Welborn was already testing my interest. I marveled at how quickly his mind was reintegrating. He functions effectively enough to attempt subtle manipulations, I observed. Good. But I must be careful not to compromise my role by offering too much. Let him exercise his judgment further and take a more direct initiative in seeking my help now that the circuit between us is connected. Whatever responsibility I can get him to assume toward his treatment from the outset will eventually make it that much easier for him to reassert his independence later.

Welborn blew his nose again and cleared his throat. "You are a psychiatrist, aren't you?" he asked. I reminded him that I was. "Do you think you can help me?" he asked meekly.

"If you feel that you can confide in me and discuss your feelings and concerns openly, I am willing to try, Mr. Welborn."

"Yes. . . . I know I need some help. I've been getting these . . . I guess you could call them spells. Things begin to seem less and less real, as if I'm not really there . . . as if I'm an observer, apart. I feel as if I'm watching myself, but I am really not part of what's happening."

"How long has this been going on?" I asked.

"For a month or so, ever since I came back to work after my vacation in August. The first day there was a meeting, and I found it hard to maintain my interest in the discussion. My mind kept wandering. It wasn't as if I were bored either; we were planning an underwriting, and it was to be my responsibility. I remember thinking that something strange was happening. As I looked around the table, something like the one over there, it seemed as if I were dreaming or in a kind of fog. I looked at everyone there; in fact, I stared at all of them, watching their faces, their mouths moving, their expressions. I became fascinated by their eyes, their wrinkles, even their warts. Then I felt distant as if I were almost observing them through the wrong end of a telescope. Even my own hands looked far away to me."

"Did anyone else notice you weren't right?"

"No, I don't think so. Someone asked me a question while this was happening, and apparently I answered him all right. But my voice sounded funny to me."

"What happened?"

"Nothing; it passed. I shrugged it off. I hadn't slept well the night before and assigned it to that. I didn't worry about it until it happened again several days later. Since then I have had a number of such episodes. I've been afraid to say anything about them."

Just then we were interrupted by Ms. Nieder, who explained that the radiologist was reviewing Mr. Welborn's skull films and wanted to take additional X-rays.

"We'd best pause and get that out of our way," I said, trying not to alarm Welborn. "We can continue our discussion later this afternoon." We rose and followed the nurse. As we came out into the corridor, Welborn hesitated, then stepped close and extended his hand. I took it and gripped him firmly. "See you around five," I said reassuringly.

I returned to the nurses' station to make some notes. Though our conversation had strengthened my suspicion that Welborn's lapses were psychological in nature, I now wavered. What if the X-rays showed something? I began to review possible organic syndromes again while I searched about for consultation forms.

An attractive woman, late thirties, thin, strands of gray showing through her dark hair, worriedly approached the desk. She hesitated uncertainly, then announced, "I am Cynthia Welborn. I am sorry to disturb you, but the nurse isn't here. I wonder if—"

"The nurse has just taken your husband down to X-ray, Mrs. Welborn. I am Dr. Jacobs. I'm glad you've found him. We tried to reach you earlier."

"The police," she explained. "They were really very kind. There was a patrol car in our driveway when I got home. Meg, our daughter, had a program at school this morning. How is Doug?"

"We're trying to find that out," I said. "So far physical examinations do not reveal anything wrong with him, but we are taking more X-rays."

"Then what happened?" she asked, perplexed. "What is he doing here in Brentwood, at this hospital?"

"I am hoping you can help us with that, Mrs. Welborn. Your husband got off the train here this morning. He seemed confused, dazed, as if he'd had a spell of some sort. Was he entirely well earlier at home, before he left?"

"Why, yes, of course. I mean, well, Doug never has very

much to say in the morning, but he ate his breakfast. He seemed himself, not sick or anything. I've had a pesty cold, haven't been able to play tennis for a week, but Doug's been fine as usual, as far as I know. He always is."

"And he's had no recent accidents, falls, or head injuries?"

"No, none. What on earth are you getting at? A spell, you say? He's never had anything like that, ever. Are you certain, Doctor? Doug was wounded when he was in the Marines many years ago in Korea. But it's never bothered him. He had some shrapnel taken from his back. It wasn't too serious, but it left some horrid scars. I hate to see him in a bathing suit or without a shirt on because of them, but there was no question of head wounds. I am sure of that."

"Has anything happened to disturb him recently?"

"Well, no, just the opposite. Doug was just made a partner in his firm," she answered.

"Did he seem pleased by his promotion?" I asked.

"What a strange thing to ask! Why, yes, of course, we were both delighted." A slight defensiveness had crept into her tone. "Doug hasn't said otherwise, has he?"

"No, not at all. May I offer you a chair?" Mrs. Welborn sat down. "I really know very little about your husband. That is why I am asking you so many questions."

"Well, Doug isn't an easy person to get to know. He's a very quiet man who keeps a great deal inside. Even when it came to this promotion, he didn't show how elated he must have felt. He isn't the sort to get excited about anything. But the partnership means a great deal to us both. It has been a struggle financially with our two oldest in college, our daughter at Miss Warren's, the club, and taxes, of course. I've even considered finding work, but there are no really interesting jobs."

"You have three children?"

"Well, no, actually four. There is Douglas; he is at Bowdoin. Andrew is at the University of Vermont; he's a skier. Hal—he should be talking to someone like you. You are a psychiatrist, aren't you?" I nodded. "Well, that boy has to find himself, that's all. He and his father used to be very close. They'd talk for hours and hours. Then, well, it just stopped. They wouldn't say why, neither one. They just became moody, especially around each other. Then Hal spent some money my aunt had left him to buy a used car, a tiny, dented Toyota, and he left. He said he wanted to travel around for a while and do some thinking. You know what young people are doing today, I'm sure. We have received exactly one card so far, from Billings, Montana. Hal's car needed repairs, so he has found a job working in a laundry to get it fixed. Oh, well," she said, exasperated. "Our youngest is Meg. She's a dear. I spoil her terribly."

"Have there been any problems between you and Mr. Welborn?" I asked.

"Heavens, no, nothing you'd call a problem really. That is, we don't quarrel, if that's what you mean. Sometimes I think it would be better if we did. No, we're happy. Doug has his work. He likes to tinker, garden, and read. I keep myself busy with tennis and Junior League and, oh, yes, my hospital work. I volunteer at Millway Hospital two days a week. . . . You are going to ask about sex, aren't you? We may have a problem there, but you'll have to ask Doug. I mean, well, he doesn't seem to have much drive, frankly. You'd think a big, healthy man, an ex-marine, a football player would, well, you know. . . . But, it doesn't bother me really, not anymore. You don't smoke, do you, Dr. . . . Dr. Jacobson?"

"Jacobs," I corrected. "No, I'm not a smoker anymore."

"Dr. Jacobs," she repeated. "I am terrible with names. I must have left my cigarettes in the station wagon, darn it!" Mrs. Welborn reached across the nurses' desk, picked up a package of cigarettes, noted the brand, and put it back with a disapproving scowl. Her brazenness surprised me.

"I was telling you about Doug," she went on. "There's nothing really to say. Until today he has seemed perfectly normal, normal for him. I guess he is content; he doesn't show his feelings. Sometimes I wonder if he has any." A hint of resentment had surfaced. "Last Wednesday Gladys Wade called to congratulate me on Doug's becoming a partner. Her husband, George, was in Doug's class at Harvard, but George has been a partner three years already. Well, I thought she was pulling my leg; she would be one to do that. I didn't know what to think, what to say. Gladys finally convinced me it was so. They had told Doug Tuesday morning, the day before, after the monthly meeting. I was furious."

"He hadn't told you?"

"He didn't even tell me when he got home Wednesday evening, not until I told him Gladys had called. God, I wish I had my cigarettes."

"Had your husband intended to surprise you with his secret?"

"Surprise me? You really don't know Doug! He hasn't surprised me ever, until this afternoon, when they told me he was here. No, he said the promotion wouldn't make any difference until November, so he hadn't thought to mention it."

Mrs. Welborn was restless now. "Tell me," I asked, "does your husband drink to any extent or—"

"Doug has no vices, Doctor. I have a couple of manhattans while waiting for him, before dinner, but he rarely drinks. He doesn't smoke either. I wonder if there is a cigarette machine downstairs anywhere. Let me tell you something about my husband. My parents have a perfectly gorgeous home on Martha's Vineyard which we are free to use in August. Doug won't stay there. He came only on weekends even though he was on vacation. Said the drought would kill his precious garden if he didn't stay home and water it. Daddy couldn't get over it. 'Doug,' he teased, 'it's indecent to move your mistress right on in the moment your family's gone. Find her a place of her own!' Mother didn't think it was funny, but I thought it was a howl. Doug being that way about sex, you know. So did my friends. . . . You don't suppose I could just run down to the parking lot for a minute, do you, Doctor?"

I glanced up at the wall clock. "It is almost two, I'll have to leave in a moment. There is nothing else you've noticed?"

"Well, no. . . . He's not crazy, is he, Doctor? I mean you just told me he'd had some sort of spell or something. But he is all right now, isn't he?"

"He is much better. I didn't mean to alarm you. Until we have reason to suspect something else, I think this disturbance is an emotional reaction, the result, perhaps, of some strain or conflict he's been wrestling with for a while. When I get back here about five, I'll spend more time with him. We may have all the tests and X-ray results by then also."

"Around five, you say. Oh, dear, I was hoping to take him home with me—if he is all right, of course. Meg is in a show at school, you see. It isn't a lead, but she has a good part. I've been there with her every night for the last two weeks. I'm responsible for costumes and props. Let me tell you, there is a lot to do. With eighteen teenage girls to organize, I have my hands full. But I love it. I was wild about the stage when I was that age. I was gorgeous, too. I had a bust and a figure when I was fourteen, but poor Meg is still a stick. Oh, well, at least she'll acquire poise and more confidence with a good role. Maybe she'll get a lead next year. Anyway, it takes about forty minutes to get down here. That's eighty, both ways, and with dinner . . . maybe I can ask a friend. . . ."

"I'll call you, if you wish, Mrs. Welborn," I offered.

"Well, that won't help, will it? Oh, I am sorry. That's very kind of you . . . Dr. Jacobs. It's 555-3316, and thank you."

I jotted down the number and quickly wrote a note to Ms. Nieder explaining that I had to leave but would return at five, when my office hours were over. Then I showed Mrs. Welborn where Room 311 was and left her dashing down to the parking lot for her cigarettes.

At ten minutes to four, while I was showing a patient out, my phone began to buzz.

"Dr. Jacobs? Is it all right now? Your service said you would be able to talk at ten minutes to the hour. I wanted to catch you before I go off duty. This is Joanne Nieder, on three north."

"Yes, Ms. Nieder, I recognized your voice. How is Mr. Welborn? Did his wife see him?"

"That's what I want to tell you about. After you saw him, he was a lot better, remember? I took him down to X-ray. His films were all negative, by the way. So were the other tests so far. We had to wait around after they took him to see if they would want more films. It was almost an hour before they let us go. I want you to know that all during that time Mr. Welborn was fine! We got to talking. He told me about his wife and kids. He asked about you and how I liked being a nurse and working in a hospital. He seemed genuinely interested, and I talked a lot, maybe too much; I guess I was nervous. Anyway, we got along well. He listened as if he cared. He was really all right; I mean, completely normal, you know? Then we came back to three north, found your note, and went to his room, where his wife was waiting."

"Yes," I interjected. "She came after you'd left. I told her she could wait there."

"Well," she went on, "you never saw such a change. One moment we were walking along talking and he was smiling and all. Then the next, in his room, it was like he suddenly had turned to wood. I mean, he took one look at his wife and went numb. Mrs. Welborn got all shook up. She smiled and tried to cover by being friendly and chatty. She even kissed him. But he just stood there, staring right through her, looking sort of blank and shut down. I didn't know whether to stay there with them or not. I could see she was embarrassed, though, so I left them alone. Mrs. Welborn stayed only about fifteen minutes. She came out to the desk and asked me for your phone number and then left right away. I could tell she was upset. Who wouldn't be? I've checked in on him since then. He's just sitting in there again, the way he was this morning before you saw him."

"Have you tried to approach him?"

"No, I felt it best to leave him alone to sort things out again."

"Fine, you used good judgment. You're been a great help to me, Ms. Nieder."

"Thank you," she said, sounding a little embarrassed. "Incidentally, I've ordered supper, a regular diet, for him. I didn't think you'd be sending him home the way things are."

I couldn't help smiling at that. She was expressing her judgment as delicately as she could. It demonstrated her interest in

Welborn, and I was pleased. Before his wife's visit with him, I had held some hope that if everything else was normal, I might gain a sufficient grasp of what troubled Welborn to discharge him, reassured and improved, to his family that evening. If that had been feasible, I would have asked a colleague up his way to see him tomorrow.

In some acute cases, not permitting the patient to retreat too far from his normal circumstances is advantageous. Treating the disturbed person in his usual surroundings keeps his problems in the foreground. It avoids the further erosion of the patient's self-confidence that so often accompanies hospitalization. Nieder's report of the interaction between Welborn and his wife discouraged this strategy. Had they related in a close, supportive manner, my plan would have received a boost. As it was, and in view of his evident setback, his retention in the hospital seemed likely.

"Thank you for planning ahead, Ms. Nieder. Let's proceed as if Mr. Welborn will be staying. If it is all right with Dr. Knapp, put my name on his chart and admit him with the diagnosis *Depersonalization Neurosis*. Also, though we have no indication so far of suicidal thoughts or intentions, and there may be none, it would be wise, until we know more, to take some precautions. Place Mr. Welborn on frequent observations; leave his door open, and tell the staff to look in on him unobtrusively. They can forgo taking his pulse, blood pressure, and temperature for the present."

"I'll see to it, Doctor. Do you think he'll come out of it again and be all right?"

"I trust so, Ms. Nieder, but then I am a therapeutic optimist. Seriously, not every disturbed person becomes a psychiatric patient. Not everyone in difficulty has the will or the incentive to undertake psychotherapy. Welborn, however, was beginning to come around; our job will be to interest and encourage him to become a patient again."

At five minutes to five Mrs. Welborn called. "Dr. Jacobs, I tried to call you all afternoon. They told me you only pick up at ten minutes to the hour, but your line is always busy then."

"I am afraid there were some calls. I am sorry you had difficulty, Mrs. Welborn."

"Well, something is terribly wrong with Doug!" she said, unappeased. "I was really shocked, let me tell you. I thought you told me he was better from that, what did you call it, a spell? But he isn't himself! You haven't given him some drug, a tranquilizer or something like that, have you? I just don't understand!"

"No, your husband has received nothing. He had shown considerable improvement since coming to the hospital, but apparently he has slipped back again," I explained.

"Well, then, perhaps you should have given him something. He's not right, I tell you!"

"Mrs. Welborn, your husband is being observed, and I will see him again in a few minutes. I understand how alarmed and concerned you are. Please rest assured we'll all do everything we can to help him. Did you talk when you were together earlier?"

"Well, no, you can't talk to someone who won't even acknowledge that you are there, can you? He's in a world of his own. Doug's having a breakdown, isn't he?"

"In the sense that he is unable to carry on in his usual way, yes."

"Dear God!"

"Please don't let your imagination panic you, Mrs. Welborn. This afternoon, before you came, your husband was quite coherent and was beginning to discuss his condition with me. I hope to learn more from him in a little while. I can report, however, that our workup, so far, indicates that he is not physically ill. Still, it would be wise to ask your family doctor to call me anyway."

"I'll do that," she promised, "and Daddy will probably call you, too."

"Mrs. Welborn, I am going over to the hospital to see your husband now. Unless he objects, I think it best that we plan on his staying there for a few days until things are clearer."

"You don't think he will refuse, do you?" she asked worriedly. "I mean, well, I've never seen him behave so strangely before. There's only Meg and me at home. I mean, I just wouldn't know what to do. . . ."

"We'll see if we can make him comfortable here. I know it is a distance for you, but it would be a good idea to get his own pajamas, his robe, some casual clothes, and his toilet kit down to the hospital for him. Does he have an electric razor?"

"Yes. . . . Oh, you don't think he'd hurt himself, do you?"

"It's just safer until we know better, isn't it?" I said.

I found Welborn sitting as before, but this time he looked up at me when I entered.

"Look, Doctor, I am undoubtedly keeping you from going home to your dinner. I am really much better now. I guess I was just overtired after all." He smiled almost convincingly. "A good night's sleep and I will be fine, I'm sure. I want to thank you for having been so kind." He rose to his feet and extended his hand.

It was all very polite and well done; I was being dismissed. Unease stirred within me. I made another decision. I nodded, acknowledging his words, but instead of taking his hand, I sat down. I had no intention of leaving. Welborn sat too. I drew my chair closer to him.

If Welborn's life was in some way unbearable before, what had changed? Nothing. The worry that I might have blocked his withdrawal and denied him his only alternative to suicide nagged at me. When a deeply troubled person suddenly claims to feel good and asserts he no longer needs help, and there has been no evident resolution of his problems, it is not a good sign. The sufferer, believing there are no answers to his dilemma, may have decided to end it all. This often brings immediate relief in anticipation of a surcease to his misery. Though he may feign and exaggerate its degree to an extent, the sense of well-being he experiences is genuine. This is why oftentimes others concerned about the individual are tragically misled into relaxing their vigilance.

I found myself committed to the unaccustomed role of imposing myself upon a reluctant patient again. This time, however, it was not my safety that was at risk; it was Welborn's life that might be in jeopardy.

"Your problems have not blown over, Mr. Welborn. I think you are merely in the calm eye of the storm right now. How long have you considered killing yourself to be a solution?"

Laymen and lay physicians often skirt this issue. They fear that by asking about suicide, they may be planting the idea in the patient's mind. Suicide, however, is not communicable, not by direct, concerned, open discussion. Desperate people are usually relieved when the question is asked because, if nothing else, it conveys a capacity on the part of others to appreciate the depth of their despair.

Welborn's facade dissolved. He shook and wept openly again. "I just can't take it anymore," he cried. "I've tried to stand it, believe me, longer than anyone knows. It isn't fair to my family. They don't need me on their necks, not this way, not the way I've been. Cynthia, all of them, would be better off without me. I'm dead already anyway. I have no desires any longer. I don't enjoy my life, and I'm ruining theirs. Cynthia is too good a person. She doesn't deserve this. She tries hard, inviting people, making parties, but I've been nothing but an albatross. Cynthia's put up with a lot. I fail her miserably. I fail them all."

I waited for him to finish unburdening himself. It would have been usual procedure to examine his statements painstakingly. Instead, I had an idea that I could forge ahead more quickly with a different approach. "Your wife told me something happened between you and Hal. Why did he leave home? Did Hal feel you had failed him?"

Welborn looked at me, surprised. My questions had caught him off guard. "Yes . . . no . . . it was different with him," he said, taken aback. "Do you know about Hal? What has Cynthia told you?"

"Only that she thought you and he had a falling-out before he decided to go. Tell me about it."

"Hal and I were close. Closer, I mean, than most fathers get with their sons. Maybe because he was the same kind of sensitive, oddball kid I had been. Maybe because he wasn't outgoing and self-assured like his brothers. I'm not sure what it was, but I felt I knew him best. He was always too concerned with what life was all about to accept things as they were, the way his brothers did, the way I've learned to do. We never had to say too much to understand each other's thoughts and moods—at least I thought so." Welborn shook his head in a discouraged, troubled way.

"It all changed, you see, when he graduated from high school last June. Hal had attended Millway High, though his mother would have preferred to see him at Prescott, where our other two had boarded. My father-in-law is an alumnus and a trustee of Prescott. Cynthia and I had a small row about it at the time, but she relented. Hal actually did quite well at Millway. His grades were better than his brothers'. So it seemed as if we'd made the right decision.

"Hal applied and was accepted at Bradford for admission to the freshman class this fall. We were proud of him, as it's an excellent college, difficult to get into. But during the summer Hal changed his plans and wrote to them requesting a year's postponement. We were surprised, but he explained that he didn't feel ready to go on with his education. He said he needed a year to mature, to come to some decisions about his direction. Bradford turned his request down. Perhaps it was too late already. We expected Hal to accept the situation and go along with it. That's where we were wrong.

"Hal withdrew from the entering class. He said he knew what he was doing, that he'd made up his mind to take some time and learn more about the world and where he fitted into it. It was strange. Hal said things I'd thought about many times and never openly expressed. I realized that somehow I had influenced him. Cynthia thought so, too, and blamed me. Naturally, she was very disturbed to see Hal throw away his opportunity. I know she also feared her father would have fits. He did."

"How did you feel about all this?" I asked.

"Well, at first, I confess that I supported Hal. He seemed to know his mind, and he is a responsible fellow. But then I was affected by how upset Cynthia had become. She was miserable with worry that Hal was keeping the truth from us. She feared something was seriously wrong with him. I know she searched his room for marijuana and drugs more than once, though I believe that he never used them. Hal didn't have a girlfriend just then. He hadn't taken anyone to his prom in June. Cynthia got this foolish notion that he might be homosexual. Finally, she made him see a psychiatrist. He said that Hal was maturing and trying to figure out his identity, that his desire to grow up before making important decisions that would affect his life for years to come was legitimate."

"Didn't you feel reassured by his opinion?" I asked.

"Yes, but Cynthia was unnerved. She felt that the psychiatrist was completely taken in. She took it all as a personal attack on her. I should explain that my wife is the youngest of three sisters. Her mother died when she was six, and she had a difficult time of it. Her father remarried, and she has two half sisters of whom she is jealous. She is, however, close to her father, and he has given her some money from time to time. There is also a small trust for our children's education to which he contributes. It is all very important to Cynthia."

"She felt Hal's actions put these ties to her father in jeopardy?" I asked.

"Exactly. Cynthia was obsessed about disappointing her father. She began to come apart. She drinks a little anyway, and well, things got quite bad. We couldn't sit down to dinner without something being said and an argument occurring. She accused Hal of hating her and of tearing the family asunder. She felt that I had influenced him and that I didn't care that this was destroying her happiness. It was hell."

"It sounds unpleasant," I agreed. "What did you do?"

"I tried to reason with Hal, to show him what he was doing. I tried to persuade him to change his mind, to reconsider and enter Bradford. I argued with him that he would grow up soon enough away from home at college. I reminded Hal that I had supported him in refusing boarding school and that he owed me this favor."

"He didn't accept that, apparently," I said.

"No, he exploded . . . said some things he must have been keeping inside him all along. . . . Then we couldn't talk to one another afterward."

"He felt you had failed him?" I asked again.

"Hal called me a Judas, a hypocrite, and a lot worse. He said I lacked the guts to admit that I'd sold myself out, that I hated the kind of life I had, that I had become a—" Welborn choked on the words—"a . . . drone!" He broke down once more, sobbing. "He said . . . that . . . my wife didn't love me or even respect me . . . I was a fool . . . that I didn't face things as they really are . . . that I had no right to . . . to pretend to know anything about life."

"That's pretty rough talk," I said solicitously.

"But what he said may be true! I don't know anymore. It's been tearing me apart for months."

"We can try to find out if you wish."

"I guess I've got to try. Will you help me? I feel I can talk to you, Doctor."

"I will do all I can to help on the condition that you renounce any thought or plan to harm yourself. I want to feel, in working with you, that I am free not to pull any punches for fear of your doing something self-destructive."

"I accept, and thank you," he said.

I got to my feet and extended my hand. Welborn rose, and we shook on it.

"I feel better now, really," he said.

"Good." I smiled. "I'll be back at eleven tomorrow morning. The nurse will have something to help you sleep tonight. I suggest you take it. Good night, Mr. Welborn."

"Good night, Doctor."

It was almost seven when I left the hospital, tired, hungry, and satisfied. A fragile alliance had been born.

The next morning was sunny and cloudless. The hills beyond the hospital were mounds of orange, yellow, and red. I walked along the path that leads to the entrance, delighting in the lingering beauty and warmth, aware that it would not last.

Welborn was dressed in a sports shirt and corduroy slacks when I greeted him at a few minutes past eleven. I had stopped first to check his chart. All the initial tests and X-ray reports were now posted and were negative. The nurses' notes recorded one gentleman visitor the previous evening and a restful night.

"I called Cynthia last evening, Doctor. I took a chance that she might be at home—lately she has been helping out with a play at our daughter's school. I was glad I called. Cynthia was home; she had been drinking and was quite overwrought. She cried and kept repeating that I didn't love her, though I told her I did, that I was all right now, and I just had a bad case of nerves from taking on too much responsibility at the office. She wasn't too coherent, but I tried to calm her. I assured her that all I needed was some rest here and your good help to be fine again. After I soothed her for a while, she did manage to collect herself, but I'm not certain I convinced her. I hope my father-in-law succeeds. Mr. Ball brought me some of my things last night, and we also had a brief chat. Has he called you?"

"No, not yet," I said.

"That's strange. He asked me what was wrong, and I suggested he speak with you. I did say that I haven't felt good for months and had fears that I was heading for a breakdown all along. I told him how fortunate it was that when my nerves finally did give out, I was brought here because I have confidence in you. I explained that you were already helping me sort things out and that I wanted the opportunity to rethink my life and my goals. . . . Well, how do we begin?"

"Perhaps, Mr. Welborn, you might start telling me your history," I suggested.

"I was born in a small town not far from the Canadian border . . ." he began.

Welborn was the second of three siblings, of whom only he and a sister, seven years younger, were living. An older brother had died of pneumonia when Douglas was two. Welborn's parents were also deceased. His mother had been an aspiring, ambitious woman whose constant prodding to improve had quickened her husband's and her surviving son's resolve to better themselves. His father was a sedentary man by nature, a scholar and a teacher. He might well have contented himself reading the classics and eking out a paltry living, but for his wife's nagging. It was she who urged him to leave the public schools and to take a position at Renshaw, an exclusive private school. There, eventually, he became headmaster.

Young Welborn's childhood was overshadowed by his brother's death and his mother's grief. The patient's earliest memories were of being alone, eating berries between boulders in a crevice he called his secret place. He played at times with the few farmers' children his own age, but his mother disapproved. When the Welborns took up residence at Renshaw, his life changed abruptly. By then his sister had been born. When his mother was not occupied with her, she drilled Douglas on how to speak and behave, refining him, teaching him gentlemanly ways. In time he attended Renshaw, where he was well accepted by the other students. This, in fact, caused certain strains.

"You see," he explained, "I was there only because of my father. Everyone else at school was wealthy. So when it came to holidays or vacations—well, off they would go to Switzerland with their families to ski. I'd be invited along, but we couldn't afford that kind of luxury on my father's income. It was awkward. My mother would inquire what my friends were doing and ask where they were going. When I told her and she learned that I had been invited along, she'd be delighted. She and my father would argue about the expense, but in the end she would always win, and somehow they would scrape enough together to buy me some clothes and send me."

Welborn paused. He moistened his lips. When he spoke again, his voice was low and plaintive; his words were measured. "I wanted those trips. God, I know I did, even though they had to scrimp and dip into their savings. I should have refused to go or gone out and gotten a job to repay them, but I was too spineless. Besides, my mother encouraged it; she kept insisting that it was important to my future to have the right kinds of friends and experiences. My future . . . I can still hear her lectures. And

I remember my father's eyes and how difficult it became for me to face him," he said, tremulous now. Welborn struggled to keep from breaking down. "I tried hard to succeed . . . really . . . not to disappoint him," he managed in a choked whisper.

"You felt you had to justify their sacrifices," I said. Welborn nodded. "Did your excursions turn out well?" I asked.

"Yes . . . and no," he answered, recovering. "You see, I was in a funny position. No one ever said anything to embarrass me; to the contrary, they did everything to make me feel welcome and comfortable. People were very generous to me. But I could never offer anything in return. My friends were able to exchange visits and favors, but I was always a guest. They spoke so casually and naturally about what they had or expected, from the finest tennis rackets to sports cars, that I was always conscious of the difference between us."

"Did you confide this also to your parents?"

Welborn swallowed. "At times, I did, Doctor. My mother was terribly eager to hear about my experiences, and sometimes I was too frank. The result often was that she would arrange to get me an expensive tennis racket or some costly skis so I wouldn't have to borrow them and feel uneasy. Her rewards came when I'd tell her that I'd been introduced to a senator or that I'd crewed with the governor's nephew. It pleased her that I was accepted socially. From Renshaw, I attended Harvard. Though my grades were not exceptional, Mother insisted I apply. I am not sure to this day how I managed to be admitted. I have often wondered whether my father asked a favor of someone in a position to help with my admission."

"What was your life at college like?" I asked.

"There was much more work, but in many ways it wasn't very different from Renshaw. I maintained my friendships with classmates who accompanied me and made some new friends. Oh, yes, I put on some weight and was cajoled into going out for football. I made the varsity team in my sophomore year, though I'm not sure why I made the effort; I didn't enjoy the game. As a third stringer, however, I did not play often. I remember one incident very clearly, though. I was sitting on the bench one

Saturday. We were so far behind that the coach decided to send me in. I don't think I'd even been following the action when there I was at left end. The whistle blew, and suddenly the game was going on all around me. I guess I couldn't adjust that quickly. It seemed unreal, as if I were some kind of robot going through the motions of playing even though they ran right at me and I got flattened. I didn't do too well. After the game people asked if I'd been jarred or dazed in that play, and I let them believe that. Eventually I dropped off the squad.

"I met Cynthia in my senior year. I had been invited to the Cape for a weekend, and she was there. Cynthia is a beautiful woman—you've met her. Well, she was young and sort of daring then. I'd never met anyone like her before. She was fond of me right away, maybe because I was different, less jaded than her usual friends. I enjoyed girls well enough, but I hadn't had too much experience. . . . Besides, Cynthia came from a prominent family. She began to turn up at parties where I'd be and . . . well, I knew she cared about me. She would listen to me talk and jabber for hours then. We fell in love and were married after graduation."

"What did you do next?"

"Mr. Ball landed me a position with Kinsey, Davenport, investment brokers. It was a great opportunity, but I found that I was very uncomfortable there. The older partners, my father-in-law's cronies, treated me too well. They would take me out to lunch and introduce me to important people. I knew the others, who had been with the firm much longer, resented this, but I was helpless to stop it. I stuck it out despite my malaise for most of a year so as not to embarrass Cynthia's father. The Korean War was on, and I counted upon being drafted. Then I learned that Mr. Ball was quietly trying to arrange something to keep me out."

"So you enlisted in the Marine Corps?"

"That's right. Cynthia must have told you. I had no intention of becoming a hero, however. I didn't really think about actually seeing action. I was just looking for an acceptable way out of the situation I'd gotten into. I was also almost twenty-three, and I knew that I'd been coddled most of my life. I thought the corps might be good for me. I needed to be on my own more, and I felt it would help me grow up."

"How were you wounded?" I asked.

"My platoons were helping to protect the retreat from the north, up above the thirty-eighth parallel. Maybe you were there or read about it. When the Chinese came, it was awesome. There were literally swarms of them like fields of locusts. All I wanted to do was withdraw our units as fast as we could, but that wasn't possible. We had orders to slow the enemy's advance. My men liked and respected me, and I felt, in return, I owed them something. So, I stayed with the rear guard. I was hit then and carried out, or I'd still be there."

"It seems as if you've been in difficult straits more than once," I said.

"Yes, that's true, but sometimes it's merely a matter of circumstances, or don't you think so?"

"I am impressed that circumstances often appear to be part of a pattern and not accidental."

"I don't understand."

"You seem repeatedly to entrap yourself trying to repay others. A sense of obligation, or guilt, always appears to keep you from pursuing your own inclinations. Wasn't that what Hal was trying to point out?"

Welborn considered this. "I think so . . . yes, I'm sure of that, but freedom can be costly. Does one have the right to do something that will hurt others and tear his family apart? Hal had pushed his mother to the point where she was becoming . . . ill over him. He had nothing in mind except having his own way."

"Nothing in mind?" I echoed. "You told me he had quite a lot in mind. Didn't you say that he kept a great deal stored inside for a long time until you urged him to give in and appease his mother—the way you had pleased yours years ago?"

Welborn paled. "Go on, Doctor," he urged soberly.

"Well, again, I wonder if your son hasn't unknowingly been influenced somehow to act out what you regret that you haven't done. He seems to be expressing his independence and his will to determine his own goals in life. Your wife may be correct in her suspicion that you are responsible for nurturing his attitudes."

"You also think that's why he left?" he asked, bewildered.

"Don't you? His attack on you, painful though it must have been, could only have expressed truths you, in some way, exposed to him. You may have set out to save him some time ago. Perhaps, after Meg was born, you began to identify with Hal. Maybe, to set him free, you revealed some of the misjudgments and compromises that you had had to make. Perhaps in so doing, you sought only to caution him to be deliberate in choosing his direction. It seems, however, that you revealed much more than you were aware and that you underestimated its impact. Hal's withdrawal from college was something you apparently had not anticipated, nor did you foresee the severity of your wife's reaction." He shook his head confirmingly.

"When Mrs. Welborn began to drink you panicked. That is when you decided to persuade Hal to reconsider. It was too late. You had given him your support, at least tacitly, then withdrawn it. Whatever his doubts and apprehensions were, he was able to divert himself from them by reacting to your fickleness. He felt betrayed. The vehemence of his denunciation of you is probably a good clue to the intensity of his unease. When he left, you continued to feel the weight of his words, brokenhearted. You began hating yourself."

"I guess you are right. I know you are. How clearly you see it all. . . . But, Doctor, even as you were speaking, I found myself struggling to pay attention, to listen to you. Is that because I don't want to face it yet? It is all true, every word Hal said. He told me my life was as flimsy as a house of cards, and he was right—look at me."

"Hal was angry—"

"No, Doctor, he was correct, straight up and down. I am weak-willed and pliable. I have always let myself be influenced. I accepted too many favors and misled people because I was unable to say no. I didn't have enough of whatever it takes to know my own mind. It was easier to go along with things. The trouble was that after a while matters became involved and complicated, and by then I had so many responsibilities, including the family, that I couldn't change directions even if I had wanted to do so."

"You started to withdraw and become depressed even before Hal left, didn't you?" I asked.

"Yes, but I still had hopes that in some way we could patch things up and work the problems out. When he drove off, however, I can't tell you how empty I felt my life suddenly was. I knew that I had finally failed in every way. I hardly cared anymore about anything. I couldn't bear to go to Martha's Vineyard with the rest of my family in August. I hated to be around people. I couldn't stand to make conversation. When I saw what I was doing to Cynthia, I felt even worse and tried to cover it up."

"And when September came, you tried to get back to work," I added.

"I hoped it would be easier working, keeping my mind occupied and busy. I deliberately took on a huge assignment. As you know, however, I just could not get my mind back into gear. When they called me in that Tuesday morning, would you believe that I thought they were going to let me go? I was certain that everyone could see that I simply was not getting the job done, that I wasn't able to do it, even though I was putting in a considerable amount of time. Maybe they did sense that I was more quiet and aloof than usual. They might have guessed that something was bothering me and thought that I was depressed about being passed over. A partnership, however, never excited me that much. I wanted it only for Cynthia. I think that the senior partners must have felt I had deserved the promotion earlier and, given the size and importance of my current project, persuaded the younger partners to accept me at this point. It couldn't have been more ironic. Here I was, winging it like a wounded duck, working hard just to keep from falling, and they elevated me."

I shook my head and smiled sympathetically. "You seem to have a penchant, Mr. Welborn, for falling upward."

"I guess you could say so." He nodded, also smiling, more at ease now.

We agreed that Welborn would remain in the hospital for the rest of the week and that I would continue to see him daily. Beyond that, we would arrange to meet in my office. In the treatment of individuals in acute crises, it is sometimes possible to make rapid strides. Anxious, depressed patients may respond quickly when it is possible to identify the more immediate sources of their distress. To mature and change, not merely to recover, would take a greater and more extended effort in psychotherapy. Welborn and I were beginning to define his problems and to relate in a productive way. I hoped he would continue to be as open and cooperative when I probed more deeply into his relationships and the conflicts of his childhood. There were delicate matters to be understood.

Psychotherapy is the process by which the therapist attempts to treat emotional disorders. Its form will vary according to the theoretical orientation of the practitioner. Whatever the framework, however, it is modified to meet the unique needs of individual patients. In my own work, I have found it useful to view psychotherapy as a fabric varying in design but composed principally of three main threads. The first consists of the attempt to understand the patient's current life in terms of his immediate problems, relationships, and goals. What is it that the patient is reacting to so stressfully? What are his coping resources, his weaknesses? How does he relate to others who are important to him? How does he reconcile his needs and aspirations with his abilities, values, and concerns? What degree of insight does he possess?

An emotional crisis arises which causes the patient to feel threatened and interferes with his functioning. There is pressure on his adjustment. He may know that he is reacting excessively or inappropriately to some stress, actual or anticipated: a move, retirement, marriage, childbirth, a visit, death, or even a vacation. Sometimes it is a disappointment, a loss, or the frustration of some cherished hope that he cannot accept. Often, however, the victim is unaware of what has caused his undoing. A person suffering a psychosis may not even realize that he is impaired as he divulges strange concerns or complains of bizarre happenings.

The second major thread concerns the patient's past. As in other fields of medicine, a thorough history is essential to proper diagnosis and treatment. It exposes to the physician dimensions of the problem that are otherwise inapparent. These aspects influence the decisions the psychiatrist makes about psychotherapy. But the patient's past history has a further role that is unique to psychiatric treatment. It is an important part of the actual treatment process itself. Reviewing it with the therapist helps bring into awareness the deeper causes of the patient's difficulties.

The patient's past reveals the circumstances that prevailed when he was young and most impressionable. It may expose influences and attitudes that helped mold his self-concept, his values, and his ambitions. What gave him a sense of security, of confidence? What inhibited, frightened or discouraged him? Knowledge of his parents' lives and roles as authorities and models, of religious beliefs, ethnic and social factors, and sibling and peer pressures is enormously valuable to understanding the patient's path in life. How did he react to the birth of a sibling, the absence of a parent? Were separations difficult? Did later experience modify or reinforce earlier conceptions? Do barely remembered or even forgotten events continue to affect the patient?

The third thread in psychotherapy is present from the moment the psychiatrist and patient meet. It concerns the character of the therapeutic relationship. The patient's wishes, fears, and expectations influence how he relates to the psychiatrist. These are both conscious and unconscious. Together, they are called the transference, because the patient is prone to transfer to the therapist attitudes he has harbored toward parents or other important figures in his early life. This thread provides the psychiatrist with a unique second sight into the patient's history. A patient, for example, who seeks constant reassurance from the psychiatrist may be revealing how uncertain he was of his parents' approval.

The psychotherapist can respond to the transference in different ways, according to his assessment of the patient's needs. He may choose to be more accessible and supportive to a patient whose anxieties are severe. With another, he may maintain a certain distance, frustrating the patient's wishes for him. In general, the fewer clues to himself that he provides, the less real he appears to be, and the more inclined the patient will be to project and to transfer. When properly developed, the transference can be a powerful means of confronting the patient with his unconsciously determined attitudes and motives.

In Welborn's case, I would have to observe to what extent his tendency to appease authority figures was emerging in the transference. Such inclinations were likely to be patterned after his relationship to his mother. These tendencies appeared to have stifled his drives and compromised his values. He might otherwise have achieved a closer bond to his father, taken a more self-determined course, and achieved more personal satisfaction in his life so far. As matters stood, he had avoided failures, but his successes seemed unearned and were ungratifying. If, as I expected, Welborn tried to please me and conform in the treatment process, I would eventually have to interpret this to him and frustrate these tendencies, to force his own drives to the surface. Otherwise, therapy would have little significance or lasting value.

As these latent drives emerged, the therapeutic relationship would become ticklish. I had a sense that Welborn might have manipulated his son, Hal, to rebel and to disappoint his mother, Cynthia, in order to satisfy Welborn's own unfulfilled wishes to have resisted his mother. Accordingly, if I managed our relationship deftly, I could encourage him to rebel and to express his true feelings openly. This would have to be handled so that he could work through this growth experience without becoming so anxious that he would bolt from treatment.

There was also the matter of Welborn's affectional feelings toward his son. There was much to suggest that he identified with Hal, regarding him with the love he may have wished his own father had shown. The breach between Hal and him was intensely painful. It would be important for Welborn to find a way to repair this relationship and regain his son's respect and esteem.

At a few minutes to five, as she had the previous day, Mrs. Welborn telephoned. I reported that her husband and I had had a long and productive discussion and that he was improved. I related our plans for him to remain at the hospital for the rest of the week and to continue in psychotherapy afterward. Mrs. Welborn made no comment. Instead, she announced, "Daddy would like Dr. Lloyd Traynor to see Doug. Do you know of him? He is the director of Whitegate Hospital in Boston. He and Daddy are old classmates, and he has agreed to fly down to examine Doug. He'll be here this evening. In fact, he is coming to dinner. Can you arrange for him to see my husband around eight?"

"Of course, Mrs. Welborn. If your husband is amenable, I'll notify the staff. Tell Dr. Traynor that I am at his disposal. He can call me, through my office, before and after he visits your husband if he wishes. I shall be delighted to consult with him."

Traynor was one of those highly visible, polished, and well-connected psychiatrists about whom the public hears in association with the problems and tragedies of the very privileged. I had seen him interviewed on television and found him remarkably adept at sounding profound. He was a tall, white-haired, handsome gentleman whose airs inspired respect and awe. It would be interesting to confer with Traynor. I called Welborn, who was already aware of the proposed consultation and was amenable to it. I arranged for Dr. Traynor to have access to Welborn's chart.

All evening I waited, but Traynor never called.

The next morning, at ten minutes to nine, Ms. Nieder called from three north. She seemed excited and distressed. "Doctor, I've been waiting to reach you! Mr. Welborn's left! He signed out half an hour ago! I tried to persuade them to wait to discuss it with you, but they wouldn't listen. They put on this big rush act and finally made him sign out a.m.a. [against medical advice]. They said they were in a great hurry to catch the nine-twenty flight from the county airport to Boston."

"Who were they?" I asked, knowing already.

"Some smooth-talking Dr. Traynor, Mrs. Welborn, and another old gentleman, her father, I believe. They really pressured poor Mr. Welborn. I could hear his wife crying in there while the other two talked to him in his room. He didn't want to leave, but they wore him down. They kept working on him right up until the moment they were inside the elevator. He is to be admitted to some hospital in Massachusetts."

"Did they make any effort to get in contact with me as far as you are aware?"

"No, Doctor. They weren't even going to leave you a note, but I had to call Mrs. O'Dell, the nurse supervisor, to approve Mr. Welborn's release and she insisted that Dr. Traynor make an entry in the chart. Shall I read what he wrote?"

"Please," I said, feeling defeated. This is what she read:

Consultation Note

The patient appears to have experienced an acute, dissociative episode with schizoaffective features. There are evidences of an incipient psychosis, and he has recently entertained self-destructive ideas. Hospitalization in a more suitably protective and rehabilitative milieu is indicated. He will be transferred to Whitegate Hospital for further observation and extended care. Thank you for your cooperation.

Lloyd H. Traynor, M.D.

"Did Mr. Welborn leave any message or note?" I asked.

"No, I thought, at one point, he was going to say something

to me, but he didn't, and we were never alone. Most of the time he just looked stricken and meek. They didn't give him a chance to think."

"I see." I was disappointed. "Did Dr. Traynor request Mr. Welborn's records or ask that I forward a transfer note or report?"

"No, Doctor. They just took him."

It took an effort on my part to keep Welborn from intruding and disturbing my concentration that morning while I saw other patients. At eleven, when I had planned to see him, I made up my mind to write to Dr. Traynor. Briefly I summarized my findings and the direction I had intended to pursue in treatment. I made no comment on my clinical views. I ended, however, with an offer to remain available to the patient upon his discharge from Whitegate if I could be of further service to him.

I never received a reply.

Three weeks went by. Then I heard again from Mrs. Welborn. It was on a Sunday. My answering service said it was urgent, so I called Millway.

"This is Dr. Jacobs. Mrs. Welborn?"

"This is Cynthia Welborn, Doctor. I want to know if you have heard from my husband."

"No, Mrs. Welborn, I haven't had any word. Is anything wrong? You sound alarmed."

"Doug has run off—eloped, as they put it—from the hospital. As you know, well, we thought he would be much more comfortable and better in Boston, so we removed him to Whitegate. Dr. Traynor has personally looked after him up there, but Doug has steadily deteriorated these past few weeks. He is really a very sick man," she said reproachfully.

"I'm sorry to learn he has done poorly," I said.

"He has changed so, I don't know what to think about him anymore," she went on. "Since he entered Whitegate, all he's done is to withdraw and sulk. He won't even answer my letters. My last visit upset me so that Dr. Traynor hasn't wanted me to see Doug for a while. He feels Doug needs electroshock therapy to snap out of this. He believes the treatments can restore my husband to his old self once more."

My heart sank. Electroshock is an effective treatment for depression, and it is indicated in a number of special circumstances particularly where other forms of treatment may be contraindicated or the patient does not respond to them. In Welborn's case, however, I felt he was an excellent candidate for an insightful psychotherapy. Electroshock could obscure the underlying sources of his discomfort, making him well but, in a sense, not better. "Was electroshock performed?" I asked.

"No," she answered regretfully. "Doug hasn't been cooperative. He wouldn't agree to it. He wanted to speak to you. My husband was under your care for such a brief time I cannot imagine what you could have done to have had such an influence on him. He seems to think you are the only one who understands him. Dr. Traynor hasn't felt your contacting Doug would be helpful, however; he has intercepted letters my husband has written to you. When he would not approve of Doug telephoning you, my husband became furious. He has been so angry and obstinate it was necessary for a time to give him strong tranquilizers until he quieted down." From her tone it was clear that Mrs. Welborn held me entirely responsible for all that she had revealed so far.

"This morning," she continued, "my son, Hal, finally decided to call home. He was shocked to hear about his father. Maybe he felt guilty also. I pointed out that this all began because of him. I told him that if he cared anything at all about his father, he should call the hospital and try to speak to him. Maybe he could convince Doug to try to get well, I hoped. But it was right after Hal called and spoke to him that Doug went berserk. Apparently he demanded to be released immediately, and an attendant who tried to restrain him was hurt. The staff tried to stop him; but Doug raced out past everyone, and before they could catch up with him on the grounds, he'd climbed over the wall and was gone. They are searching everywhere. Do you know where he could be?" she asked worriedly.

"No . . . no, I can't imagine," I said, wondering where Hal had promised to meet his father.

Weeks later, around Thanksgiving, I received a letter from Welborn. He thanked me for my efforts to help him and reported that he was working in the office at a famous Idaho resort. It seemed as if Welborn had discovered his own Shangri-la. He had not solved his problems, but perhaps he would work them out yet. There was no mention of his family or of his plans regarding them. I wondered what kind of Thanksgiving they would have. I placed the letter in my file and moved on to other urgent matters.

I had taken a few days at home over the Christmas and New Year's holidays and was returning to my office the first Monday of the new year. It was an unusually bright, windy, bitter day. I hurried from my car toward the entrance to my building. Perhaps that is why I failed to notice a tall figure emerge from a car off to my right.

"Dr. Jacobs! Dr. Jacobs, wait up a moment! It's Doug Welborn!" he called. Surprised, but determined nonetheless to get out of the wind and to gain the shelter of the lobby, I pointed ahead and went inside. He opened the door a moment later. I smiled and stepped forward to shake his hand. "Hello. I'm surprised to see you in these parts. How are you?"

"Fine, just fine, Doctor." He smiled. "I am really quite well again. How are you? You seemed a mite cold out there. Ha, this isn't even a chill compared to Idaho. . . . I know you probably have a patient coming in to see you shortly, so I won't detain you. But I do wish to talk to you. Is there some time, maybe later today, I could come back?"

"How about five o'clock?" I suggested.

"Splendid. It's very generous of you to make time to see me this way on such short notice. I think I'll just leave my car here then and walk to the railroad station. I can probably catch a train back out of the city around half past three and be here by five."

"Good," I agreed, taking notice now of his business suit under the open overcoat he wore. "I'll see you then."

Welborn nodded. "I have a lot to tell you. I'll explain at five," he promised. Then he turned and pushed back out through the front door.

I ushered Welborn into my office. He took the chair a short distance from my desk and sat looking about and rubbing his hands for a moment. His ears and cheeks glowed with wind-burn. "You have an attractive office, Doctor. I haven't been here before," he reminded me.

"That's right," I reflected. "I saw you only at the hospital, didn't I?"

"Yes. Well, that's all water under the bridge now. I would just as soon forget all that happened back then. It is nothing but a source of embarrassment to me now, landing in your hospital over there and then breaking out of Whitegate like some convict crashing out of prison. I don't know what came over me. It is fortunate no one on the staff up there decided to press assault charges against me. But Dr. Traynor is a good friend of the family. He saw to everything, thank God."

"I see," I said, sobered. "Tell me, how did you wind up in Idaho?"

"Well, my son, Hal, the prodigal, promised to meet me in Billings, Montana. He had been there before and knew a place where the two of us could stay inexpensively for a short time. I thumbed my way out there. It took me five and a half days riding in trucks for the most part. I was terribly cautious, never traveling more than a few hundred miles with any one driver for fear I could be traced otherwise."

"So you did meet Hal. I thought you might have," I said.

"Yes, we spent about two weeks together. Hal taught me how to survive on my own out there. I even worked as his assistant for a week installing carpeting for a furniture store. Then I got the idea of going to Ketchum. I visited Sun Valley once with friends when I was in school and loved it then. I wrote to you around that time."

"Yes, you sounded very happy."

"I was, Doctor, but I realized soon afterward that I could not just run away from my problems. So I decided to return and settle matters."

"What have you decided to do?" I asked.

"Well, Cynthia has taken me back, but of course, it isn't the same as it was. I couldn't expect it to be after all I've done. We have separate rooms now. It's really all right, if she prefers it that way. I am going to stay at least until June, when Meg is finished with school. In the meantime, I am giving business one more try. Between that and my marriage, I'll see what happens."

"You have some important decisions ahead of you," I said.

"I've done a great deal of thinking, Doctor, especially on the things we talked about. I don't know if you remember, but I had worked myself right into a corner and felt trapped until—"

"Until you realized you could turn around and find a way out," I said, deciding it best to keep matters on the surface.

"Exactly. I feel different now. I've told Cynthia I am going to give this six months, no more. If by then I feel comfortable here, fine. If I don't, then I'll know it isn't meant to be, and I'll accept it and do something else."

"How does Mrs. Welborn feel about this?" I asked.

"That is what I want to ask you about. She says she understands, but I don't think she really does. I asked her to come in with me to see you, but she refuses. I don't know why, but she doesn't seem to trust you."

"I am sorry she feels that way. I suspect your disturbance a few months back and the differences in your attitudes now may be associated in her mind with our sessions. Change can be very threatening."

"Cynthia is very insecure. I can see that now. She has always had her way because of it. I never could risk upsetting her before. I can't let myself live that way anymore, however, and I am afraid it is taking a toll of Cynthia. She apparently drank heavily all the time I was out West. It's reached a point that I am not only worried about her, but also becoming quite concerned about the bad effect it is having on my daughter, Meg. Cynthia is becoming an alcoholic. She has fallen several times, and she's broken her left wrist. She is covered with so many bruises it looks as if I beat her. What can I do?"

"Have you discussed it with her father?"

"Mr. Ball blames me; he isn't very much help."

"Perhaps if you suggested that he and you take Cynthia up to visit Dr. Traynor for some advice, he would listen," I suggested.

"That is a terrific idea. Cynthia has a great deal of faith in Lloyd. She might accept that. If he could help her at Whitegate, I can manage things at home. I've become pretty capable since being on my own."

We talked about Welborn's recent experiences, and I was impressed with his newly found resourcefulness. He made no request for further appointments before we parted, but he promised to call.

About a week later Mrs. Welborn entered Whitegate Hospital. She remained there for sixteen weeks. A short time after her discharge the Welborns separated. Mr. Welborn did not return to the West. He left his firm to go with another located in a smaller city upstate, not far from his boyhood home. I hear from him periodically.

WHY SPIDERS CRY

Dolores Kenwick

O ne could tell immediately that trouble had come to four west. Equipment had accumulated in the hall, and too many of the hospital staff were in evidence. I stepped from the elevator and started toward the nurses' station. The ward clerk was standing behind the long counter, holding a telephone, looking worried. She bit her lip as she waited for a nurse to finish counting out red capsules and distributing them in little paper cups. Nearby a laboratory technician gathered up a handful of colored forms and paused to frown at the wall clock, obviously delayed and bothered. I moved aside, making room for two nurses wheeling a cart of instruments and dressings to bustle by. Farther ahead down the corridor I noticed a blue-uniformed security aide standing, arms folded, leaning against the wall. Everyone looked strained and tense.

I had been summoned to the hospital earlier in the afternoon by Earl Hanon, a surgeon. It is unusual for surgeons to call psychiatrists, and I was especially surprised to hear from Earl. In the seventeen years both of us had been practicing in Brentwood, he had called only once before, and that had been for a contribution. Earl was a huge, broad mountain of a man one is likely to find alone reading in the medical library or sitting in his green operating room pajamas quietly having a sandwich by himself in the snack bar after surgery. He was a gentle, private man, thorough, methodical, and dedicated to his craft. Though highly regarded for his work, Earl was known for his cautious and deliberate ways. Today he had been businesslike and hurried.

"Jerry, I have a problem on my hands, and I need your help," he began. "It's a patient in four-nineteen. I have only a few minutes to tell you about her. Can you listen?"

"Go ahead, Earl. I am free at the moment; tell me what the difficulty is," I said, picking up my pen.

About a month before, a Mrs. Dolores Kenwick, age twenty-four, had been referred to Earl for surgical consultation. Mrs. Kenwick had suffered from abdominal pains and belching for about a year. Despite treatment by her internist, who had prescribed various bland and soft diets, antacids and antispasmodics, the young woman's complaints persisted, and she lost weight. Food, which often provides some temporary relief to sufferers from peptic ulcers, only aggravated her distress, and the effect of positional changes, which might have suggested the presence of a fault or herniation of the diaphragm, was equivocal and undiagnostic. Blood tests and urinary and fecal analyses disclosed no evidences of abnormal function of the liver or pancreas, nor were X-rays, including a gastrointestinal series and gallbladder studies, revealing.

Hanon and a radiologist administered a barium meal to Mrs. Kenwick and fluoroscoped her as the radiopaque material passed through her upper gastrointestinal tract. Just beyond the stomach, they discovered an abnormality. A barium-filled sac about four centimeters, or slightly more than an inch and a half in length, extended from the descending duodenum, part of the first segment of the small intestine. Outpouchings of the intestine, diverticula, are not common in this area, but when they are found, they are usually asymptomatic. In Mrs. Kenwick's case, however, the barium remained trapped in the small fingerlike projection more than six hours, and that was unusual. The delayed emptying time of the distended sac identified the diverticulum as the probable cause of Mrs. Kenwick's difficulties. Hanon discussed his findings with the patient and her husband. He reassured them that their principal fear, cancer, was not involved. He recommended, however, that surgery to remove the diverticulum be performed and that in view of the patient's pain and weight loss, about fourteen pounds, it be done soon, before Mrs. Kenwick's stamina declined still further.

"When did you operate on her?" I asked.

"Fourteen days ago," he answered. "Everything went beautifully. I excised the diverticulum and repaired the defect in the duodenal wall; there were no problems. The first day post-op she vomited a little—that's to be expected. The second day she spiked a fever of one hundred three and really gave me a scare. I started her on antibiotics immediately. Then I learned that her daughter had come down with a sore throat, positive for strep. Well, we got that under control, and she seemed to be picking up. I started her on clear fluids. The trouble was that her gut was lazy. The intestines often react to being tinkered with, you know, by shutting down temporarily."

"You mean paralytic ileus?" I asked.

"Exactly," he went on, surprised. Physicians who have little contact with psychiatry are apt to forget that psychiatrists have had identical medical training before taking additional preparation in their chosen specialty. "By the seventh day," he continued, "I took out the skin sutures. The wound was clean and beautiful, but Mrs. Kenwick still had no bowel sounds. Her stomach was full and becoming distended by then. I had to pass a tube down to relieve her. She didn't like that or the intravenous I kept her on, but I had little choice; I had to try to keep her hydrated and nourished. For the next six days there was no improvement. A repeat GI series showed no passage of barium through the duodenum. I was quite worried. I thought I would have to operate again and create a temporary bypass, which would mean yet another operation later. Besides, she was weaker now, and I hated to go back in at all."

Earl's case was interesting, but I was beginning to wonder again why he had called me. I thought I would remind him. "I'm glad we psychiatrists don't have that kind of problem to wrestle with, Earl. What happened?"

"This morning, thank God, she passed gas. Let me tell you, it was the sweetest sound I ever heard."

"She should be out of the woods then. Her intestines are functioning again. What's wrong?" I asked.

"Plenty, but it's not in her abdomen this time! That's why I'm calling you. Mrs. Kenwick's apparently become deranged. She has been fighting the nurses all morning, won't let them near her. She pulled out her last IV, and she has been mumbling incoherently and watching us like a hawk. It is really bizarre. She urinates in her bed and sits and rocks on the floor, singing lullabies to herself. Can you possibly see her today and give us some help?" he pleaded.

I stood in front of the nurses' desk for a few moments, waiting to inquire about Mrs. Kenwick. The laboratory technician departed. Ms. Gordon, the nurse who had been counting pills, was busily talking on the telephone now and tracing her finger down a list of doctors' orders. The ward clerk seemed to recognize me, but she fled abruptly into the small office behind the nurses' station. Now she reemerged, followed quickly by Mary O'Dell, the nursing supervisor.

"Oh, Dr. Jacobs. I am so glad you are here—*at last,*" she said, pretending to be angry.

I had to smile and explain that until my scheduled patients had been seen, I was unable to come to four west. Mary was always her patients' advocate, pressing to have their needs and interests served first. She was a handsome woman about fifty-five with a reputation for being not only a highly competent professional but also a frank and plain-speaking person. Mary sometimes overstepped the invisible line of authority between nurses and doctors that most nurses who rise in administrative responsibility tactfully observe; she was known openly to criticize physicians, as well as her own staff, when she felt circumstances warranted it. I admired her and valued her integrity and judgment. We had always been on warm, confiding terms. She motioned me into the little office she had come from.

"Thank God, you were able to come." She sighed. "The girls have been worried about that poor child for days. She's been doing little things, talking to herself and acting strange. The other day she stripped her bed completely and arranged the blankets and the sheets in a big cross on the mattress. Then she lay on it as if she'd been crucified until the other patient who was in there woke up from a nap and called us. Mrs. Kenwick wouldn't move. Said she knew she was going to die, only she hadn't known it would be this way. Over and over again she kept repeating the same thing, that she didn't realize it would be this way. We finally persuaded her to let us straighten up, but we haven't been able to keep any other patient in there with her since then. Some of the time she seems all right, but I think often that's just for our benefit so we'll leave her alone. At other times she will scream or find excuses to have someone stay in there with her as if she's deathly afraid to be by herself. The girls have tried to tell Dr. Hanon, but he was probably too concerned about her nonfunctioning bowels to pay much heed. You know Earl—when something is worrying him, you simply can't communicate with him. He just nods and smiles as if he's listening, but nothing sinks in. Well, Mrs. Kenwick finally got through to him all by herself this morning. She almost ruined Earl. When he tried to examine her, Mrs. Kenwick lunged and almost bit off two of his fingers. He didn't tell you that, did he?"

"No, he was rushed when he called me."

"He certainly was. He called because I wouldn't be put off any longer. Mrs. Kenwick has been impossible. Hanon may have thought all her problems would clear up when her bowel activity resumed, but she's been worse than ever, mentally. The poor thing is still scared out of her mind. She sits on the floor in a corner or hides under the bed and kicks and screams when you try to help her. This morning, after Earl left the floor, she wandered into Mr. Kaplan's room across the hall; he is just down from coronary care with a new pacemaker. There she knelt, reciting her rosary in front of the old gentleman, naked as a newborn. She was begging him for his blessing when we found her.

"Well," she continued, "I couldn't allow this to go on any longer, not when it puts other patients in jeopardy. So I marched myself up to the OR and looked for Hanon. He was scheduled for a hernia repair at one o'clock. Earl had just finished his scrub and was waiting to be gowned when, you might say, I bumped into him. It was an accident, you understand." Mary winked conspiratorily. "I am afraid I contaminated poor Dr. Hanon and broke his scrub. Well, of course, I apologized to him, but since he had to start all over again anyway, and his hernia case could wait five minutes, I suggested that he might save a few hours' delay and call you first. I was standing there holding the phone for him when he spoke to you."

"Mary O'Dell, you are diabolical," I said. "I am sorry I couldn't come sooner. After all that, I only hope I can help."

"This child needs psychiatric attention desperately, and we can't get anything done around here with her out of control this way. I hated to do it, believe me, but on Hanon's orders we put restraints on her until you could come," she said. "Her husband is here now. He is furious about her wrists and ankles being strapped to the bedrails. I explained that they were necessary, that the only alternative was to sedate her, and then you wouldn't be able to examine her properly. I didn't get very far with him, I'm afraid; he is threatening to have his wife discharged and transferred to another hospital. He is a nice young man really, but he is frightened. Incidentally, he happens also to be a lawyer, though he isn't talking about suing anyone. He just wants his wife well again. They have two little ones at home. This whole thing has taken longer than anyone expected, and now, on top of everything, she has become psychotic."

"I'll talk to him," I promised.

The charge nurse, Ms. Gordon, Mary, and I entered Room 419. A worried young man in his late twenties was seated beside the bed nearest the window. On it rested the still, small, child-like figure of a woman. Her pale, fine-featured face was framed by long dark hair. Her hands lay clasped on her chest; her dark eyes stared fixedly at the ceiling. Were it not for the slight motions of her breathing, she could have been taken for a corpse. Mr. Kenwick put aside the magazine that had been on his lap and rose to meet me. Thinning blond hair, tortoise spectacles, and a pipe protruding from his tweed jacket gave him the appearance of a young professor. He did not smile or extend his hand. He was angry.

"I took those leather cuffs off my wife's wrists and ankles," he declared. "They are on the floor of the empty locker. I don't see why she had to be tied down like that. I won't permit it!"

"I am Dr. Jacobs, Mr. Kenwick. I hope I can be of some help."

"You're the psychiatrist?" he asked. I nodded. "Well, Doctor, I don't know what is going on here. Dolores has had a rough time; they've probably told you about it. She is not a strong girl." He turned to look down at his wife for a moment. She continued to stare as still as death at the ceiling. "She has been through quite an ordeal," he continued, "but now . . . she is really upset." His voice broke. "She isn't herself. I . . . I can't get any sense out of her. Dolores just lies there like that, staring at nothing and mumbling to herself from time to time. I don't understand this. Will she be all right?"

As he spoke, Ms. Gordon slipped past him and went over to his wife. She carefully lifted a limp wrist and took the patient's pulse. Then she gently raised Mrs. Kenwick's head and puffed the pillow beneath it. The patient never stirred.

I avoided answering Mr. Kenwick's question directly. I assured him, instead, of my intention to study her condition very carefully and to do all I possibly could to assist her. Mary O'Dell, tactfully and sympathetically, explained once more why the restraints had been necessary and that they had been meant only to protect his wife and the other patients. She did not criticize their removal. Meanwhile, I watched Mrs. Kenwick. I had a sense that though she looked for all the world like a fairy princess under some magic spell, she was really alert and interested in our conversation.

"She's never been this bad before, Doctor. She had upsets after each of our two children was born. Postpartum blues, I think they are called." His voice quivered. "She never had to see a psychiatrist. It just took her a little while to adjust to the babies. Dolores snapped out of those moods after a few days. So many women seem to go through similar problems that we both just shrugged it off afterward."

He started to go on, but I stopped him. I am averse to discussing a patient in his presence when he is not participating. If the subject is unable to contribute to the conversation, it is an insensitive practice. The patient, already anxious and apprehensive, is further suffered to feel dehumanized. It appalls me when some nurses and physicians do this. I gestured for Mr. Kenwick to step outside. He followed me out into the corridor, where we talked for a moment. I suggested that he might wait in the solarium while I attempted to interview his wife. Kenwick explained that he had to depart. His baby-sitter had to be relieved and his children fed. I promised to call him later.

I reentered 419. Mrs. Kenwick and I were alone now. The late-afternoon sun shone in the large hospital window on the other side of her bed. I crossed the room and stood leaning against the windowsill, blocking the sun. It was a habit I had learned as a result of an experience years earlier in my residency. Called to see a patient one afternoon, I unintentionally terrified the poor man because the sun's rays, entering through a window, reflected from my eyeglasses and fell upon him. When he looked at me, what he saw were two burning orbs of light focused on him. Ever since then I try to make certain not to face a source of light when I am in a similar situation. Mrs. Kenwick, however, did not turn or follow me with her eyes.

I looked at the patient, trying to think of how to begin. The practice of psychiatry in an art, much of which is intuitive. Each set of circumstances is unique. What a painter once told me often comes to mind when I am confronted with this problem. He confided that he always began each of his works by studying the canvas. They are never quite the same, he explained. Little differences in the texture of the surface stimulated his ideas.

"They are all gone now, Mrs. Kenwick," I said quietly and simply. I had decided to act as if her strange behavior were neither mysterious nor alarming to me. "It's all right now, really; they are all gone," I repeated. A large tear slowly formed and rolled down her face. Mrs. Kenwick sniffled. More tears appeared. Was she in contact, as I suspected, or merely responding coincidentally to some unrelated, private thought? I tried again. "It is difficult to lie there so still like that. You controlled yourself perfectly, Mrs. Kenwick, not only your body, but your feelings also. You played dead very well. . . . I am Dr. Jacobs, and I'll see to it that you are safe now."

Many people will tend to regress when exposed to sufficient stress. Mrs. Kenwick's bed-wetting and her recurrent fear of being alone were evidence of this. If one assumes that the conduct of severely disturbed persons is purposeful, despite its primitive form, then their acts may be regarded as a kind of sign language intended to communicate and be interpreted. Mrs. Kenwick's resistance to care, her attempts to hide and pray, and her present cadaverlike repose all suggested that she was experiencing great terror. Perhaps she was trying to communicate, as Mary O'Dell had suggested, that she was "scared to death."

Her eyes flicked over and looked up at me. I nodded and smiled to emphasize that she was secure now. Mrs. Kenwick sat up and looked at me full face. Her tiny black pupils seemed to pulsate as they struggled to relax. "I have to fight them," she confided ingenuously. "Millicent said that if I want to get well, it's up to me; I have to fight for it."

"I see. . . . Well, you have certainly put up quite a struggle," I said.

"The one called Gordon, she's really the leader. Did you see her come over and fuss with me, pretending to be nice? She always manages to come in the afternoon while George is here." Mrs. Kenwick leaned toward me and whispered, "They are not really nurses, you know. They just put on those white uniforms so people will think they are. They are trying to kill me." She lay back down.

"What makes you think that?" I asked.

"It's because of George. They're jealous. Poor George. If I tell him, they'll harm him also." She began to cry. "I tried to fight them . . . but there were so many," she said, sobbing. "They held me and strapped me down. I'm sure they would have hurt me, but George came before they could. He untied me. Now they'll be angry at him, too."

I picked up a box of tissues beside me on the windowsill and offered them to Mrs. Kenwick. She blew her nose and thanked me with a weak smile. "They are trying to make it seem that George and I were never even married. Why, Doctor? Why are they doing this?"

"Which nurses do you mean?" I asked. Mrs. Kenwick gave me a sharp look. When her distrust eased, she seemed disappointed and confused. She had expected me to know already who her enemies were. Asking had dealt a blow to her confidence in me. While I did not want to encourage her delusions, my slip had undermined our rapport. I tried to repair the damage. "Who, I mean besides Ms. Gordon, do you feel is against you?"

"The fat one, the one with red hair who comes at night, she is with them and . . . oh, I don't know all of them. I hear them talking about me in the hall outside."

"I see, but perhaps there are some you do trust?"

"Mrs. Bloom, Doctor, she is good to me. She never hurts me . . . and the Chinese nurse is nice, too. She hardly ever comes in to see me anymore. I don't think they let her because she likes me."

"Well, Mrs. Kenwick," I said, standing up, "you have been a big help. I am going to need your assistance to put things right again. We've made a good start. I'll see to it that things begin to change now that I've been called in on your case. You are safe now, and you'll feel even more secure when you are stronger," I added confidently.

"Do you always wear eyeglasses, Doctor?"

"Yes, Mrs. Kenwick. Why do you ask?"

"Gordon took mine away. She's given them to someone else. I've tried to find them in other rooms on the floor, but they always catch me and bring me back," she said.

"I'll do what I can to get your eyeglasses back to you. Things certainly will look a lot clearer then." I smiled warmly. "Meanwhile, you get some rest. I will send someone in shortly to stay with you."

"All right, Doctor." She sighed and closed her eyes as I left the room.

Psychotherapy had begun. The brief interview had accomplished my immediate goals: to evaluate the patient's mental state and to lay the groundwork for a relationship in which she could trust and confide in me. To achieve my purpose, I had not challenged her distorted views and fears. I had accepted her delusions and, to an extent, even exploited them to gain an alliance with her as a protector. I fully intended to do away with further restraints and to have someone with her at all times instead, so my promise to her would be fulfilled. I wasn't worried about that. What did concern me was the fact that I had "entered" her psychosis and was now part of a grotesque game whose rules were not yet clear.

I asked the ward clerk to summon Mary O'Dell and sat down in the office behind the nursing station with the Kenwick chart. It had a brief, relevant history and physical examination, which revealed nothing more than Hanon had summarized on the telephone. I read his synopsis of the operative procedure, the pathology report, and the laboratory results recorded in the back of the chart. Mrs. Kenwick's most recent tests disclosed normal values for her hemoglobin and those critically important concentrations of plasma electrolytes: sodium chloride, potassium, and calcium. Her acid:base values were average also, and the amount of urea in her blood, a measure of kidney function, was not excessive. I found no physiological abnormalities consistent with Mrs. Kenwick's disturbed mental condition.

Next, I scanned Hanon's progress notes tracing her course since surgery. Until this morning there was no mention of her psychological state, and then there was a reference to her being "confused and uncooperative." Finally, I read through the voluminous nurses' notes in the front of the chart. It was here that I expected to learn most. Because entries are made during each of the three shifts of staff every twenty-four hours, variations in the patient's mental condition at different times of day and night become apparent. These differences can be diagnostically significant. Patients developing brain dysfunction of a physiological or organic type tend to have diurnal changes in their mental capacities. Though at first they may still manage relatively well during the daytime when cues are commonly available, their acuity and discriminatory powers deteriorate as they fatigue. As night comes, reducing the number of orientating stimuli, confusion may set in. I looked for evidence that Mrs. Kenwick misidentified people or mistook her surroundings after dark. I found no consistent pattern.

The notes suggested, however, that she had been very apprehensive at the time she entered the hospital. She had delayed her admittance, balking at the last moment, until her husband agreed not to go on to his office afterward but to stay with her. Neither this nor her refusal to let him leave at the end of visiting hours could have endeared her to Ms. Gordon and the already-burdened evening staff, I thought. Later that first evening before surgery, after initially refusing sleep medication, Mrs. Kenwick called home several times, disturbing her roommate. Finally, after midnight, she was persuaded to accept sedation. After this inauspicious start, the patient did reasonably well, despite discomforts, during the immediate postoperative period. It was not until the persistent inactivity of her intestines endangered her, requiring further treatment, that her psychological disposition changed. From that point onward her behavior was variously described as resistive, uncooperative, and strange.

Mary O'Dell entered the office. "Well, how did it go? Would she talk to you?" she asked.

"Yes, Mrs. Kenwick spoke to me when we were alone. I learned a few things that should help, and she has a degree of trust in me." Mary smiled and shook her head in mock amazement.

"Do you think we can keep her here?" she asked.

"I don't know yet. It's risky, but it certainly would be worthwhile trying. If we have to transfer her to another hospital, it will disorient her still further, and she will not have the opportunity to resolve all the delusions she has developed here with our personnel."

"What do you think has caused this?" Mary asked.

"I don't know, but perhaps there were significant underlying emotional conflicts in her life before all this. Her husband indicated that she had periods of disturbed moods twice before, following childbirth. She was quite apprehensive about this admission when she came into the hospital. If she had made a normal, quick recovery from surgery, her psychological defenses might have held up. Things would have seemed all right or at least as well as they had been before. But day after day, as she grew weaker when she had expected to feel stronger, she must have begun to doubt Dr. Hanon's reassurances. Maybe his growing concern became evident. Mrs. Kenwick could have lost confidence in him. Instead of receiving less and less care as she recovered, she began to get more and more attention and felt worse. There were blood tests and X-rays again. Tubes were inserted to relieve her distension. Intravenous feedings began. Instead of continuing to walk her, as they had during the first few days after surgery, the nurses told her she was too weak and began trying to keep her in bed. I imagine she became very frightened. No one could explain to her exactly why she was not progressing. She was getting sicker, in fact."

"The strain was too much then," Mary commented.

"I think so. With her life in apparent danger for so many days, Mrs. Kenwick's psychological defenses began to collapse. Look at it this way. Suppose a country is menaced by enemies that threaten its borders. As the siege progresses, dissatisfied, dissident factions inside seize the opportunity to rise up and take control. Chaos and confusion result; it is no longer easy to distinguish which dangers pose the greatest threat, those from without or those from within."

"Well, what do we do, send in the Marines to restore order?" she chirped.

"No, because we know that the external threat has subsided. What we have to do is help her realize that she is safe. Then, perhaps, her confusion will lift, and she can start resolving the strife and conflict that came to the surface from inside her mind during the crisis."

"What do you suggest?" Mary asked.

"First, I want three nurses who are comfortable with psychiatric patients, one for each shift. If Mrs. Bloom or a Chinese nurse on your staff that Mrs. Kenwick mentioned is available and willing, that would be great. These nurses will special the patient so that she is not confronted by an array of different faces or by those she distrusts, especially Ms. Gordon and a red-haired night nurse. Incidentally, find Mrs. Kenwick's eyeglasses and return them. Ms. Gordon took them, probably to prevent their being broken. With nurses assigned to be with her around the clock, the patient can have more freedom to move about. That will lessen her fears. She probably should be ambulated anyway. Have the nurses mention my name in some way when they come on duty, and if she gets upset about something, they should encourage her to tell me."

"Are you going to medicate her?" she asked.

"Yes, we'll use Thorazine. Everyone here has probably had experience with it, so they won't be watching her with peculiar interest. Besides, it will enable us to adjust the dosage up and down quickly over a wide range, and I want that freedom with her. We want to be able to calm her without sedating or depressing her, so the least effective dose will be our rule. Try to administer it in liquid form. It doesn't taste that great, but she is more likely to swallow a liquid. Suspicious patients like Mrs. Kenwick often think they are being poisoned, so they pretend to swallow a pill but, instead, spit it out when the nurse is not looking. If she refuses medication, however, no force is to be used. If she is violent, call me at any time.

"I want no night sedation given. It will only addle her the next day. Sedatives exert too much of their effect on the higher brain centers, dulling the patient's capacity to discriminate and integrate, impairing judgment. Tranquilizers such as Thorazine primarily block excessive activity in the lower brain centers, where the crossover between psychological phenomena like mood and thought and physiological reactions like increased pulse rate and blood pressure occurs. It is here that we want to intervene, so that Mrs. Kenwick can gain sufficient freedom from her response to fear to be able to identify its true origins. For insomnia or restlessness use more Thorazine. I'll come in twice a day. Tell the staff that I read the nurses' notes carefully, and I value their observations."

"You'll put all your orders in the book before you leave, won't you?" she reminded me. "Meanwhile, Dr. J., I'll see who I can find to special her."

"Fine, thank you. I'll finish writing this up, call Mr. Kenwick to inform him, and then, I promise, I'll remember the order book."

The following day I visited Mrs. Kenwick in the morning and again in the afternoon. She was calm on both occasions and seemed to have accepted the presence and attention of the special duty nurses. I learned that she had taken her medication and had eaten for the first time since her operation. According to her nurse, however, she was still confused and easily frightened.

My efforts to converse with Mrs. Kenwick were not successful. She offered nothing spontaneously. When I said something, her response was to repeat my last words. "I see you have your hair in braids now" elicited only "braids now," for example, while she continued turning the pages of a magazine. Repetition like this can be evidence of generalized brain dysfunction, and I was immediately concerned. But after several such exchanges, I sensed that it was willful. I was being childishly teased.

I glanced at the warm, grandmotherly nurse, who raised her eyebrows and shrugged, surprised at the patient's playful game, confirming my suspicions. I had to find a means of discouraging Mrs. Kenwick's resistance and prevent a power struggle. I decided not to confront her directly. Instead, I suggested that she might be burdened, having so many thoughts on her mind that she had not yet decided to tell. At that, Mrs. Kenwick looked up from her magazine. She gave me a searching scrutiny. Whether I satisfied her, or she regarded me as insignificant, I could not tell, for after a moment she smiled to herself and went back to her magazine.

Unproductive as they were in some ways, these brief sessions were important. Mrs. Kenwick, though regressed and childlike, had dared challenge me. She had done so openly, yet in a controlled manner, testing my patience but not jeopardizing our rapport. She discovered that she could do this with impunity; she was not defenseless. Her grin suggested that she savored her power even more knowing that I was aware of it. I was disappointed, but I had hopes that if Mrs. Kenwick felt less vulnerable, her confidence would return, and she might cooperate.

That evening Mr. Kenwick visited the hospital again. This time his wife was more responsive to him. They talked and watched television together. Before he left, she stroked his head affectionately and kissed him. He called me, excited to report her improvement and greatly encouraged. I tried to caution him not to be too disappointed if her progress proved to be only temporary. I told him that the tranquilizer she was receiving might well be masking the intensity of her disturbance. I explained that her upset represented, perhaps, an upwelling of latent conflicts triggered by stress and the exhaustion of her psychological controls. The medication and the measures we were taking were giving his wife the opportunity to rebuild her defenses, but her inner turmoil might break through once more. I talked to Mr. Kenwick until I felt he understood.

It is difficult for laymen and for physicians who are not psychiatrists to grasp easily the rationale and goals of psychotherapy. There are many differing psychological ideologies, each cloaked in its own jargon. Psychological principles are complicated and are often made to seem obscure. The main reason for confusion, however, probably lies in the historic, popular concept of illness. This specious reasoning, which serves to reassure the unaffected, holds that illnesses are maladies visited only on the unfortunate or the deserving by outside forces: the capriciousness of an unkind fate, the revenge of an offended god, a curse, hex, or malign intruder. If the affliction was madness, the sufferer was likely considered to have fallen victim to an evil spirit, dybbuk, or demon; he was possessed, suspect, an instrument of dark forces. The disturbed were regarded with awe and were feared. They were turned out, avoided, even persecuted and burned as witches.

The revelation of the nature of infectious diseases—the roles of pathogenic microbes, invisible to the naked eye—modernized but did not alter this universal attitude that an otherwise healthful individual who becomes mentally disturbed has been attacked from without. The discovery that the bacterium treponema is responsible for the dementia of syphilitics strengthened this view. It is not surprising, therefore, that thousands of psychiatric casualties of the First World War were believed to have been shell-shocked, brain-damaged, by concussive explosions when they were actually victims of fear.

Treatment of the mentally ill reflected the prevailing wisdom of the times that alien forces were responsible for disorders of mood and thought. First there were incantations, ritual exorcisms, purges, forced fasts, and the drilling of holes in the skull to drive out and release possessing spirits. Then came more technological approaches. Ingenious devices were invented to dip the afflicted into ponds or to spin them in special chairs to whirl away their madness, and there were other practices which seem cruel and simpleminded today. Eventually, however, there were more benign approaches. "Moral management" attempted to restore a sense of personal dignity to mental patients and various sanitoriums emphasized the healing values of nutrition and rest, or "Dr. Diet and Dr. Quiet."

In the modern era, notwithstanding the contributions of Freud and psychoanalysis, other developments in medical science which have had impact on psychiatry have been more comprehensible to the laity and to the medical profession at large. The use of the hormone insulin to treat schizophrenia was widely accepted. Electroconvulsive therapy revolutionized the management of depressive illness, and antibiotics all but eliminated syphilitics from mental hospitals.

More recently, tranquilizers, antidepressants, and lithium have become the order of the day. The advances of psychopharmaceutical medicine have been spectacular. They have elevated the nonpsychological therapies of psychiatry to levels of sophistication approaching treatment in cardiology and endocrinology. Psychiatrists now have an array of potent mood- and behavior-modifying drugs in their armamentarium and enjoy a new respect among their medical brethren.

A noted professor of pharmacology has bluntly observed that the practice of medicine in general concerns itself largely with the treatment of symptoms, not disease. We can do more to treat hypertension or appendicitis than we can to alter an individual's resistance to them; we are still far from knowing what susceptibility to disease really means. In psychiatry too, remedies command increasing attention, though the causes and prevention of emotional disturbances are still poorly understood. It is simpler to comprehend that a metabolic malfunction in the brain may produce neuroses, psychoses and even criminality, and to treat that disorder relatively cheaply with chemicals, than it is to spend time with patients in psychotherapy trying to understand and sort out numerous variables in their developmental experience which are responsible for their suffering.

This raises the difficult question of whether pragmatism is masquerading as science. The psychiatrist who views emotional suffering as a manifestation of hidden conflicts and is not content merely to treat symptoms may be chided for being "unscientific." He may appear to be inventing difficulties others do not perceive, especially when medicines suppress symptoms and produce apparent recoveries. In Mrs. Kenwick's case, her progress would soon require a judgment as to whether I should pursue her underlying problems. The risks of exposing her to the stress of confronting her latent conflicts would have to be weighed against her potential resources to face them when she was stronger.

For a week Mrs. Kenwick made steady gains. She seemed a little more self-assured each day, and her physical condition improved dramatically. She advanced to a normal diet and gained four pounds. The staff observed none of the bizarre symptoms present earlier. When I visited her, she thanked me for the return of her eyeglasses. Mrs. Kenwick was friendly but guarded. She clearly wanted to avoid any probing into her inner thoughts. I did not press her and kept my visits brief.

"She is really very chatty these days," the day nurse reported.

"What does she talk about?" I asked.

"She goes on a lot about her children, little Donna and Steven. I've seen pictures of them—they are adorable. She tells me things about her new home and about how good her husband is to her. It's strange, though, how in the middle of saying something she will stop now and then, as if someone suddenly threw a switch in her head. She'll be quiet then, though I can't tell whether she is really thinking about something or even thinking at all. When she realizes that this has happened, it seems to upset and embarrass her. I don't ask her about it or call it to her attention if she says nothing, but if she apologizes, I make little of it and tell her things like that happen to me sometimes. Am I doing the right thing to handle it that way, Doctor?"

"Mrs. Kenwick probably finds your acceptance and casual reassurances very helpful at this time. But tell me, have you noticed, by any chance, whether there are particular topics on which she blocks?"

The gray-haired nurse shook her head and frowned. "No,

Doctor. I'll try to pay closer attention to that if it happens again this evening. But I—"

"Yes?"

"It's nothing, just a feeling I had. It's not important." She shrugged.

"Please go on," I urged. "Your impressions have value. You say you had a feeling?"

She smiled self-consciously. "Well, I wouldn't know what to call it, but there is something funny about that young lady. It's in the way she talks about things. . . ." She paused to reflect a moment. "Yes, it's definitely in her manner, not in what she says. Mrs. Kenwick will be quiet for a time. Then, as I said, she'll start to chatter about her family and such. Now I don't doubt that what she tells me is true. She's shown me her photographs, cards, and letters, and I have met Mr. Kenwick. He is an attentive husband, just as she says. Still, whatever she says has a way of sounding made up, like a nice story."

"Something true, yet something not quite real to her?" I asked.

"Exactly, Doctor. It's not only with me. I often hear her talking on the telephone or speaking to her husband, telling him about her day, relating something that I know is so because I was with her. When I hear her tell it, it comes out like boasting. It's as if she has some kind of need to make everything sound pretty and nice—as if she's trying to convince herself that's the way things are. Do I make myself clear?" she asked frettingly.

"Yes . . . yes indeed. Your observation is quite interesting. I haven't picked up the attitude you're describing in my brief visits. Thank you. You've given me something to think about."

"Doctor, I am going to be able to stay with Mrs. Kenwick only through my shift tonight because I have another case I promised to take on before Mrs. Kenwick came along. I think she'll be all right, though, and you may not need to replace me. She seems to have overcome her fears enough to be friendly with all the regular floor nurses now. She'll smile and say hello to them when we take strolls in the halls."

"That's encouraging, but please don't underestimate your

significance to her. Be sure to tell her, and be open and reassuring. It is important that she understand why you are withdrawing and has a chance to accept the idea and express her feelings about it. You've really done a terrific job for all of us here. Thank you again, and good luck with your next patient."

Earl Hanon was delighted by Mrs. Kenwick's progress. "Jerry, I have to hand it to you. She's been a new patient since you came."

"Well, let's say a different patient, but thank the staff, not me. I've hovered, but actually, I've purposely avoided exposing her problems. They are covered over by a thin, opaque scab. I'm not at all sure whether any real healing has taken place under it. I've been waiting for her to recover from her surgery before testing her adjustment."

"From a surgical point of view, she is largely recovered and ready for discharge. She can convalesce at home now. It is up to you when she leaves. I've talked to her husband about that already. His in-laws are coming in from Columbus, Ohio, to help out. Mrs. Kenwick's father is a retired admiral. Did you know that? It's quite a coincidence, but I actually served under him down in Guantánamo Bay many years ago."

I smiled and remarked, "It is a small world, after all, isn't it?" Earl left to continue his rounds.

I had known about Admiral John Linette, but he was not Dolores Kenwick's real father. Her husband had revealed in strictest confidence that his wife's origins were a mystery, of which even she seemed unaware. He had learned this shortly before he married her. One evening, his future in-laws had invited him to dinner alone to disclose and explain certain things to him in secrecy.

Dolores had been born in Cuba. Her father had been a wealthy and prominent person in prerevolutionary Cuba who subsequently disappeared. Before he and his wife vanished, however, they managed somehow to have their only child spirited out of Cuba to the United States and delivered to the Linettes, whom they had known socially, though not well. They had entreated and authorized the admiral and his wife to adopt and to bring up Dolores as their own daughter, pledging them to secrecy for the child's future safety.

The Linettes, who had two adult sons and were already grandparents, honored their friends' extraordinary request. Mrs. Linette, who had always yearned for a daughter, became a devoted mother to Dolores. Mr. Kenwick knew few details of his wife's childhood, but recalled being told that she had been so frightened and withdrawn a child initially that the Linettes feared she was retarded. She did not speak and had regressed to thumb-sucking and bed-wetting. It had taken great warmth and encouragement to overcome her shyness and to help her readjust. But the gentle, loving efforts of her new parents had finally won her over and succeeded. It was curious, however, that Dolores never again spoke in Spanish, her first language, and that she seemed not to remember having lived anywhere but with the Linettes.

It was five-thirty on an overcast afternoon, the following day. I had dismissed the special nurses after the last shift had ended at seven that morning and was eager to learn how well Mrs. Kenwick had managed on her own. When I entered her room, it was unlit and dim. She was sitting alone in an easy chair alongside her bed, braiding her hair in the gloom. I noticed immediately that she was wearing a striped cotton hospital robe and gown instead of her own bedclothes. She did not look up as I approached and sat down on the edge of the other unoccupied bed.

"Good evening," I said. If Mrs. Kenwick heard me, however, she gave no hint of it. Instead, she hummed softly to herself and continued dividing her hair and twisting the strands. As she finished with one side, she began on the other. Then she would undo the first braid and methodically begin all over again. She was deliberately disregarding my presence. I waited. I tried to speak to her once more, but she hummed still louder, shutting me off. Why? I wondered. Had I done something to offend her? I could think of nothing. Why was she acting this way?

I began to review all I knew of her current situation, searching for a clue to what was disturbing her. I had scanned her chart on my way in. The nurses' notes reported that she had a normal night and slept soundly. This morning she had showered and washed her hair. She was cheerful and friendly until my visit earlier. Afterward she had remained in her room. The nurses recorded no further observations.

Quickly, silently, I reviewed our conversation that morning. Had I missed something? We had discussed Dr. Hanon's encouraging report of her progress. She seemed pleased by her recovery. I asked whether she felt apprehensive about coping without her private nurses. She told me no, that while she would miss their companionship, she was much more concerned that another patient might be moved into her room with her. We talked about that. She explained that she didn't feel up to making conversation with a sick roommate who might be in distress and need attention. I thought that somewhat self-centered but felt it more odd that in light of her apparent recovery, Mrs. Kenwick had not asked how long she would have to remain in the hospital. She was aware that her discharge was now my responsibility.

Could that be it? Was she anxious about her release? Her retreat into hospital clothes might indicate she feels threatened about going home. Also, her indifference to me is significant. She may feel disappointed and angry with me. Perhaps I have failed her in some important way. All my promises to her had been kept, but maybe she had expected me to resolve her other doubts and problems. I decided to find out.

"Recovering from your surgery, Mrs. Kenwick, has not solved other matters that upset you. Unless I am mistaken, you do not feel ready to go home yet. I don't plan to discharge you either, not until you communicate to me that you are all set to face it." The humming stopped. She finished her braid and looked up, shifting her gaze from one of my eyes to the other, searching to see something in them. I went on. "Both of us know that some problem deeply troubles you. We have put off discussing it until now so you could regain your strength without becoming more upset. Perhaps the time has come for us to consider whatever it is, together, in confidence. You must decide whether or not you can trust me enough to tell me about it."

Without taking her eyes from mine for even a moment, Mrs. Kenwick began to rotate her hands, one over the other, like a paddle wheel. She spun them forward, then backward, reversing direction frequently. Now she also began twisting and rocking from one side to the other rhythmically, bizarrely like a life-size mechanical doll. She was becoming increasingly agitated. I tried again. "You are having difficulty deciding what to do, which way to go, where to turn."

Abruptly her motions halted. She broke off her stare and dropped her eyes. "Will my parents be here tonight?" she asked quietly.

"I believe your parents are arriving today," I said, recalling Hanon's remarks. "Do you want them to visit you here?" She didn't answer but began twisting again. Her ambivalence was apparent.

I told her that I didn't think she felt ready to see them yet. "Suppose," I suggested, "that I tell them I would prefer to have them come at some later time. I do. Then you can discuss it with me, and I'll ask them when we've agreed to it."

Mrs. Kenwick closed her eyes and sighed. A thin, elusive smile formed on her lips. She seemed relieved. After a few moments she looked up at me again.

"Do you know whether spiders cry?" she asked.

"No, I don't know if spiders cry."

"They do sometimes," she said seriously. "John, my father, told me so. On our porch once, when I was little, I saw a small white moth caught in a spider's web. He struggled and struggled, but he couldn't get free. Then the spider came and was going to eat him. I was afraid of the spider, but I snatched the little moth away and set him free."

"That must have taken courage. I'll bet you were pleased with yourself," I said.

"John laughed. He said, 'Now the spider will cry because it has no supper for its babies.' "

"I suppose it isn't always easy to know what is right, is it?"

"I don't want to get well anymore. I want to die," she announced suddenly.

"You must believe then that there is no answer to your problem," I said, hoping she would go on.

"At first, you know, I was certain I had cancer and they weren't telling me. Even when I saw Dr. Hanon and he found the diverticulum, I didn't believe that the operation would cure me. I was terribly afraid, but George wanted me to have it; my parents did also. So I agreed and had the surgery, convinced that it wouldn't help. When I didn't improve afterward and got sicker, I was positive everyone was lying to me. I . . . I was confused and angry. I thought they had cut me for nothing . . . to make me suffer . . . to punish me. I was sure then that they were going to kill me. I remember, I was afraid to fall asleep. I had to watch for their tricks. I didn't know how they planned to do it. I was mixed up. . . ."

I listened to Mrs. Kenwick describe her psychosis, amazed anew at how extraordinary the human mind is. While her thought processes seemed to jump about in time and skip from one thing to another, I sensed a continuity in their emotional content. Here she was, initially disturbed by the prospect of going home from the hospital but ashamed, perhaps, and unable to tell me. So she acted it out in such a manner that I could interpret it to her. It became my idea; she never said it.

We repeated this charade about her parents' visit with the same result. Again I obliged her and made the actual decision, sparing her the burden of her ambivalence; her statement about wanting to die suggested that her adjustment was too fragile to risk exposing it just yet. Perhaps I had erred in referring to a problem she had yet to face. A person who must manipulate the therapist into uttering his thoughts and taking responsibility for his wishes is often unprepared to confront his conflicts. Dolores Kenwick's desire to die might reflect a wish to avoid facing her problem at all costs. Nevertheless, I had to find a way to bring it out carefully, or it would remain to threaten her again in the future.

She continued. "Then Millicent talked to me. She was angry with me because"—Mrs. Kenwick flushed noticeably—"I made a mess on the floor. She scolded me and said I shouldn't behave like that, that if I wanted to get well, I had to pull myself together and fight for it. I believed her; I felt I had finally found someone who was telling me the truth, someone I could trust."

"And apparently you put up quite a fight. You seemed to have taken on almost the entire staff single-handedly when I was called," I said, smiling gently.

"Millicent gave me a rosary, and I began to pray. I was born a Catholic. She said that God would answer my prayers. When you came, I believed that God had sent you. You seemed to understand without my having to tell you. And I started to get well. I believed you would take care of everything."

"I suspected as much when I came in before and found you looking so disappointed and angry. You feel overwhelmed that after all you've been through, you still face problems, is that it? I guess I've let you down as an angel, Mrs. Kenwick. Maybe now, however, you will let me try to help you as a psychiatrist."

Mrs. Kenwick smiled weakly. "I don't know if I can be helped."

"Tell me about yourself, Mrs. Kenwick."

I learned that Dolores Linette Kenwick was aware that she had been adopted, but beyond that, she seemed to have no knowledge of her background. She had been brought up in a manner that bordered on adoration. She had been protected, pampered, and indulged. Both her new parents delighted so in her that they virtually resented sending her off to school because it deprived them of her for hours.

Dolores had few close friends and seemed to have difficulty in relating to her peers. As the Admiral's daughter, however, she was invited to and entertained at lots of parties. What friendships she made were short-lasting owing to frequent moves. But Dolores did not miss friends or feel lonely. Her parents, especially her mother, were her pals and companions.

"Wherever we went, people would remark that they'd never seen such devoted parents, that I was really lucky. I was. I don't remember ever wanting anything I didn't get, but I was good, too. I did whatever my parents asked of me. They were really good to me. They still are. And so is George. That's the problem. I'm so unworthy of their love. . . ." Mrs. Kenwick put her face down and covered it with her hands. She began to cry.

Just then the telephone began to ring. I went over to the nightstand and picked it up. It was Mr. Kenwick. "This is Dr. Jacobs, Mr. Kenwick. I'm visiting your wife just now. . . . I see. Well, she is a little depressed this evening. As a matter of fact, I was going to call you to suggest that her parents not visit for a while, just yet. . . . That's right, perhaps in a few days. Mrs. Kenwick is going to stay on here a little longer. . . . No, her physical condition is fine. . . . Dr. Hanon has essentially discharged her, but I think, after this ordeal, she can use a little more time to sort things out emotionally. . . . Yes, I'll continue to see her."

I gestured to Mrs. Kenwick, but she shook her head. She didn't wish to speak. "I am going to give Mrs. Kenwick a chance to call you later if she isn't too tired. . . . What's that? . . . Just explain to him that here I'm sort of captain of the ship, and my orders are the law. But say it with a smile. Things will work out. . . . All right, I'll tell her that you love her and you will take care of things at home. Fine. Good night, Mr. Kenwick."

"I am very tired now, Doctor," Mrs. Kenwick said.

"Yes, I can see you are. We can continue our talk tomorrow. Good evening, Mrs. Kenwick."

"Good evening, Doctor."

I left Room 419 and proceeded toward the nurses' station. Along the way, I ruminated about my speculations that underlying problems, like subversive forces, had taken advantage of Mrs. Kenwick's overtaxed defenses to threaten her from within. The apprehensiveness she displayed about leaving the hospital to return home and resume her normal life was evidence of their existence and their power. For now that the danger to Mrs. Kenwick's life had passed and her recovery was assured, she was not only still anxious, but depressed.

I debated whether to change her medication in light of this development. The Thorazine, useful earlier to calm her when she was terrified, resisting care, and out of control, was no longer suited to her present condition. Thorazine is somewhat depressant and now could be contributing to her distress. I wrote a new order restricting its use, specifying that it be given only at night in the event Mrs. Kenwick became agitated or extremely restless. I gave some thought to placing her on antidepressant medication but discarded the idea; it would take days, perhaps even weeks to become effective. It could also excite and reactivate her psychosis. From our session it was clear that Mrs. Kenwick still had a marked tendency to act out her feelings and impulses. I wanted a drug that would continue to support her controls without deepening her depression. I decided to switch to a different, less depressant, yet potent tranquilizing agent as the mainstay of her drug therapy. I explained my aims to the charge nurse and prescribed a moderate dose of the new medication to be given at intervals during the day. It was important, I emphasized, for the staff to keep a watchful eye on Mrs. Kenwick because of her mood. While there was some risk in leaving her relatively unattended, I was reluctant to reinstitute full special nursing care and procedures. At this point I felt such measures would be an overreaction that could panic Mrs. Kenwick.

The following morning I took advantage of every moment between patients that I normally use to write up my impressions to check my notes for a talk I was scheduled to give to the nurses at the hospital. I also telephoned to see that Mrs. Kenwick understood I would be in to see her later than usual. Before I left for the conference, however, I had a call from Mrs. Linette.

"Doctor, I hope you won't mind my calling. I just hope I can help in some way," she explained.

"Not at all, Mrs. Linette. I'm afraid I can't speak to you at length this morning, but I am interested in learning as much as I can about your daughter."

"Well, I can't tell you how concerned my husband and I have been. Dolores doesn't bear up to stress all that well, and we've been sick with worry that with all that's happened, she would break down. She has that tendency, you know."

"Tell me what makes you feel that way," I said.

"Dolores had a frightful time as a very young child. My son-in-law has told you her background. I needn't go into it more than to tell you that when she arrived on our doorstep, my husband and I were totally surprised. We had no idea she was coming; we had hardly known her parents and didn't even know Dolores existed until then. I cannot begin to imagine what it was like for them to part with her or what she was told. Perhaps she was warned to say nothing, because she was a terribly frightened little girl. She wouldn't speak for the longest time despite all our efforts to coax her. It wasn't until a pediatrician wisely advised us to stop trying so hard, and not to speak Spanish, that she began to respond and answer us."

"Mr. Kenwick said your daughter recalls nothing of her life before."

"That is correct. Dolores was five and a half when we adopted her. She was such a pathetic, beautiful child. John and I felt we had to keep her. We wanted to give her a home. She seemed so lost and in need of affection that we probably overdid it. You see she was so unsure of herself, so insecure that we gave her affection unstintingly and unconditionally, to make her feel accepted. Dolores could do no wrong. Unfortunately she became a clinging, rather spoiled child as a result. I don't think she has ever really grown up emotionally. She has never learned to accept criticism or failure, I'm afraid."

"She had difficulty making decisions then?"

"Oh, yes. She always had a way of involving us whenever she had choices to make. Somehow her frustrations always became our fault. Whatever we suggested she would deride and then complain that we weren't helpful. Believe me, Doctor, John and I made plenty of allowances and put up with a great deal because of her insecurity. We felt that because my husband's assignments required us to move fairly frequently, we were at least partly responsible for her difficulties in adjusting. Dolores, however, never seemed to mind moving; in fact, she tended to be enthusiastic about it. She made friends quickly wherever we went. Now that I think about it, though, she never became very close to any of them. I can't remember her ever mentioning that she missed someone, nor did she try to keep up with any of her friends after we moved."

"Her involvements were superficial then," I observed.

"Yes. Dolores didn't seem to interest herself greatly in anyone else. She was always too involved with herself, I guess. She had fantasies of becoming an actress and achieving fame. Her room was cluttered with magazines about the movies and theater. But it actually was very difficult to get her to participate or try out for parts in plays or school programs. There was always some excuse: The director had his favorites, there wasn't sufficient time to learn the songs for a fair tryout, term papers were due, and so on."

"I see. You sensed that she really feared to test her talent," I said.

"Exactly. Though Dolores was pretty, she had no real confidence in herself. She preferred to believe that other, more successful girls had advantages or belonged to favored cliques. If we tried to discuss it with her, she'd become upset and hurt. When she finished high school and was accepted at the Taylor School of Dramatic Arts, she was thrilled, and so were we. We hoped that at nineteen, being on her own in Boston would help her grow up. Unfortunately it didn't work out quite that way."

I looked at my watch and saw that I would be late for my lecture if I continued the conversation. Yet I wanted to know more. Mrs. Linette was providing helpful history. "What do you mean?" I asked, deciding to go on for another few minutes.

"Dolores floundered on her own. She started out up there full of enthusiasm. However, once classes were under way and she saw how talented others were, her self-assurance rapidly waned. Dolores became involved with an instructor at the school. He was coaching her, and they began seeing a lot of each other. He claimed to be separated from his wife. It was her first serious romance, and she thought she was in love. I wonder if it wasn't partly just a diversion to take her mind off her constant fear that she wasn't going to succeed at Taylor. Well, anyway, he must have tired of Dolores and dropped her. She never told us exactly what happened, but suddenly there was no longer any mention of Kevin in her letters. She was doing things and going out instead with her roommate, Anne, and her fiancé, who I gathered were trying to cheer Dolores up. All we began to hear about was the fun she was having with Anne and George."

"Your son-in-law?" I asked.

"That's right. Dolores attached herself to them. She became more and more dependent on George. Anne didn't recognize what was happening at first, but eventually Dolores caused their breakup. In a real sense, she snatched George away from Anne. My husband and I were very uneasy about all this, of course, but they seemed so taken with each other that it was easy to rationalize that if George had married Anne, it would have been a mistake. Now I'm not so certain."

"Haven't your daughter and her husband been happy?"

"Yes. On the surface, anyway. George has been just marvelous to her, but now and then I have the impression that Dolores isn't satisfied. After each baby I sensed that she felt trapped and couldn't admit it. Incidentally, for your information, she wouldn't see us for a while afterward then either. It was as if she had to put herself together first and present a picture of success and happiness to us."

"Mrs. Linette, thank you. I must go now. You've given me a helpful insight and been most cooperative."

"I hope you can help Dolores, Doctor. I love her very much. We all do."

I raced across the street to the hospital, five minutes late. Some sixty or seventy nurses were assembled and seated in a lecture room, listening to Mary O'Dell tell humorous anecdotes about me. As I approached the lectern, she turned and, in a loud, mimicking voice, said, "Well, Doctor, you've kept us waiting, haven't you? I wonder how significant that is. . . ."

My lecture concerned the management of postoperative psychoses; it lasted forty minutes, and then I answered questions. My talk drew upon material from several cases, but not that of Mrs. Kenwick since her case was still in progress. Some of those present, however, were aware of her and prevailed on me to summarize briefly and explain the salient features of her course and treatment. I ended my remarks by telling them, "All in all, this combined team approach has so far succeeded in restoring the patient to a more tractable and amenable attitude. With her better able to cooperate now, psychotherapy directed at her underlying problems can proceed." If only it were as simple as that, I thought. Mrs. Kenwick's condition was still unstable and unpredictable. She had yet to be mobilized to confront her life and adjust to it once more.

"Good afternoon, Mrs. Kenwick." She sat up in bed.

"Hello, Doctor," she said, scowling slightly. "I expected you this morning."

"I had to give a lecture earlier. I'm sorry that I forgot to mention it yesterday. But didn't the nurses tell you and explain that I would be in later? I telephoned to make certain you'd be informed."

"Um . . . well, it doesn't matter really," she said, still dissatisfied. "I know you must have many other patients and responsibilities. I'm not all that important." As she spoke, she finished applying tape to the back of a torn photograph. Her hostile, dependent attitude suggested, though in a negative way, that she had accepted our relationship as important to her. It was evidence of a transference, and I was quick to exploit it.

"You seem to feel some resentment toward me," I commented.

She burst into tears. "Oh, go away; I don't need you. Just leave me alone. Please go," she cried.

I sat down. After a moment I quietly said, "I rather think this is a time I should stay and try to understand how you feel."

Mrs. Kenwick wiped her face. "You'll be angry with me now. You'll think I'm selfish and self-centered."

"You seem to believe either that your feelings will be disregarded or that if you are disappointed and angry, others will retaliate." Mrs. Kenwick stared at her knees for a moment or two. Then she reached over and adjusted the control, so that the head of the bed rose to support her in a sitting position. She looked at me now.

"What do you mean, Doctor?"

"I just wonder if you aren't manipulating matters now to avoid expressing something you are reluctant to say."

"And what would that be?" she asked, coloring a little.

"That perhaps you aren't entirely happy with your life as it is."

She didn't answer but turned toward the window and seemed to think for a long time. Finally, she looked down at the photograph she had pressed to the bed beneath her hands. She took it up and showed it to me. It was a picture of a pretty, smiling little girl holding a handsome, reluctant younger boy. The photograph had diagonal tear lines where it had been mended.

"You have lovely children, Mrs. Kenwick," I said. "Why did you tear their picture?"

"They are good children, Doctor. They deserve a better mother than me. I don't love them the way I should."

"What do you mean?" I asked gently.

"I became pregnant soon after George and I were married. I didn't want to continue at the school I was attending—I had been studying acting. There wasn't anything else I was any good at, and jobs just didn't interest me. I guess I also was uncertain George would stay after he got to know me better, that he wouldn't become annoyed or bored and leave me to find someone else. Then Donna was born.

"I tried to pretend that I was happy, but I became very depressed. I knew I didn't really love her. I was worried about the stretch marks on my stomach, and I was angry that I might not be able to wear my cute bikinis anymore. I was jealous also of all the attention the baby received. To be perfectly honest, it took me weeks to accept Donna and get over that. Then, after a few months, my parents and George seemed to think we should quickly have another child so Donna would have a sister or brother, close in age, with whom to grow up. So I became pregnant again, figuring that I'd have two and be done with it. When Steven came along, however, I got depressed once more. This time it was even worse. I . . . I had fears of hurting the children. That makes me pretty horrible, doesn't it?" she asked, looking into my eyes.

"It isn't very pleasant or easy to admit such things. I appreciate your candor, Mrs. Kenwick."

"But you find me selfish and disgusting just the same, don't you?"

"Many other troubled young women have related similar emotions and fears regarding their babies to me before they solved problems. They found it helpful to acknowledge their feelings of guilt and self-hatred in working through their ambivalency about motherhood."

Mrs. Kenwick bowed her head. When she looked up her eyes were bleak. "The thing is"—she dropped her voice—"after the operation, when I started to get so sick and became confused, it happened all over again. It was as if everyone knew I was rotten, that I cared only about myself. I thought I was being punished, that the children would be taken away from me. That's when I did this." She held up the mended photograph. "Millicent was my only friend. She saw the torn pieces in the trash basket and put them back in my drawer. I'm glad I have them now."

"You seem to be working on the guilty fears that made you so vulnerable. The inhibitions which usually prevent you from expressing your true feelings, however, deserve our attention. It must be burdensome to play a role all the time."

"Not really." She smiled affectedly. "I'm used to it; I've been an actress all my life."

We talked for the rest of the hour. I suggested that her dissembling probably led others to misinterpret her needs and wishes repeatedly. Mrs. Kenwick acknowledged that she lived in constant frustration and disappointment, afraid to reveal herself, yet resentful and despairing because no one really knew and accepted her. She was her own best friend, her only one. Even that narcissistic self-love, however, was ambivalent. She saw herself, with reason, as selfish and self-centered. "I knew what kind of person I was, but I couldn't change just by wishing I were different," she said. "So, Doctor, I tried to live the way I was. . . ."

It was a productive session. At the end we made an appointment to continue the following day. My brief, frequent visits were no longer necessary, and we agreed that hereafter it would be better for us to meet once daily for longer sessions. I left Mrs. Kenwick, encouraged that our talks were becoming increasingly insightful.

The narcissistic personality is one in which the self is the primary and almost exclusive object of the individual's affection and interest. When I deal with a narcissistic character, I find it helpful to differentiate two principal types. I make the distinction primarily on the basis of whether the affected individual perceives that he "suffers" from a personality disorder. Those lacking sufficient insight share with psychotics distorted views of reality. They may be uninhibited, demanding, and even charismatic, bending and rearranging the truth with unconcern. In several ways they resemble newborn infants in their almost total preoccupation with themselves, their own wishes and needs.

They assume that those about them are there to serve them; they lack humility and appreciation. Such individuals see other persons as extensions of themselves, mere means of affecting and obtaining their own gratification, or they disregard others as irrelevant. Whether these personalities develop as a result of prolonged overindulgence in early life or are predisposed, narcissists of this type feel all-important in a world that was meant to be theirs.

When a narcissistic individual has sufficient insight to recognize that he is afflicted with an undesirable and unwanted trait, such as self-centeredness, I place him in another category. Such a person's affectation is compulsive in nature; he resembles the neurotic. That is, he cannot resist his abhorrent tendencies without experiencing anxiety.

These unfortunate persons view the world as a threatening environment for which they have been ill-equipped to cope. Many blame their parents for this. They take refuge from their feelings of weakness and fear in self-pity and self-indulgent behavior. They feel their inadequacies keenly and are envious of those who manage effectively. They become manipulators and dissemblers. Their moods oscillate between self-loathing and resentment toward persons who seem more capable. Periods of depression occur when self-hatred prevails. At other times they project their own hostile attitudes onto those they resent.

I do not know what produces this form of narcissism, but I view it as probably taking origin in a childhood trauma such as that which Mrs. Kenwick endured when she was separated from her parents. I believe that if love and trust, essential to a child's healthy psychological growth, are betrayed or withdrawn, certain children will thereafter react to that catastrophe by minimizing their emotional investments in others. They may be capable of caring to a degree, but the depth of their feelings is shallow. They find themselves unable to love, yet they may be self-conscious enough to feign it. To love deeply risks arousing anxiety that their past trauma will recur. Mrs. Kenwick would have to discover that her narcissism was a defense and confront the trauma she had repressed if she hoped to change significantly.

It was Saturday morning. When I entered Mrs. Kenwick's room, I found her husband with her. He and I exchanged pleasantries, agreeing that the patient looked very well. She did. Although Mrs. Kenwick still seemed to prefer hospital clothes to her own, her hair was attractively combed, and touches of color had been added to her face. After a few moments I tactfully suggested that Mr. Kenwick leave to permit his wife the opportunity to resume therapy in private. He rose and was beginning to go when Mrs. Kenwick called him back.

"I want George to stay, Doctor," she announced. "I asked

him to be here this morning because there is something I want to say." I nodded agreeably, and we all sat down together again. Mrs. Kenwick reached over and pulled a small yellow envelope from her nightstand drawer. She tore off the end, dropped a small silver wedding band into her palm, and studied it.

"George," she began, "I don't think I love you." Kenwick was taken aback, his eyes widening in surprise. A nervous half grin formed on his lips, and he glanced at me. "I'm sorry, George, but it's true. I didn't love you when I married you." She looked up, facing him now. "I don't feel whatever it is that people in love . . . that *you* feel." Kenwick started to speak, but she shook her head, adding, "It's not your fault in any way. You've been wonderful. You are a truly good man, but I don't love you. You should have married Anne."

"I loved you, Dee!" he protested. "I still do and always will."

"You don't understand. This is not something that just occurred to me. I've known it all along. I don't know if I really love the children either. I'm not sure what I feel about them. All I am certain of is that I've made a mess of our lives, yours and mine. I think I should leave you and the children and go away. We should separate and probably divorce. Maybe everyone will be better off that way. You and they deserve someone who can give one hundred percent, the way you do." She held out the ring to him.

Kenwick folded his hand over hers. "Keep it, Dee," he pleaded. "I don't want anyone else, honey. I want only you."

"Look, George, I loved Kevin more than you, and he was half the person you are. When I couldn't get him, I took you away from Anne. It was a rotten thing to do."

"Don't you think I know how you felt about Kevin, dear? But you've gotten things twisted. When he and you broke up, I began to realize that I loved you more than Anne. I was the one who kept suggesting that we invite you out with us, remember? It was I who let Anne down, not you. I told her so, and she agreed I caught you on the rebound. I knew you didn't really love me, but I saw my chance and took it. I hoped you would eventually. I'm still eager to gamble that you will someday. Don't leave us, Dee; we need you." Kenwick rose and pulled his wife to her feet, and they embraced.

The emotion filling the room began to ebb. I thought it inappropriate to proceed with a psychotherapy session after what had taken place and decided to leave the Kenwicks alone together. Mrs. Kenwick had just taken a courageous step—if she was sincere. "I think you two should be alone now," I said, rising and retreating toward the door.

"Thank you, Doctor," Mrs. Kenwick called. "I needed you here to say what I did. I'd like to see my parents this afternoon if that's all right."

"Of course, Mrs. Kenwick."

"Oh, and, Doctor, do you think I could go home tomorrow? I could come and see you at your office on Monday if that's all right. I am going to need a lot of help to see things clearly."

"Monday at eleven—the same as our appointment here," I reminded her. "I'll arrange for your discharge. Dr. Hanon may want to examine you again before you leave." I could tell, watching her, that Mrs. Kenwick was disappointed that I had not commented on what had occurred. I thought of saying, "It sounds as if you've decided to become the person you want to be, Mrs. Kenwick," but chose to say nothing. Time would tell.

I wrote a discharge order and left a prescription for a lower dosage of the same medication she had been taking to be taken at home. Various aspects and events in the case came to mind as I penned a discharge summary. They were beginning to gel. The crisis had passed; further progress would come more slowly now. The therapeutic challenge to bring about some enduring shift in the patient's personality was still ahead. On my way to the elevator I passed a scrubwoman wringing her mop out into a pail. As I went by, she looked up and spoke to me.

"Ah, Doctor?"

"Yes?"

She wiped her palms on her smock and extended her right hand. "*La pequeña*, the little one, in four-nineteen, she likes you very much. She's a lot better now, no?"

I shook the woman's hand and agreed, "Yes, I think she is going to be fine. Mrs. Kenwick will be going home tomorrow."

"I'll go and say good-bye when I'm finished here then. She and I are friends. I'm Millie Fernandez; she calls me Millicent."

"Oh, so you are Millicent!" I said, surprised.

"That's right. I visit Dolores every day. She practices her Spanish with me."

"She's been speaking in Spanish?"

"Oh, yes, *sí.* She was born in Cuba, you know."

"So I understand." I nodded and extended my hand to shake hers again. "Millie, you have been a great help on this case. Thank you."

Millie flushed and smiled proudly. *"Gracias."*

I entered the elevator and went down to the snack bar for a cup of coffee. Earl Hanon was there and waved me over. "Earl, I'm discharging Mrs. Kenwick tomorrow. I told her you might want to check her again before she leaves."

"No, Jerry, she's fine. She has a follow-up appointment at my office. But thanks for telling me anyway. I'll stop by and say good-bye to her. I really appreciate all your help on this one. I was sure we'd have to send her off to a funny farm for a while. But she's going to be okay now, isn't she?"

"I hope so, Earl," I answered, "I really hope so."

Mrs. Kenwick slung her shoulder bag into the chair nearest me and settled down in the other. She looked unhappy and bothered. I waited for her to speak, but she seemed reluctant to begin. Finally, I commented that she seemed to be disturbed about something; that drew a scowl.

"You didn't believe me on Saturday morning," she said flatly. "I could tell you thought it was all a performance I staged."

So that was it. She was angry that I failed to commend her courage for the scene in her hospital room. "Were you acting, Mrs. Kenwick?" I asked calmly, making no effort to dispute or to appease her.

"Couldn't you tell?" she asked pettishly.

"Could you?"

For a second or two she continued to stare at me, mute and smoldering. Then she reached over and retrieved her bag. I thought for the moment I had gone too far, that she might get up and leave. But she merely removed a handkerchief. "Everything I said on Saturday was true, you know." Her tone had eased and was less certain now. She leaned forward, removed a pair of contact lenses, and exchanged them for eyeglasses in her bag. "I have to get used to my contacts all over again," she complained.

"You were saying," I started to remind her.

"That you don't think I was serious, that I would have gone through with it and really left George and the children, do you?" She found no answer in my face. "I don't actually know myself," she admitted with great deliberation. "I can't always be certain how sincere I am. Would I have offered to go if I had not been positive George wouldn't let me?" She looked directly at me now. "Can you believe, Doctor, that I really do want to be able to say things and earnestly mean them?"

"Yes, I can easily accept that," I assured her.

"Then help me!" she pleaded. "I can't stand being the way I am. I don't want to spend the rest of my life like this, thinking only of myself. My children weren't even glad to see me when I came home. For two days now they haven't come near me. If I try to hold them, they pull away as if I were a witch and run to George or to my parents."

"They will need a little time to readjust and to trust you again," I advised.

"They're angry because I left them for so long. That's it, isn't it?"

"I suppose so.

"But we explained everything so carefully to them before I left the house."

"You were even older when your parents sent you here to the United States. They surely gave you a careful explanation also. Do you remember it?" I took advantage of the present situation to reveal Mrs. Linette's phone call and to stir the patient's memory. Mrs. Kenwick nervously twisted her handkerchief around a finger and bit on it. She drew a deep breath and began to shake her head vehemently. "Well, there," I went on, "explanations are not always remembered. A child—"

"No!" she interrupted. Her voice snapped back with a violence that surprised me. "There was no explanation; they lied to me! I was told I was going to visit my uncle Pedro!" she gasped, and began to cry.

"You do remember," I said.

She nodded and struggled to regain her composure. "My name . . . is . . . really . . . Dolores María Melendez," she said chokingly.

I poured her some water from the carafe on my desk. "You weren't ever supposed to tell, were you?"

She sipped from the cup and shook her head. "No, this is the first time I've told my name to anyone or ever heard it spoken to my knowledge. I was not even to think of it again. In the hospital, things came back to me. Millicent, the cleaning lady with the Spanish accent, helped me remember. At first, I had the strangest feeling that I had known her before, a déjà vu. It started me thinking. Then I remembered one or two occasions when my parents, Matilda and John—the Linettes—tried to sit down with me to explain things to me. I couldn't stand to hear about it, however. I'd become hysterical, throw a fit, and make them stop."

"What do you recall?"

"Mostly the little they managed to tell me. I know that Mother and Dad knew my real parents, though not all that well. Can you imagine that? If they wanted to be rid of me, they could just as well have left me on a doorstep somewhere," she said bitterly. "They didn't send along even one thing for me to have to remember them."

"One might easily conclude from their extraordinary efforts just the opposite, that they thought everything out quite carefully and took rather extreme and unselfish measures to protect you."

"You are just saying that to make me feel better about it," she said accusingly. "It won't work."

"If you prefer," I replied evenly.

"It isn't that I would want to be ungrateful, but I find it hard to accept what you suggest. Besides, even if I did," she argued, "what difference would it make now? It is over and done with. I don't know them, and I certainly don't love them anymore. Even if they are living and would want it, I am not sure I would wish to meet them today. That is all done with as far as I am concerned."

"But is it?" I asked. "Consider once more the qualms your children are experiencing after your relatively brief absence, even though you made an effort to prepare them."

"It's not the same at all," she protested. "They have their father to look after them. They know that George, at least, loves them."

"Perhaps you are right," I conceded. "I think your circumstances were far worse. You must have been infinitely more insecure alone, with no one, having been deceived and transported to a strange land, where a language foreign to you was spoken. All your children would have to contend with might be the fear that you alone had discovered something in them so awful it caused you to abandon them. I wonder how damaging that might prove to be to their capacity to relate lovingly and confidently to others."

"You think that's what is wrong with me?" she asked.

"I've heard you describe yourself as 'rotten,' " I reminded her.

"Well, I am selfish. I know that's true. I am not a loving kind of person."

"People who already feel they are bad and unlovable probably have little incentive to be otherwise."

"I don't know. All this is too new for me. I'll have to mull it over."

We discussed Mrs. Kenwick's resumption of her normal role in her household. At the end of the hour we agreed to meet twice weekly.

I continued to see Mrs. Kenwick for several months. She came to understand how she expressed herself as an unlikable castoff through her selfishness and how this behavior also compensated her. I gradually reduced her medication and withdrew it. She was more confident that she cared for others with interest and affection when we terminated our sessions.

Would Mrs. Kenwick maintain her apparent gains? The results of psychiatrists are generally less conclusive than those of other physicians. Surgeons, for example, are much more directly involved in affecting changes in their cases. The psychotherapist, on the other hand, is more of a catalyst whose role is to assist in the patient's efforts to understand and change himself. Even when the therapist feels he has succeeded, a good outcome is always the result of the patient's efforts.

* * * * *

The work of a psychiatrist resembles that of a detective in a number of ways. He, too, is an investigator. Each of his cases, like those of the sleuth, starts out when someone consults him with a problem; it is usually the victim who calls. Like his counterpart, the psychiatrist begins by investigating the circumstances surrounding and preceding the complaint; he probes into the victim's background for clues to what has happened and why.

He is a careful observer and a methodical inquisitor, disciplined to be cautious and to doubt. He listens patiently, perceptively, sifting through what is said, alert to every telltale pause, inconsistency, equivocation, or hint of ambivalence. No gesture or slip of the tongue eludes his notice as he traces the victim's path, studying his behavior, learning about his relationships. He will examine even remote, seemingly irrelevant, long-past events, searching relentlessly to uncover hidden feelings, disguised motives, masked identities. These efforts will discomfort his client, for in psychiatry, the victim and the culprit are one.

THE COOL CAT WITH NINE LIVES

Fred Emory

It was nearing the end of a mild, sunny afternoon early in April, a respite from the cool spring rains. My last patient of the day had departed. I finished my notes and had just left my office when the door to the outside fire escape opened and a young man stepped through into the corridor before me. He had short blond hair and was dressed casually. He weighed, perhaps, a hundred and forty pounds.

Quickly he scanned the empty hall in front of us, quietly easing the heavy door closed behind him. He turned now, blocking my way. "Dr. Jacobs?" His voice was hushed.

"Yes?"

"I know you are leaving now, Doctor, but could I talk to you in your office? It would mean a great deal to me if you could spare me just a few minutes. I got your name from Judge Farrow. I'm Fred Emory."

He sounded about as sincere as a magazine salesman pretending to be working his way through college. He smiled weakly and stuck out his hand. I clasped it; it was moist. Fred Emory was anxious. For an instant I considered telling him to call me another time for an appointment, but his tenseness and my curiosity triumphed. I agreed to listen to him. Harry Farrow, whom I had met socially, is a local magistrate, active in civic affairs. Though we were friendly, we had many differences. I knew he did not hold psychiatry in high esteem. I was surprised and interested to meet someone he would refer.

I turned to open the door to my office once more. The noise of the elevator nearing the floor came from the far end of the corridor. Fred Emory gasped. I stepped aside to let him precede me; he fled into my waiting room. Cautiously I followed, taking care not to close the door behind me completely. Fresh chips and scratches around the latch reminded me of a recently at- tempted break-in. Fred Emory's furtiveness made me uneasy and suspicious.

The office I occupy is relatively isolated at the end of a long hallway on the top floor of a professional building. It is four long flights up from the parking lot behind. Fred Emory was not winded. He had been waiting for me.

I watched his eyes dart quickly around the room, noting the windows and doors. Though he was jittery and apprehensive, there was a sly, canny look about him. A faint tic flicked in his left cheek, and the trim little mustache beneath his nose was laced with beads of perspiration. His face was dotted with nu- merous small pits and acne scars. The wan smile, present before, had vanished.

"Do you know Judge Farrow well?" I asked, deciding to take the initiative.

"Well, uh. . . ." He hesitated, taken off guard, and avoided my glance. "Judge Farrow didn't actually send me to you," he admitted. "I mean, he doesn't know I am here. Nobody does. I heard the judge holding forth over in the post office. He was raving about something or other and mentioned your name. He said you were the only psychiatrist he had met who seemed to have his feet on the ground. So I decided to come to see you."

"You came on an impulse then?"

"Well, I called first, but I only got your answering service."

"You left no message with them. . . . I wonder if you merely wanted to learn my schedule. Did you intend to catch me after hours this way? Was that it?"

He nodded, self-satisfied, pleased that I appreciated his cleverness. "Yeah." He smirked. "I didn't want anyone to know I was coming here. I'm keeping out of sight just now until I figure out what I'm going to do. That's why I need your help."

Footsteps echoed in the corridor outside. Fred drew back, startled; his sardonic grin vanished. He chewed his lips nervously, listening, waiting. The sounds paused; a door slammed; then the footsteps resumed, closer now. Fred looked scared. He wiped his palms repeatedly against his thighs.

A doorknob rattled close by, followed by the click of a latch being engaged. Suddenly the knob in my hand was twisted, and the door to my office was wrenched open. I heard a muffled cry and motion behind me as I turned, off-balance, to confront my second unexpected visitor.

"Gee, I'm sorry, Doctor. I didn't know you were there." It was the janitor. "Since the burglaries in the building, I go around checking all the offices and doors every afternoon about this time before I begin cleaning up downstairs. This exit door wasn't shut properly. Anyone could have just come in from the fire escape. That's why I come around to make sure."

"I'm grateful you do, Bill. I'll be in my office a little while longer. There's someone in there I want to talk to; then I'll lock up."

"That's all right, Doc, stay as long as you wish. But if you go out the fire door, please make sure it's really shut."

I closed my office door again. Fred Emory had disappeared from the waiting room. I found him kneeling on the floor, crouched over my wastepaper basket, trembling. I reached down and gently pulled the cowering young man to his feet. He was pale, gulping air and quivering about the mouth. "Come," I urged, guiding him back to the waiting room and into the small lavatory which opens from it. I helped him over to the commode and stepped back. He bent forward, supporting himself with outstretched arms against the walls, and retched.

"There are cups, water, and paper towels to your right, Fred. Come back into my office when you are ready." He bobbed his head. I returned to my desk and telephoned my wife. I told her I would be delayed, that I had an unexpected, sensitive consultation. I hoped I had succeeded in alerting without alarming her.

I could hear Fred washing. In a moment he reappeared in my doorway. "Why don't you sit down and tell me what this is all about?" I asked, gesturing at the chairs. "I've called my wife and told her I am here seeing someone, so that she won't be concerned if we talk for a while." Despite his desire for secrecy, I thought it prudent to tell him I had made a call and that yet another person was aware of our presence.

Fred entered the office and sat down heavily. He mopped his face. His pulse beat visibly on both sides of his slender neck. He bent forward, pulled the sweater he wore over his head, and tossed it in a heap onto the empty chair nearer me. His carefully combed hair was disturbed.

"What kind of trouble are you in, Fred?"

"I, uh . . . I'm nervous. I'm so tensed up I shake inside all the time. My stomach is tied in knots." He glanced toward the lavatory. "I can't eat and hold anything down. None of the junk they sell in the drugstore helps. The pharmacist said I need a prescription from a doctor to get anything stronger. And I've got to get some relief. I am so nerved up I can't even sleep at night. I don't drink whiskey ordinarily, but now I take a shot, sometimes two, before I can doze off—and then I wake up again in a few hours. I've never been like this before."

Fred was telling me how he felt, listing his complaints rather than answering what I had asked. I decided to go along with him. "How long have you been feeling this way?" I inquired.

"How long have I . . . ? Two days . . . maybe three. What's the difference? You can see I feel lousy. Jesus! You do sound like a headshrinker." He was insolent and picking a quarrel now. Whatever else Fred Emory feared, it was apparent that having to ask for help also threatened him. This was going to be difficult.

"Look, Doc, I don't have much time, you know? I'm cracking up, understand?" His tone was querulous. "Look." He held his hands out before him; they trembled. "My hands shake, right? I run to the john all the time, and all that comes out is slime like spit, okay? My heart beats so damn hard I think I am gonna have a heart attack. Man, don't just sit there like an asshole playing shrink. I mean, I need help."

It was a demand, not an appeal. I leaned back in my chair and looked directly at him. "I am trying to learn how to help you, Mr. Emory," I said, my voice calm and unaffected.

"Oh, shit!" he exclaimed, and bolted out of his chair. He paced around the room. "What the hell did I come here for? I don't want any of this psychiatric bullshit. . . . Jacobs. . . . You're Jewish, I bet. Most shrinks are. . . . I hate all you smart-assed, educated, liberal pricks. I hate niggers, guineas, and queers, too. Christ, I hate myself for being such a friggin' coward—for being scared. It sucks. You understand?"

He held out his left hand and dug his fingernails into the back of it until he winced and drew blood. Then he shoved his clenched fist forward over my desk to show the wounds he had made. "See that?" he asked. "I hate my goddamned self for being afraid. You have to give me something, understand? I have to get it all together before I snap and something bad happens."

Fred Emory didn't need threats to convince me he was frantic. He was desperate, almost out of control, yet like some hunted, wounded animal, he was dangerous. A paroxysm of tremors seized him; he dropped back into his chair, then leaned forward to grip his knees and stop their shaking. He was at his limits; his defenses were strained and failing.

Quickly I considered how to proceed. Here is a young man beside himself with a need for help, yet quarrelsome and threatening to the object of his appeal. He insults me and lashes out inappropriately and provocatively, risking my rejection, demanding, not requesting my assistance. Apparently, he cannot endure being needful; the passive dependent position must be intolerable to him. If I appease him and submit to his bullying, it may encourage him to make further demands. On the other hand, he is clearly in distress and potentially dangerous. I have to find a way to relieve him and defuse the situation.

How can I ease him without appearing to be intimidated? If he gets the idea he is frightening me and at the mercy of his own impulses, he may really panic. I must assert my role as a physician and impose control until he regains command of himself. In assuming the role of an authority, however, I risk becoming the object of his rage. I harbored no illusions that it would be easy to subdue him if he became violent. The strength of individuals driven by maniacal fury no longer amazes me. I decided to offer him the help he sought but on my terms. I would confront him, indicating I was unafraid and unaffected by his insults. It was a gamble. Demonstrating my judgment and control, when his were crumbling, might make him feel more secure; he might become more tractable.

"I can see how desperate you feel, Mr. Emory. Anxious people often blame others when they see no way out of their problems. Unless your bigoted views relate to your immediate predicament, however, we won't have to discuss them further right now. Instead, if you'll answer my question and tell me what's wrong, I'll try to determine how to help you."

Fred stared at me, open-mouthed. I lectured him in a firm, open manner. "It's apparent that you came in here terrified and in some kind of jam. You can either waste my time and cheat yourself trying to provoke me, the way you've been doing, or begin cooperating so the two of us can figure out how to help you. Make up your mind. If you intend to benefit in any way from seeing me today, then begin telling me about yourself and what has happened to you."

I paused at this point, took a few moments to search for a pad, turned and sharpened a pencil, and made myself comfortable. When I felt he had had sufficient time to consider my words and to leave if he wished, I confronted him again. "How old are you, Mr. Emory?"

Fred Emory had pulled out a comb and was passing it through his hair. His image seemed to concern him once more. He sat there sobered, calmer now.

"I was twenty on my last birthday, February seventh," he answered.

"Where do you reside?"

"At Forty-three Old Oak Lane, across town, near the parkway." I knew the section. It was one of the older, less affluent neighborhoods. "My mother and my stepfather live there. I also have a ten-year-old stepsister. But I have my own place. I fixed up an apartment for myself. It's separate—over the garage. I can come and go as I please. I even have my own refrigerator, but I don't cook or eat there. It's loaded with soda and beer," he boasted.

"You seem pleased to have a place of your own," I observed.

"Yeah," he agreed. "Say, Doc, what I said before . . . I didn't mean anything personal, you know? Like you said, my nerves were shot." I said nothing. "But, Jesus," he continued, grinning, "you don't take any crap, do you? Judge Farrow was right about you." There was a measure of respect in Fred's last remarks, but I disregarded them and solicited the background to his current problems. . . .

Two years before, Fred revealed, he had dropped out of high school late in his senior year. He quit apparently on a whim at the time his classmates began receiving acceptances to college. Since then he had worked in the family business—a furniture store. On several occasions he had minor scrapes with the police. He was proud of his reputation with them as a clever troublemaker.

"Trouble and me seem to go together like bacon and eggs," he bragged. "It's like a game to me; I always figure a way out. I'm kind of a genius at it."

Complaints that Fred was a nuisance and mischief-maker

were never sufficient for the police to hold him on any charges until one of his pranks misfired and led to his arrest for grand larceny. He had stolen a costly candy vending machine from the entrance to a local movie theater. He hauled it to the grandstand at the park to use for his personal convenience when he watched the football team practice. Despite his arrest, Fred again squirmed out of trouble when the charges were reduced. He got off with a severe warning and was placed on probation for a period of two years, which was almost up. That was part of his present problem.

"You see, I am a terrific con man," he explained. "I can usually snow almost anyone except maybe you, Doc." His respect was not reassuring, but I sensed an acceptance in his confidence.

Before this past Christmas, Fred had managed to purchase a bloc of tickets to a popular concert in the city. He was reselling them profitably at the gates when he encountered Tina. He persuaded the pretty sixteen-year-old to go to the concert with him. After that they saw each other frequently. Fred succeeded in impressing the inexperienced girl and took Tina to several events during her Christmas vacation. She became infatuated with him.

"I fed her a lot of bull," he boasted. "I even made up a story that I had an older brother who was killed in Nam. I told her I was going to join the Marines myself in a few months, to take his place in the corps. I fed her so much crap about how great he was and how I wanted to be like him that I had her practically in tears. I even promised to show her his grave someday. It was all part of a con, see, to make it with her. She was a virgin, one of those built, nice, nice little Italian birds who goes to church every Sunday, listens to her mother, and gets home by twelve on Saturday nights. She was ripe, you know what I mean? She never had met anyone cool like me before—no one with class.

"I made it with her on New Year's Eve, which is what I had planned all along. She cried and kept asking me if I loved her. They always want you to say you love them and stuff. Anyway, after that, she followed me around like a puppy. It really got boring. I used to put her down—I mean, really humiliate her—just for kicks. Man, I dumped all over that dumb broad. I'd pick a fight with her over nothing, and she'd try everything to please me. I mean, she'd do anything I asked just to make up. I jerked her around like a puppet.

"Finally, I couldn't take her whining anymore, so I told her I had enlisted and had to go to Quantico for basic. You should have heard her bawl and carry on." Fred reached down the neck of his shirt and showed me a gold link chain. "She bought me this—it's not one of those cheapies either. . . . Tina begged me to write and made me promise to send her a picture. That's where I screwed up.

"I got this guy I know, Jimmy, to lend me his uniform—he's in the Marines—and I took this color picture with some of his buddies when they were all in on a pass. Then Jimmy mailed it to her from base with a letter I wrote about how proud I was to be a marine. We even fixed it so she could write to me there; he got the letters. I leaned on her to send me a sexy picture, and she did. If I had it on me, I'd show you. I used to get a lot of guys breathing hard when they'd see it—especially with the inscription I had her write on the back.

"Then, three weeks ago, everything hit the fan. Pow! Tina took off from home and showed up in Virginia, at the base, pregnant and looking for me. Everything would have been cool anyway, if it weren't for that friggin' snapshot I sent her. But someone from the Red Cross and an SOB chaplain down there located one of the guys in the picture. He put them on to Jimmy, who tried to cover for me. He called me and said he wouldn't tell them anything. He was scared, though, and I could tell he wouldn't risk getting court-martialed because I screwed some kid. Jimmy was supposed to call me again if it all blew over, but he didn't. Now I don't know what's going on. That ain't cool."

"So that's why you're so nervous, because of your probation."

"No, man. What happens down there doesn't bother me. That shit will slide. What can they do to me for taking a picture to impress my girl, you know?"

"I don't understand. What is it then?" I asked.

"Someone's been around looking for me." He shuddered. "A big, curly-haired gorilla named Marty. It's Tina's brother-in-law. Jimmy must've given them something. Now Marty's after me. He's been nosing around the store and the house. I've seen him. He even showed up at Kelleher's and Neeley's Cozy, where I hang out. The old bartender at Kelleher's said he's a real mean type. I've been hiding out, but I'm scared shitless. I mean, this is my town, where I live. I've got nowhere else to go. You've gotta help me."

"What exactly is it that you want?"

"You're a psychiatrist, aren't you? You know about nerves. I need a tranquilizer or something to calm me down. I'm shaking all the time like a junkie who needs a fix. I have to be able to use my head to think. All I do is sneak around, checking people out all the time. Marty might not be alone; he might even know people here. How do I tell who he's talked to? Maybe they even tacked that picture of me up on the wall at Saint Cecilia's."

"Fred, even if I gave you some mild tranquilizers, it would—"

"No!" he interrupted. "I need something strong, something that works. Listen, Doc, I am not asking for charity or favors. I'll pay you for your time like any other patient. I have lots of bread." He dug into his pocket and produced a roll of bills.

"That's not the point," I said. "Taking pills for your nerves won't make Marty go away, will it? It won't solve your problem. Pills wear off. You need something more than a few hours' relief. Besides, even if Marty left town, he could always come back again. Hiding out indefinitely isn't the answer either. There ought to be a better solution. Sooner or later you will have to confront the problem more directly."

"No way!" Fred cried, jumping to his feet. "I can't go up against a guy like Marty. There wouldn't be enough of me left to scrape together for a funeral! Never!" He took out a handkerchief and wiped his hands and brow with it.

"You misunderstand me, Fred. Until now you've always managed to wriggle out of trouble being clever. You've come to rely on your cunning, and it's given you a certain confidence. In one situation after another you've lived by your wits, and you're proud of it. But I doubt that trouble was ever really a game as you've claimed. You didn't win even when you didn't lose. Now you may have violated your probation, and you also have Marty to worry about."

"I thought about that, like I said, but I haven't been charged with anything. . . . Do you think I ought to worry about that?" he asked.

I nodded. "You don't seem to understand the game you're playing very well."

Fred screwed up his nose. "You're right, Doc." He snickered. "I probably have a complex or something."

"Tell me, do you know an attorney in whom you have confidence? Did one handle your trouble before?"

"Not that bastard, he ripped me off!"

"An attorney could represent you in this. He could contact Tina's family and see what you might do to make amends. Perhaps there is some way you might be helpful and settle matters. A lawyer could also protect your rights if there is a legal problem because of what you've done," I explained.

"Man, people like that don't talk to lawyers. It's a blood thing with them—a vendetta. They don't use their heads like you and me."

So he and I are thinking men now—we're on the same team, are we? "Look, Fred, don't deceive yourself. You could overlook something useful." Why was I trying so hard to help him? I wondered.

"Okay. Okay," he said, spreading his arms in mock humility. "I've got nothing to lose, right? I'll get Harvey Eller to do it; he's cool and smart. Jew lawyers are the best anyway, aren't they?"

I was off his team again—just the water boy. He had put me in my place again. He provokes and manipulates cunningly so that he is never in a position of receiving or owing. Fred has to be the taker, the plundering victor. He really views everyone as basically selfish and unfriendly and goes out of his way to bait and antagonize others so they will seem that way.

"That last remark, Fred—you seem to have trouble showing gratitude. Do you always have difficulty accepting help?"

"All right, Doc, don't be so sensitive. I thought I could say anything to a psychiatrist."

The clever bugger. Never mind, it was important to meet his gibes squarely and face him or we would get nowhere. He must respect my strength, or he'll become anxious again. I was catching on to his tactics, learning his pattern.

Fred sat down again. He was grinning at something; it was the same triumphant smirk he had had in the waiting room when he was proud of having got in to see me. "You have to admit it, Doc"—he chuckled—"I was smart to come here to talk to you. I got more than I expected. . . . You never met anyone like me before, did you?"

"No, Fred, not exactly like you."

"You could learn a lot from a case like mine. You're probably eager to talk more, but I've got to split now. So give me the prescription you promised me and I'll be on my way. Maybe we can talk again some other time."

"Let's get something straight, Fred. I didn't promise you anything. In fact, I've decided not to give you tranquilizers. It wouldn't be wise or safe for you to use them while you're in danger. Fear is an appropriate reaction to real peril; it keeps you alert and on your toes. The mouse shouldn't relax while the cat is chasing it. Tranquilizers could lull you into a false sense of security, and that could mean disaster."

"But—"

"Instead, I'll give you these few tablets to help you get to sleep and rest at night." I took a card with samples of a mild sedative from a drawer and handed them to Fred. "There are only six here. Don't take one if you drink—and that includes beer. Otherwise, one should be enough to help you relax and get a good night's sleep."

Fred pocketed the pills and stood up before my desk. "You don't like me, do you, Doc?" he asked seriously.

"I don't admire the things you've done or the bigoted re-marks you've made, Fred. I can't help wondering what they really tell about you and the impulses that drive you. In a way, you remind me of someone who doesn't know how to dance. You move to the music, but you don't feel the beat. Everyone else seems out of step, but it is really you."

He stared at me. His lips parted as if to answer, but then he decided against it. I walked with Fred out into the hall and watched him leave, stealthily, like a thief, the way he had come.

Driving home, I mused about my strange encounter with Fred Emory. He was not typical of the patients who come to see me. Individuals like Fred normally do not voluntarily seek the services of a psychiatrist. They are more often examined by forensic specialists, psychiatrists who act as consultants to courts and parole boards. Fred reminded me of men I had interviewed as part of my military duties, years before, in a prison stockade when I attended soldiers convicted of serious crimes and offenses. He appeared to be one of those persons whose peculiar defects in character cause them to function without regard for the values of others. Once such individuals were called constitutional inferiors and moral imbeciles, as if conscience were an inborn quality they lacked. Today psychiatrists usually describe them as psychopathic personalities and view them as products of disturbing childhood experiences.

The strictures that govern the conduct of others in the community neither concern nor restrain the psychopath. He is not unaware of them, however, and is apt to exploit the moral habits and innocence of others for his advantage. The psychopath usually knows right from wrong but is unaffected by the distinction except when he is in a position to accuse others of hypocrisy and wrongdoing. He may commit antisocial acts from mischievous vandalism to serious felonies without contrition or conscious guilt and cast the blame on others, lying adroitly.

One might anticipate that an individual capable of such behavior would be an unattractive thug; some are just that. Often, however, the psychopath appears quite presentable and is possessed of an ingenuous, deceptive charm. He may be engaging and friendly, but the psychopath keeps few, if any, friend-ships. His relationships are usually too exploitive to endure; he is notoriously devious and disloyal. He may seem ambitious and full of promise, but seldom does he experience the satisfaction won through perseverance toward honorable goals. Such a per-son is likely to cheat, swindle, and connive to gain immediate, temporary advantages. Beneath his facade, the psychopath is a true loner, a dyssocial stranger, an impostor, always acting.

I recognized that Fred Emory was psychopathic from his antisocial behavior, attitude, and manner of relating. His lack of self-restraint, insight, judgment, empathy, and interpersonal sensitivity all pointed to it. Fred's interests were entirely egocen-tric. He displayed no remorse for impregnating the girl, Tina; what became of her did not seem to concern him. Only what threatened him was on his mind.

It was clear that Fred failed to see that the root of his pre-dicament lay, not in the photograph he had sent Tina, but in what had motivated his behavior toward her in the first place. In this respect, how different was he from those who also seek help at a time of crisis, not recognizing the source of their distress? Fred, too, had come for relief, not for insight.

People do not consult psychiatrists or enter psychotherapy merely to understand themselves. Despite intellectualized ex-cuses and rationalizations that emotional problems are just like any other illness, they come because their lives have become unwieldy and their efforts to cope so costly and futile that their emotional adjustment is undone or endangered. They may ex-pect the psychiatrist to serve as their confessor, judge, mentor, or healer. The role of the psychotherapist, however, is neither to forgive, nor to punish, nor to teach, nor to cure. The therapeutic goal is to learn the nature and the causes of the patient's prob-lem and to bring self-understanding into the patient's aware-ness. The psychiatrist strives to accomplish this so that the pa-tient can loose his adaptive binds and free himself to function in a more self-directed, effective way. Progress in psychotherapy is more synonymous with maturation than it is with cure.

The psychiatrist's techniques, his questions, comments, and

interpretations, all are directed toward the therapeutic goal. The success of his efforts, however, depends largely on the patient's awareness that the therapist is trying to help him. This knowledge encourages transference, and it is also an important source of support when, eventually, the patient must attempt to implement his new insights. Having reexamined his life and gained new understanding, he must act upon it to derive benefit. This will require the patient to apply his insights to everyday problems, to employ his new perceptions actively, experimenting with his role without relying on repeated past behavior. Longstanding habits must be altered or abandoned at the risk of feeling awkward. During this uneasy process the patient draws strength and encouragement from his relationship to the therapist.

Fred Emory was an unlikely candidate for psychotherapy. It was doubtful that he recognized any need to examine the disorder in his life, to investigate his motives or behavior, or to think of changing. If there was any chance at all that I had stirred his curiosity, my relationship with him was hardly promising. He had openly suggested I didn't like him. Had I succumbed to my contempt for his bigotry and destructive ways?

Can a psychiatrist successfully treat an individual he dislikes? The answer is not simple. He must examine his negative feelings toward the patient so that finally his prejudices can be set aside. The therapist must not deceive himself or the patient, or his efforts will likely fail. The patient accepted for therapy must be seen as a sufferer, a victim, no matter how reprehensible his acts or repugnant his viewpoint.

Persons seriously disturbed in the way I suspected Fred to be do not usually offer psychiatrists the chance to treat them. They are prone to be capricious and unreliable. They have difficulty relating in a consistent and intensive manner adequate for psychotherapy. I was determined, however, to try again with Fred if he presented himself a second time. I had the advantage of knowing more about his ways now. I knew his modus operandi, and it was bound to be repeated.

Three weeks passed before I heard from Fred again. Then, one morning, he telephoned.

"Hi, Doc. How are you?" a voice inquired.

"I'm well, thank you, Fred," I replied, certain that he would be pleased I recognized his voice.

"This is Fred Emory," he announced, ignoring my recognition, denying me it.

"How are you, Fred?" I asked. I wondered what he wanted this time. Whatever it turned out to be, it would be interesting to see how he would maneuver to obtain it without seeming to ask.

"I thought you would like to know the way things worked out with my trouble, Doc. Am I right?"

Fred was up to form. It would appear he was calling for my sake, to relieve my curiosity. The real reason behind his call remained hidden. "That's thoughtful of you," I answered noncommittally.

"Well, when can you see me?" he asked.

"I don't understand. Do you want an appointment, Fred?"

"C'mon, Doc. I can't tell you on the telephone. Give me some time. . . . Don't worry, I'll pay you for it," he taunted. "I owe you money for the last time, too, remember?"

His tactics were transparent. He made it appear that I would see him only to learn what had happened and to get paid. He was doing me a favor. Fred had to be in a position to take, not to receive what he wanted. "Fred, I am interested in your problems, but I cannot, in good conscience, spend treatment time with you merely to talk. There are too many people who need every hour I can devote."

"C'mon, Doc. I need you, too. You're someone I can level with, you know? Maybe you could even straighten me out?"

"Fred, I don't want to mislead you. I doubt that I can straighten you, or anyone else, out. That's not my job."

"But . . ." he started to protest.

"If you want my help to figure yourself out, all right, but you'll have to be willing to talk about yourself openly."

"Dr. Jacobs," he said, sounding earnest, the way he had when we met, "that is exactly what I want."

I had few illusions about Fred's sincerity. How smoothly he could shift his position. Whatever his motives, I had decided to see him again if only to convince myself that psychotherapy for him was probably futile. We arranged to meet in a few days.

I had been waiting several minutes when Fred arrived, sporting mirrored sunglasses.

"Hello, Fred, you are late for our appointment."

"I had to finish my smoke before I came in. . . . You don't have ashtrays in here."

"There are no ashtrays here because I prefer people not to smoke in my waiting room or office. It wouldn't be fair to me or to my other patients to have to breathe it. Our time, however, is valuable, and it's limited. We've already lost almost ten minutes."

Fred shrugged and pulled a wad of bills from his pocket. It was an impudent gesture to remind me he had reserved and would pay me for my time. "How much do I owe you for last time and for today?" he said with a sneer.

I discussed my fees briefly. Fred peeled off a few bills and dropped the money on my desk. I picked them up and counted them deliberately. Then I scribbled a receipt for him. "Is that what you usually charge, Doc? You know I pay a good hooker the same," he gibed, grinning.

"One of us is a bargain, Fred." His grin faded. "Now, why do you want to see me?"

"Why do I want to see you?" he repeated. Asking himself my question, he apparently felt more in control. "By the way," he interrupted himself, "do my shades bother you, Doc?"

I shook my head. He was still searching for means of directing our interview. I wondered how many of these ploys he would use before he felt confident enough to proceed.

"Do you remember the little broad who got me in trouble?" he inquired, reversing roles, becoming the questioner.

I let the distortion pass, not wishing to break the flow, but

I wrested my authority back. "Yes, Fred, tell me what happened," I suggested.

"Harvey Eller, my lawyer, got through to her family. It wasn't easy. They had moved because of her being knocked up, but Harvey found them. He made it sound like I had been trying all along to locate them and had spent a lot of bread, hiring him just to find them. He told them I had a nervous breakdown worrying about Tina and was seeing a psychiatrist because I was so shook up. I think the son of a bitch made me sound crazy to them, but I don't give a damn. He offered them three hundred bucks to get her fixed, but they wouldn't take it. What do you think of that?"

"What do you think of it, Fred?"

"They're small punks. They're dust, that's what they are." Fred raised the back of his hand and blew across it to make his point. "All they did was scream a lot of garbage about me to Eller. He told me what they said. That wasn't cool. If they had any friggin' brains, they would've taken the money and asked for more. Then they could've yelled their heads off. They're stupid. I hate those simple creeps. I should've offered them shit!" Fred pulled his sunglasses off and jammed them into a pocket.

"You felt you had been generous," I said.

"Damn generous. I didn't have to give them a cent."

"But what about the fellow who was after you, Tina's brother-in-law—" I was about to point out that the money was really a bribe, but Fred cut me off.

"I'm coming to that, Doc. Harvey was really cool. I was smart to think of him. He listened to them curse me out. I think the bastard probably agreed with them. Then, after a while, nice and calmlike, he told them he understood their anger and pain. I think he meant it. He said he had a daughter himself and knew what they were feeling, but that he was only interested in trying to make amends for a sick person who couldn't speak for himself. He told me that was exactly how he put it. He warned them that Marty was after me and would wind up in prison if he laid a hand on me. 'There's been enough misfortune already,' he said. He's good with words, Harvey is, the best."

It was a grudging tribute. "What was the result?" I asked.

"The mother said she'd stop Marty, and the father finally agreed on two conditions: one, that I keep away and, two, that I continue to see a psychiatrist to get my head on straight."

"How do you feel about this, Fred?"

"I'm here, aren't I?" He smirked. "I feel terrific. Are you kidding? I never planned to see that little pig again. I should have had Harvey make them promise to keep her away from me. As for seeing a shrink, I don't mind coming here for a while to make Eller happy. He gave his word—that's not my problem—but I owe him it. He wouldn't let me pay him; he said to pay you with it. So I am."

"You are only here, then, at your lawyer's request?"

"No, Doc, be cool. I like talking to you; I learn things. Look, didn't everything turn out swell? Well, didn't it? I told you it would slide, man, and it did," he said triumphantly.

"How did it turn out for Tina?" I asked.

"That's incredible. You want to hear something really far-out? I mean weird? She wants to have the kid, and they're gonna let her keep it. Now you tell me who needs a headshrinker, them or me? Why would they do that? Why the hell would she want it? I can't figure it out, Doc. It doesn't make sense."

"You think it would be easier to have an abortion or, if it's too late for that, to give the baby over for adoption?"

"Sure, don't you? I know other broads who've been knocked up—even married ones—and gotten rid of it one way or another," he confided.

"It may seem unusual to you, considering the circumstances, for Tina to keep the baby, but she must have reasons. You don't seem to have known her very well. Perhaps, since it is Tina's baby, she and her parents want her to have it, to love it." Fred made a face and uttered something under his breath. He seemed annoyed. "Since your offer to help pay for an abortion was refused, why does it bother you, Fred?"

"It does, that's all. I don't want her having my kid. It's mine too, ain't it? Who the hell is she to have a kid of mine without my say-so?"

So that was it. Fred couldn't stand the idea that Tina had something of his—even something he had discarded. Did it matter that it was a child? Was he grudging and envious that Tina's parents had accepted her back loyally and supportively?

"Fred, it's apparent from your attitude that despite your relief to be free from retribution and further responsibility in this, you aren't happy with the way matters were resolved."

"Yeah. . . . Well, that's how it goes, right?" He shrugged, signaling he had no wish to discuss it further. I persisted, however.

"I guess you didn't foresee your experience with Tina coming to all this. I wonder if you aren't the sort to act on whims too quickly, without adequate thought to the outcome."

"That's me," he agreed. "I don't like to think a thing over too long. I never do. I'm not like that. If you think it, do it. That's how I operate," he boasted. "It's the way I get my kicks. If I have to think too long about something, it's no good."

"What do you mean, Fred?"

"It's no good, that's all. I get turned off."

"Is it that you simply lose interest or that you become uneasy and unsure, worried?"

Fred nodded. "It's like I get shook figuring out what comes next. I lose my nerve and chicken out." He hunched his shoulders and shook his head in self-disgust. "I can't take that, you know? That's a bad scene."

I was onto something, a crack in Fred's armor, a defect he could acknowledge with some insight and appropriate concern. Unlike his fear reaction, which had been focused primarily outward on a reality, Marty, this was something Fred recognized within himself. If it could only be exploited . . . I tried to widen the breach with a display of concern. I shook my head and frowned worriedly. "I wouldn't want to be in your shoes, Fred, yanked around by every impulse, unable to think a thing through to see where I'm going. To me that sounds like trouble."

"Yeah, well, I've gotten along pretty well so far, Doc," he

said. "I'm naturally lucky. I'm just like a cat. I always land on my feet, and I've got nine lives, too." He chuckled confidently.

I remained solemn and unaffected by his bluster. "You know, Fred," I said gravely, like a caring father, "luck is a tricky and uncertain partner. You may pretend you have nine lives if you like, but we know you don't. When Marty was after you, you couldn't risk losing this one."

Fred's mood grew sullen and restive. He reached into a pocket for his cigarettes, then remembered, and shoved them back, bothered. "I don't think kids ought to be brought into this friggin' world without a mother and a father and a home that's right. What kind of a home is she going to give him with her folks telling her what to do? They didn't do such a good job with her or she wouldn't've gotten herself knocked up, would she?" he blurted, projecting responsibility for what had happened onto Tina's parents. "That dumb birdbrain. What the hell does she or her dopey family know? She'll have the kid all right, but after a while she won't want to stay home and be with it, right? He'll be a little bastard, won't he? He'll start getting his ass kicked before he even knows. Shit!" He exploded. Fred rose and walked to the window.

His outburst had taken me by surprise. For the moment, at least, I had a glimpse of the inner man. I wondered what chord I had struck to unleash his tantrum. Perhaps my fatherly concern had helped to catalyze it. I wondered if I could lead him further into a transference relationship.

"You seem to feel strongly about this, Fred. Would you care to sit down again and discuss it with me?" Slowly he turned from the window, returned, and sprawled back in his chair. His face was reflective, sad, and bitter.

"What do you want to know?" he asked.

"Tell me about your life . . . from the beginning." I opened my pad and took up my pencil.

That was how it began. For the remainder of the hour and for several sessions afterward, over a number of weeks, Fred talked about himself, giving me his history.

Frederick Henry Emory was born in Brentwood. His parents, Harriet and Gilbert Emory, moved here a few years after their marriage to take over a floundering furniture store from an ailing relative. The Emorys, especially Harriet, worked hard to salvage the failing business. Mrs. Emory, a sturdy, dispassionate woman, rapidly developed into a highly competent, effective businesswoman. It was largely her levelheaded determination and imperturbability that reassured their creditors and turned the store once more into a profitable enterprise.

Gilbert Emory recognized his wife's abilities and relied heavily on them. Her proficiency stirred resentment within him, and the respect accorded her by others aggravated this. Fred surmised that his father's desire to displace his mother and gain a freer hand in running the business prompted him to demand that she start a family. Apparently, despite misgivings about having children and allowing her husband to take over the store, she finally yielded and agreed to have a child.

Fred was born after an arduous, long labor which was finally terminated by cesarean section. Fred grew up hearing the tale of his difficult and perilous birth told and retold to customers who admired him as a tot playing on the floor in the rear of the store. It seemed to him, later, that his mother emphasized the ordeal of his birth as an excuse to refuse further pregnancies. Harriet Emory was not content to remain with Fred in the apartment over their store but brought him with his bottles and diapers down below, where she could continue to supervise business matters.

Gilbert Emory was a poor manager and, according to his son, a bullheaded, obdurate man too impulsive, stubborn, and uncompromising to succeed at trade. When it became obvious that he was alienating customers and suppliers and harming the business, he began to cooperate in his wife's devices to keep him out of the store. That also served to keep him away from his son—a circumstance Fred welcomed. His father had an intimidating, gruff way that frightened Fred. Gilbert Emory delighted in scaring his son, then taunting the timid boy with gibes of "sissy" or "mama's boy."

"Once in a while my old man and I would play a game. It only happened when he was half loaded. He'd stink of beer and carry on like he was doing the greatest thing any father ever did. He would sit down at the table to play Chinese checkers with me and go through another six-pack, getting up every other minute to go to the john. The games took so long I used to cheat to make it fun. He'd accuse me of doing something, but he was so far gone he never could figure out what I had done."

"Did he drink to that extent regularly?" I asked.

"He could put it away. Actually, I liked him better when he was crocked. He was nicer. He would put his arm around me and get sloppy. Sometimes he would ask if I loved him and then give me a quarter. He'd try to talk to me, but his words were all slurred and hard to understand. A couple of times he just held onto me and cried. I couldn't figure it out. . . ."

Fred fared little better with his mother. Harriet Emory saw to it, with her usual efficiency, that her son was fed, clothed, and presentable; beyond that, she had little time or affection for him. It was as if she thought Fred another of her husband's impulsive vagaries that she had to tolerate. At an early age she pushed him out of the store to play on the street, where, in the commercial district, he found few companions. Fred remained timid and insecure, acquiring neither the skills nor the confidence to compete successfully in the games other children his age played. When he entered public school and had more opportunity for peer contact, his inexperience was a disadvantage. He was usually the last chosen for a team. Often, to avoid this humiliation, he would hide or act uninterested until others no longer encouraged him to play. Then he would watch, envious of them and resentful. Companions thought him moody and difficult to know. He became a morose, sour child whose disposition earned him the nickname Mopey, which he hated.

Fred was nine when his father deserted. Gilbert Emory made his move on the first Friday of the month, when the receipts and cash were greatest. He took them, drew a sizable draft from the checking account, and left in the new family car for California—with a waitress from the diner nearby. Harriet Emory was calm and steadfast in the wake of her husband's treachery. For years, it seemed, she had providently accumulated a secret nest egg; it was now to see her through. She filed for divorce, and as soon as her husband could be found to sign the agreement, she became free of him and sole owner of the business to which she was devoted.

Gilbert Emory was not missed. Fred found it easier with him gone. Others no longer teased him about his father's indiscretions. He was trusted with his own key to the apartment and had only minor chores and responsibilities; he was never called to account. Harriet Emory took perverse pride in doing almost everything herself. Each afternoon Fred was free to watch television or read magazines without interference. His father wasn't there to drop in and taunt him because he wasn't athletic and sought after by other boys. Fred's ennui lasted until he was fourteen, when his mother remarried.

"We were getting along fine until my mother met this creep, Walter. I couldn't believe that after my father she could take another loser like him seriously. Why did she need him? I was helping more in the apartment and even getting supper started every night. He didn't have any money, not even a good job. It nearly drove me up the wall when she told me they were going to get married and we would be moving."

Walter Murray was forty-three, a year younger than his bride, but the paunchy, lugubrious widower seemed older. He and his nine-year-old daughter, Jeanne, became part of the family the month Fred started high school. They all settled down together in the Murray house at the edge of town. Fred was bitter about his dislocation from the stimulating downtown area. He was also jealous and contemptuous of his hapless stepfather and stepsister. He waged a campaign of sabotage and harassment against them. He stole money and credit cards from Walter's wallet, siphoned gas from his car, and mutilated or hid his newspaper. Methodically he emptied and refilled Walter's sinusitis capsules with powdered sugar and gloated about the poor man's discomfort. Fred baited and bullied Jeanne mercilessly.

Fred enjoyed my interest and attention as he told his history. It gratified him to talk about himself, relating his life story as if it were a series of episodes in an adventure novel. He showed no guilt or remorse about his misdeeds; he seemed proud of them, as if they were heroic forays in an endless war. I was careful not to condemn his behavior and, from time to time, highlighted Fred's motivation for revenge. I suggested mildly that he seemed to have a burdensome need to compensate for his low self-esteem. Fred seemed to take little notice of my comments. It was my plan to hear him out, not only to learn his background but also to encourage his trust and strengthen our rapport. I accommodated his need to be in apparent control by listening attentively. As a result, he became complacent and increasingly open, revealing vague feelings of loneliness.

"Fred, you certainly have stories to tell."

"I never told any of this before, Doc. I couldn't trust anyone. My own mother doesn't know what I've been into. She wouldn't believe it."

"It must be lonely to go along having no one with whom you can share things."

"Um," he murmured.

The results of my efforts to promote a relationship between us were not always encouraging. On one occasion, Fred mused, "Someday, maybe soon, I'm going to do something really spectacular like assassinate some big pinko lawyer or dynamite some place I know about, where a couple of broads are living together. I think they're queer, and they are teachers, too. You'll be the only one who'll know I did it, Doc. But if they get me, you can tell the world my story. How about that, Doc? I'll make you famous telling about me on TV." The thought made me shudder, but in Fred's maniacal way, he was expressing a kind of positive feeling toward me. I appealed to his egotism, suggesting that his wish to achieve fame and importance could provide incentives toward more constructive goals. I pointed out that only small, inadequate persons resort to sensational stunts, and they do this to obscure their inadequacies. I wasn't certain, however, that I had dissuaded him.

In high school Fred's behavior became more decidedly antisocial. His puberty was delayed; nature conspired against him to aggravate his self-consciousness. His hairless chest and puny size made the gymnasium locker room a hell for him. The onset of the usual adolescent social-sexual interests among his peers left him in an even more uncomfortable position. Though he joined in the locker-room chatter about girls, they held no fascination for him. When finally his voice deepened and the fuzz on his face turned to stubble, the changes were accompanied by ugly pimples and pustules.

Fred was sensitive about his appearance and suffered considerably because he was small and acned. He spent extravagant amounts on clothes and wore special shoes to make him taller. Despite this, he avoided school dances and made excuses the few times he was invited to parties. He developed no close friendships, though he yearned to be popular. Finally, he found he could attract attention in a way that seemed particularly gratifying. Fred became outspoken in a comic-insolent manner in his classes. He was the bane of many of his teachers.

At about the same time Fred began committing acts of vandalism against the school building and equipment. He learned how to open lockers and stole money and other items from students. Sometimes he spitefully slashed jackets, sweaters, and sneakers stored there. He destroyed notebooks and term papers. Once he was questioned about a smoke bomb in the girls' rest room, but the evidence was insufficient to accuse him.

"Every day I pulled something," he boasted. "It was unbelievable how I was able to get away with things. I had a streak, one term, in which I never let a day go by without pulling something. I practically turned the whole high school upside down without getting caught. It was the only thing at school I really cared about. I went there every morning knowing that sometime during the day I'd get a chance to do some trick. I'd slip a condom over the teacher's pointer, tip over the janitor's pail, or slit the back of some guy's pants. Once I even peed over all the paper supplies in the storeroom. It was my private war."

In his senior year, it became apparent that Fred was not college bound like the majority of students. Nevertheless, he preferred to associate with those who were. He made excuses about college. Fred invented stories of opportunities he intended to pursue first. He was a facile liar. The faculty found him an enigma. They had difficulty accepting the fact that a student who seemed quick-witted could do so little work and be content merely to pass. Some tried to talk to Fred but found him evasive. Those who criticized him soon found themselves victimized by his disruptive and vengeful antics.

Fred respected teachers who maintained their distance and set firm limits. Some of the least popular members of the faculty were Fred's favorites. He was pleasant and solicitous to them. Guidance teachers and advisers could not reconcile Fred's apparent potential with his record. They tried to encourage him, assuring him that he had the capability of becoming anything he desired. In this way they flattered him, contributing unwittingly to his self-deception. Fred never possessed the ability and untapped potential that people assumed he had.

After quitting high school, Fred obtained several promising jobs. But he did not last through the training program at the bank or at the insurance and telephone companies. His mother finally put him on at the store, though there was little need for him there.

"It was boring in the store. No matter what I did for kicks, it got on my mother's nerves. So after a while I took off. She didn't object. I just hacked around town, looking for good vibrations all the time."

There were no regular girlfriends in Fred's life. He made showy but insincere overtures to women in bars, especially when others were on hand to laugh and enjoy his teasing. But he had less interest in females and in sex than anyone would have suspected. Fred was also wary of venereal infection and felt malaise when any of his barroom pals would elaborate in detail the symptoms of his latest bout with gonorrhea or crabs. Fred's only sexual experience, before Tina, was similarly with an uninitiated adolescent girl.

In the weeks between the first greening and the full bloom of early summer, the chronicle of Fred's wayward life and misadventures lengthened and grew. He bragged of being a chronic scofflaw who delighted in ignoring parking rules. When he was finally caught and forced to pay fines, he took retribution by slashing tires and spray-painting cars in a vengeful spree. It was difficult to listen to him and not recoil from the loathsome deeds he confessed so easily and guiltlessly. I struggled to hold to my purpose to focus on Fred's motives and feelings, despite the repugnant acts he disclosed.

By no means was I always convinced of the truth of what Fred told me. I knew him to be a braggart and an adroit faker. At times he sensed my skepticism; it goaded him to bring in news clippings and other corroborative evidence that the events he described had actually occurred and that he indeed was responsible. There were photos of the library doors defaced with swastikas. Once Fred brought in the missing hand from a statue on the village green.

The most outrageous and frightening deed of all, however, was the derailment of a commuter train. Fred had Polaroid snapshots taken before and after the event to prove that he singlehandedly had jammed a switch by wedging stones into it. He also displayed a collection of related newspaper accounts. The incident, fortunately, resulted only in considerable inconvenience; there were no injuries. Still, I could not dissemble the horror I felt at his temerity.

"Why, Fred? Why would you, an intelligent person, do such a harebrained thing as wreck a train carrying innocent people?" I asked disconcertedly.

"The cruddy train was never on time, that's why! I missed an appointment with a guy in the city because of it; it cost me big bucks!"

"But—" I started to interrupt.

"What about the passengers? Who are they? I don't know

them." He scowled, reacting to the shock which must have been evident on my face, and moderated his tone. "Think about this, Doc. Those poor slobs have to go to work riding those lousy trains every day. None of them got hurt. I didn't wreck the train; I derailed it. I just got my revenge, and I got back for all of them, too. That's what I did." He grinned.

Fred was proud of himself; his reaction was scary. He felt justified in his actions and even had illusions that he was almost a public-spirited sort of fellow. It was frightening that he could regard the safety of others so cavalierly and recklessly. His apparent rationality made it all the more chilling. For here was no frenzied madman but a pompously conceited young man who might well have been boasting about his golf score or a successful business deal. Beneath his surface, however, was a bitterly alienated, implacably and obsessively vindictive individual. Fred Emory was a very dangerous man.

"When you think back about it now, Fred, doesn't your behavior strike you as rash and impulsive? Wasn't your wish to satisfy a grudge out of control?"

"Geez! Don't tell me you really care about the railroad, Doc? You don't own stock in it or something like that, do you?" he scoffed.

"You're evading the issue, Fred. People could have been killed or maimed. It is important for you and me to grasp whether or not you are able to anticipate consequences before you act and, if not, to understand the nature of that impairment before you and others get hurt."

"Don't be so serious, Doc. I know you're trying to help me." He grinned. "You mean, did I think of people getting hurt and all the lawsuits that would come of it? No. Actually, it never occurred to me till you asked me. That would have been terrific!" he crowed, teasing me.

"And the victims?" I persisted.

"Look, no one got hurt," he argued, still untouched. "Besides, afterward, they inspected the tracks and probably fixed up other things wrong with them, too."

"You're still ducking the issue of responsibility for your

deeds. You didn't sabotage the tracks to protect the riders. That would be like starting a forest fire to help people lost in the woods."

"Hey, that's a good one. You have a sense of humor after all, huh, Doc? It really bugs you about people getting hurt, doesn't it? Why? Who are they anyway? What do they mean to you?"

I realized that in spite of myself, Fred's callousness had affected me, and I had allowed my own concern to intrude and obscure the point I wished to pursue about his impulsiveness. "The people on the train were just ordinary, fellow human beings, Fred," I said, defeated. "They're just like me."

"Yeah." He sniggered. "But I don't know them, and I like you, Doc."

Fred's estrangement from humanity was striking. Session after session, he regaled me with stories of his unsavory escapades, trying to impress but exposing, instead, more of his malevolence and spitefulness. I was not untouched by his invidious tales; they were heartless and loathsome. I found sufficient self-command, however, to listen without betraying my repugnance. My early image of Fred, as a dangerous, wounded animal, came back to mind frequently; he was lashing back insensibly and reflexively like one who had been painfully hurt and remembered it. To have permitted myself license to censure each of his odious tricks not only would have been futile but would surely have stiffened his resistance and driven him beyond reach. Rather, I made a deliberate effort to remain on good terms with him. I tried subtly to assuage his need for admiration and simultaneously to redirect his attention inward, working toward a time when I might find him more interested and receptive to insight. . . .

"Fred, the things you reveal astound me. I am amazed at what you've done. But there is also something disturbing and puzzling to me. Again and again you reveal yourself to be quick-witted and resourceful, but your whole life sounds as if it is devoted to getting even. I cannot see, however, what has so aroused you. Do you feel a strong drive within you to avenge something?"

"Sort of . . . it's like I enjoy screwing the whole friggin' world," he admitted.

"Do you know why you do?" I asked.

"Maybe the world deserves it," he said.

"Come on, Fred," I smiled, twitting him. "Come off it. Tina was innocent. And what did the kids at school, the teachers, and others do to you? What did you have against the library or the town itself, for that matter? I've been listening to you all these weeks, and most of the time your motives are a mystery. It's hard to see what arouses you to do the things you've done. Is it because of something you were denied?"

He looked at me uncertainly. "What do you think?" he demanded.

"Well"—I grinned—"you sure carry a big chip around with you as though you feel deprived and cheated. All it seems to take to stir you is someone with something you lack or envy, and you are antagonized and goaded by your feelings to attack them to even things up."

"What of it? I'm not crazy," he insisted.

"I'm not suggesting you are. I am pointing out that certain emotions are, to use your words, 'jerking you around.' That's a weakness. It's dangerous to you and to others. I'm reminded of an old story. I'll tell it to you.

"A lonely, tired salesman lugging a heavy case of wares was walking along a hot, dusty road. He hadn't had much luck selling, and his thirst was killing him, when he saw a house high up on a hill with a few trees and a well. Though he was exhausted, he decided to trudge up the hill, hoping to quench his thirst and rest in the shade. All along the way he couldn't help remembering having been turned away from other doors all that day. He struggled to think of something friendly to say, so this time he wouldn't be rejected. Finally, he reached the house, and a man came out to greet him. Before a word could be uttered, however, he suddenly punched the startled fellow in the face and walked away, as thirsty and miserable as before, muttering to himself,

'He can keep his shade and water; no one is going to make me beg.' "

"Right on," said Fred, grinning.

"From what you've told of your life, Fred, you received little attention and affection as a child. The memory of being unloved and unvalued seems to have lingered and may help account for your attitudes and behavior toward others." Fred gazed up toward the ceiling and yawned impressively. He turned, looking around the room in an airy, unconcerned, almost foppish manner. I pursued it. "What was it the other kids called you . . . Mopey?" He pretended not to hear, but his face flushed. I've reached him, I thought. "Your needs, when stimulated, seem to stir unpleasant memories which influence and direct your actions, not permitting you to benefit from later experience or more mature judgment." He started to protest but thought better of it. "Do you recall how, like the salesman in the story, you acted in here the first day?" I asked.

He didn't answer; he stared hard at me, trying to decide whether I was censuring him. I went on. "It would be a shame to allow circumstances in the past, over which you had no influence, to continue to control and ruin your life, directing your reactions in such an automatic, repetitive, and senseless way. They are making you a bitter, lonely outsider whose only satisfaction is to spoil things in a wasted effort to get back."

A tic began to twitch below Fred's left eye. He rubbed his face and wrinkled up his nose to combat it. Then, in a haughty, you-be-damned manner, he took out a cigarette and lit it. Careful not to appear put out or condescending, I poured some water from my coffeepot into the bottom of a paper cup and set it in front of him for his cigarette.

Fred drew twice more on his cigarette, then dropped it ceremoniously into the cup. He looked over at me now and slowly shook his head, smiling broadly. "You are serious, aren't you, Doc?" he asked superciliously. "Look, you know I like you. You're my friend, okay? But don't give me that crap about my awful childhood causing me to be this way. . . . I don't buy it. Life is one big con game, and you know it. If you don't get yours, someone else will. You better believe it, Doc. You've been reading too many books and sitting there listening to losers too long. Remember what I'm telling you," he lectured, "you got to be realistic. I wouldn't want to see you get taken, you know what I mean?"

After the session I wondered if anything I had tried to tell him had penetrated or simply been deflected. I also worried that I'd gone too far and thought there might have been a hint, in his last remarks, that he was saying good-bye. My sense of discouragement played tricks with me. Fred did return and continued as unperturbed and intransigent as before. I, for my part, redoubled my efforts to make him cognizant that his childhood's broken promises were relevant to his current life-style.

Gradually my interpretations seemed to carry some weight with him. Fred appeared to accept the relatedness of his past to the present. I was, however, disquieted because he did so in an almost rote and unaffected way. By the end of the summer I realized that my efforts to help him comprehend himself were failing. My interpretations were ineffectual. Fred had become inured to my comments. Like a germ that develops immunity to an antibiotic and begins to thrive on it, he prized my analyses in a curious, vain way. Their accuracy seemed irrelevant to his interest in them; rather, Fred seemed to value them only as evidence of my devotion.

Our sessions became very amiable. No longer did Fred scoff or trouble to refute me. All traces of his former impudence disappeared. He became increasingly amenable and eagerly contributed additional evidence and material from his experience to support my inferences. On the surface, it appeared that our relationship was flourishing and that we had found a productive, cooperative partnership. I worried, however; it was as though Fred were no longer my patient but had become my collaborator. This kind of participation in therapy is spurious. It is a form of resistance particularly troublesome since it tends to put the therapist who frustrates it in apparent opposition to the patient's efforts to cooperate in his treatment.

I had doubts about the efficacy of continuing therapy. Was it futile? In spite of Fred's warning, had I perhaps allowed myself to be taken in after all? Should I end the treatment? It was a time to take stock. Was Fred merely coming and paying to make a mockery of me and of his treatment? We had come a long way in our relationship from distrust to acceptance, but was it a therapy? Fred experienced nothing of an insightful nature spontaneously; he now listened to my words and repeated my ideas about his life almost dutifully, like a catechism. Was it foolish to assume he benefited from this in any real way?

Then it struck me. Like an overzealous, myopic detective, I had overlooked the most obvious clue of all. That Fred had become friendlier and closer to me was paramount. It was the most significant development since treatment had begun. Perhaps he was sincere in his attempts to be helpful even though he lacked any meaningful self-understanding. Had I misconstrued the motive behind his efforts because I was disappointed at his lack of insight?

At the outset Fred was demanding and exploitive; now he was taking pains to be friendly and to assist me, even though he didn't believe in what I was doing. It was I who was now the cynic and was succumbing to doubts and distrust. My zeal to straighten Fred out—something I had explicitly confessed I was unable to do—had led me astray. I had underestimated and misjudged the transference. For it now came to me that I had perhaps become the object of Fred's most deeply felt needs for approval and had neglected to realize it.

I felt the same sense of shock a person experiences when he has momentarily fallen asleep at the wheel while driving. I knew I must take heed. If I ignored his fondness for me, I would fail Fred and tragically repeat the trauma of his past. He would be hurt and withdraw behind his defenses again, convinced anew that his hopes for affection and acceptance were merely weaknesses.

I could hope to influence Fred only by continuing to demonstrate my interest and loyalty and by accepting his efforts graciously. Fred's personality was damaged, and his expectations in interpersonal relationships were distorted by the need to cope with parental indifference and disregard. I could only strive to provide consistent attention and understanding and hope to revise his poor self-image. Then perhaps he would no longer feel and act like an outcast but could go on through a second childhood and adolescence to become a whole and social being. It might be a goal beyond reach.

Every individual tends to behave in conformity to his self-concept. A person, such as Fred, inadequately cared for as a child and repeatedly victimized by unfavorable circumstances is bound to have a poor self-image. By the time Fred's mother forced him out onto the streets, his peers were already more confident and experienced. He was unable to participate or to compete successfully. He became cunning and devious, employing his intelligence largely for defensive and retaliative purposes. A strong tie to someone dependable, whom he respects, could disarm him perhaps. . . .

"My mother wants to know what we talk about here," Fred announced one day.

"I gather, then, that you've told her you're coming," I said.

"Yeah. Once in a while I say something. She doesn't like me seeing you. She doesn't trust psychiatrists. My mother thinks you've got some easy racket. She keeps asking me if I'm still coming and how long I am going to continue. You'd think she was paying for it, not me."

"How do you feel about her views?"

"I know what I'm doing. If I'm finding out about myself, why should she care? What bothers her is my asking questions about when I was little. You know why? Because she doesn't remember a damn thing about me, that's why. It's amazing. I ask her this or that, and she can't give me an answer. All she can do is tell me how tough everything was for her. Then she gives me a lot of jazz about how I shouldn't let you put ideas into my head about her."

"Apparently your mother is concerned that I may influence you. Certain parents feel that because a psychiatrist tries to learn what went on during a patient's childhood, he is conducting a witch-hunt. What he really wants, of course, is to understand, as much as possible, what affected the development of a person's attitudes about himself and his ideas about the world around him. I shouldn't think it would benefit you to blame your mother, or anyone else, for your troubles. The point of understanding your life is to be able to see how to help yourself achieve your goals more effectively.

"You know, Fred, you might imagine that many people tell me that all their problems come from unhappy childhoods, but the truth is they don't. Most people have difficulty realizing that their childhood was special or unusual in any important way. Children tend to accept their lot early, before they're capable of making any meaningful comparisons. They assume, on the basis of their closest relationships and circumstances, that life is that way, and they try to cope with it accordingly. All too often they grow up with distorted notions about themselves and the world, rejecting evidence to the contrary or becoming confused by it. If, for example, you were, as you suggest, not given very much affectionate care and support, can you see how helpful it might be to deny this so the truth couldn't hurt you? You might well take a sour-grapes attitude toward better relationships when you found they existed."

"Maybe, Doc. I don't think much about it."

"If you had grown up in a community where everyone was treated as you were, your way of life would not seem so unusual. But here I'll bet you were the only child at school whose parents didn't come to see you in programs and assemblies. Am I right? Did your folks take you to Cub Scout meetings the way the others did?"

"Come on, you know they didn't," he grumbled.

"It's painful to be different in some ways. It makes one jealous and resentful. Not until your father left did you find any benefit in your circumstances, and then it wasn't particularly wholesome. You spent your time watching television, reading magazines, and hoping perhaps your mother would come to appreciate you more. But then she remarried, changing everything, and you began to act up, striking out in different directions, expressing your rage and getting back at everyone."

"For chrissakes! You make it sound like I was some kind of maniac. I was just having fun; it was like a game to me. I'm not crazy," he argued.

"No, you're not, not in the ordinary sense of the word, Fred. But what you did was no game to the kids at high school whose lockers you raided and whose clothes you ruined. It wasn't one to Tina whose life you rearranged. Nor was it such fun for the strangers on that train with whose safety you gambled. Haven't you deceived yourself long enough about its being a game? You invented that myth to cover up the actual emotions you experienced. You created a role for yourself to explain your actions. You see yourself as a cynical, tough guy, the antihero who prefers to go his own way, but it's merely a ruse to hide the real truth that you were out of control. Your drives were running away with you even as you pretended you were in charge. The cool cat with nine lives who always landed on his feet was just a disguise to make it seem as if you were all together."

Fred stared at me worriedly. "You say I'm not crazy. Then what am I?"

"Let's find out, Fred. There are a lot of things to suggest you are a fellow with a deep-seated grudge that is self-destructive and dangerous. I am hopeful you can gain enough understanding and confidence to bring yourself under control and begin to use your abilities in an effective way to achieve something for a change instead of squandering your talents and energies the way you have."

"Okay, Doc, you made your point."

I was beginning to feel at last that Fred had begun to recognize the nature of his disorder and was seriously interested in mastering it. Despite occasional supercilious lapses, he seemed earnest about examining his life and displayed more insight in our discussions. Another factor also encouraged me. Without being conscious of it, Fred began to imitate me. He used more and more of my words and phrases, aped my gestures, and postured in his chair the way I do. I found him tamer, more reasonable and reflective. The flaming bigot I had first encountered seemed to have mellowed and reformed. I realized that I had heard no boasts of new mischief in months. At the end of August, when I took my holiday, I left with fewer qualms about Fred but no real conviction that he had changed.

Fred missed his first two appointments after I returned. When the week had passed without his contacting me, I assumed he had dropped out of therapy. Then, one morning, my answering service reported that Mrs. Murray had called and asked me to telephone her late in the afternoon. I wondered why his mother, not Fred, was calling me. Perhaps I would learn the reason from her for his disappearance.

It is always a delicate matter to receive an unanticipated call from a relative or someone else close to a patient in psychotherapy. This is because it is crucial to preserve the exclusive and confidential basis on which the therapeutic relationship depends. The relative or friend who calls even for simple, mundane reasons, for example, to relay information that some unforeseen event prevents the patient from keeping an appointment or to request a receipt for insurance purposes, is curious. He wants to hear the psychiatrist's voice.

The sound of the therapist, this specter who has materialized importantly in the life of the patient and, therefore, sometimes into the affairs of the caller, gives him corporeal substance. It sharpens the focus of the caller's fantasies about the psychiatrist. The caller has also invariably felt left out and is alert and sensitive to further rebuff. Even when he is not consciously resentful, he must be dealt with discreetly to avoid pitfalls. The therapeutic relationship can be damaged easily by an injudicious comment to a friend or relative of the patient.

Particular care must be taken when persons call to volunteer information regarding the patient. Though the caller may believe himself entirely sincere in his wish to help, such calls often have a conspiratorial quality. They may create problems for the therapist. At the risk of seeming irresponsible to the concerned informant, psychiatrists must discourage such revelations and disclose them judiciously to the patient, even when it seems untimely. To do otherwise imperils the patient's basic trust and confidence in his therapist.

The prudent psychiatrist will listen with interest when persons close to the patient call with complaints about the treatment. These infrequent calls often prove especially enlightening. I have learned to take some pains to listen and think about them. They may reveal significant deficiencies in the treatment. The patient may be exploiting therapy as a justification to act out and to intimidate those who are close to him. On the other hand, he may have minimized the pressures to which he is subjected. Thus, occasionally I have encountered an overbearing and thoroughly disagreeable individual on the telephone of whom a depressed patient spoke lovingly, presenting a false picture.

More often, persons who telephone about a patient respect the privacy of the therapeutic relationship while seeking reassurance for themselves. They are apprehensive about the extent that changes within the patient are likely to affect their relationship.

"Mrs. Murray?. . . Good afternoon, this is Dr. Jacobs."

"Oh . . . thank you for calling back, Doctor. I know you were seeing my son and that you've been away." She had an unaffected, businesslike manner.

"Yes, Mrs. Murray. But I've been back for a week already." I wondered if she knew Fred had not been in to see me.

"Doctor, are you aware that Fred was seriously hurt and in the hospital?" There was a captious, chiding quality in her tone now.

"No, Mrs. Murray. I'm sorry to hear it. I was puzzled when he failed to keep his scheduled appointments and didn't call," I admitted. "It's not my practice to check up on patients who do not continue. I leave the responsibility for coming entirely in their hands, so I had no way of knowing. Please tell me what happened."

"Hmm . . . well, I wondered frankly if you cared, Doctor. After all, Fred's been seeing you for a long time." My explanation had not appeased her.

"I assure you, Mrs. Murray, I am quite concerned."

"There was some trouble . . . a riot," she said uncertainly. "Fred was mixed up in it and injured badly. In fact, he was shot. He had to have emergency surgery to stop the hemorrhaging. We almost lost him. If it weren't for Dr. Talcott . . . But I'll let Fred tell you since you're supposed to be the only one who understands him."

"You seem to disapprove, Mrs. Murray. Are you opposed to Fred's seeing me?"

"He's a grown man now; it's not for me to say," she said, hedgingly. Then, however, as if she could restrain herself no longer, she went on. "But if you ask me—and I'm only his mother—you aren't about to do Fred one bit of good. People like us don't need psychiatrists like your wealthy patients. We have *real* problems. Besides, Fred's been sneaking around, lying and getting into trouble and out again almost all his life without needing help, thank you. But now that you've got this hold on him, he acts as if it's my fault he's that way. Well, let me tell you, I had to struggle just to see he had a bed to sleep in and a roof over his head. How many other mothers and fancy ladies had to do the same? Fred was a weak, lazy boy, not at all like me. He takes after his father, unfortunately."

She paused, giving me an opportunity to reply, but I sensed she would not be pacified, and I was right. As soon as I started to respond, she continued her tirade. "You're turning my son against me. I know you are. I've seen it before where psychiatrists couldn't get people better, so instead, they just turned them against their families. It's wrong. Since Fred's been coming to you he hasn't been himself around me. We always got along. No matter what Fred did—and I'm not making excuses for him—he was always polite and obedient to me. I brought him up to know his place as a son and to show respect for his mother. But you think I did everything wrong, it seems. I wish others outside his home, especially his teachers, had done as good a job. He'd be a lot different if they had.

"Now, however, because of you, all I get are flippant, smart-alecky answers when I ask him what he's been up to. He accuses me of not caring. Where did he get that from? I suppose I'm to let everything I've managed to accomplish in my life just slide because Fred, who never did a real day's work in his whole life, has something on his mind. Something you put there more than likely."

"I—"

"I'm not finished, Doctor. I want you to know I gave that boy as much as I could, and that was a lot more than I ever had when I was a child, one of eight, with a father who drank himself to death and couldn't support us. It was my misfortune to marry a man who wasn't much better as it turned out. Fred's father was worthless. He failed at business and ran off, leaving me with debts and his son. I worked seven days a week, shopped, cooked, and scrimped, and managed just the same to get Fred off to school looking decent every day. I think I did pretty darn well, considering. Why don't you blame his father? How is it Fred never points a finger at him? Maybe if he'd been half the man he should have been, instead of depending on me, then I could have had time to bake brownies for the PTA or attend luncheons like the other mothers Fred now compares me to."

Mrs. Murray's anger and excitement abated. I did not think it wise, however, to defend myself or to become embroiled in a discussion about Fred that could have repercussions on his relationship with me. When she had finished upbraiding me and her recriminations had subsided, I spoke. "Mrs. Murray, I am sorry you've been so distressed. I assure you I have listened to your complaints. It is not my aim to alienate your son from you. I regret that he has been disrespectful lately, but I also want you to understand that his complaints are also important, and they affect him more when he keeps them bottled up inside and doesn't express them to you. In the end, I think it will prove worthwhile to encourage Fred to communicate more openly to you, even though you may find his feelings disturbing."

"It isn't so simple as you make it sound, Doctor. I have a husband and a stepchild to consider also. They and Fred don't get on. Besides, you may have time to sit around all day and listen to that kind of thing; you get paid to hear it. But I have to work to earn my living. In fact, now I'll probably have to pay Fred's doctor bills. He's managed until now to pay for you and other luxuries out of his own pocket. That brings me back to my purpose in calling you this morning. I'd put off telephoning for a week already and delayed you from calling back most of today deliberately."

"Why, Mrs. Murray?"

"Fred wants to see you again. He asked me to get in touch with you as soon as you got back, but he has been so much more pleasant and like himself again since you left that I dreaded the time you'd return. He can't call you himself; he's in the intensive care unit. Now he's caught on to the fact that I hadn't kept my promise to call for him, and he's threatened to have Dr. Talcott get in touch with you if I don't. I know it's probably useless to ask you this, but couldn't you leave him alone for just another day or two?"

"No, Mrs. Murray. You may have acted as you have out of conviction, but I think you've done your son and me a disservice. Despite the lateness of the hour, I intend to visit Fred this afternoon, shortly. I have a professional responsibility to fulfill."

"I thought you'd hide behind that," she said caustically, and hung up.

Later that afternoon, after my last patient, about the time Fred had first appeared outside my office months earlier, I visited him. He lay in a bare little cubicle off to one end of the intensive care unit.

"Hello, Fred. I came over as soon as I could. Your mother told me about an hour ago where you were. I had no idea." He shook his head weakly and smiled. "What happened to you?" I asked. "She said you'd been shot."

"You look great, Doc," he answered, evading my question. "I bet you had a terrific time . . . up on that houseboat in Canada." He grinned proudly.

So he'd managed to ferret out where I'd gone from my answering service or some colleague. Was he back to his old tricks again? I didn't have to wait long to find out. "You shouldn't have left when you did, Doc. Maybe none of this would have happened if you hadn't taken off just then. We were doing swell." He smiled sardonically.

"What happened, Fred?" I repeated. I would deal with the intimation that I deserted him and was derelict later, when I knew more. Again, however, I was put off.

"I'm not supposed to talk so loud, Doc. It tires me, and I have to rest. If you want to pull over a chair, though, I'll tell you about it." I did as he asked and leaned close to Fred. He pointed to the television camera in the corner of the ceiling and whispered, "There's no need for anyone else to hear this. You, I can trust, you're my psychiatrist, right?" I nodded.

"Like I said, I think you were really helping me, Doc. I didn't mess up or get into any trouble while you were taking care of me, did I? All along, though, I was dealing. You didn't know that. It was only small stuff, grass, acid, and some uppers."

"I didn't realize you were selling drugs, Fred."

"Sure, I know that," he chaffed. "If I told you, it would have made a problem, wouldn't it? But I paid you in cash, every visit, remember? It had to come from somewhere."

"You had your job at the store—"

"That job was mostly bullshit. My old lady put me on the books for a hundred seventy-five a week. But ask her what she gave me"—he snickered—"a crummy twenty-five as a kind of allowance. The job was a tax gimmick, dig? I always had to hustle what I needed on my own one way or another." He coughed and spit into some tissues.

"Anyway," he continued, "some guy I knew came to me, right after you left, with what seemed like a terrific deal." He edged over to the side of the bed, lowered his voice even further, and spoke almost directly into my ear. "I got my hands on cocaine, enough to make a bundle. I mean, I could've seen you every day for five years with that kind of dough." I cringed. "I hunted around," he went on, "until I found two guys who handled smack, you know, heroin. I figured they were big enough to take the stuff off my hands so I wouldn't have to deal it myself all over the streets. They even gave me two Cs up front. We set up a meeting over on Tyler Street behind the old school bus garage."

"In Brentwood?"

"Yeah, you've probably never been over there. It's across the bridge, on the other side of the train tracks where the warehouses and the recycling dump are. When I got there, those bastards jumped me. They took my stuff and beat the shit out of me because I didn't have the two hundred bucks they gave me in my pocket."

"Who are they?" I asked, then bit my tongue.

Fred gave me a queer look for a moment. "It doesn't matter, there's nothing to be done about it. These guys are connected, you know what I mean? You don't do anything if you want to go on breathing. I must've passed out while they were working me over. When I came to, it was five-thirty. I was supposed to meet Le—, the guy who put up the bread for the deal in the first place, over at Neeley's Cozy. What could I do? I was all messed up, like. People would ask questions. Besides, I figured if I told this guy what really had happened, he would have been stupid enough to do something silly and get us killed. He's a hot-tempered nut—he ought to see you. Anyway, I got this idea, you know. I drove over there just the way I was, with my clothes all ripped and blood on my face and stumbled into the place like I was pulling my last breath. Man, everyone got excited and asked me what happened." Fred grinned. "I told them some niggers pulled me out of my car when I stopped for the light over on Davis Street. I conned them with a lot of crap about being dragged out and stomped. I said, I was told to warn other whiteys not to come around there anymore.

"Everybody seeing me the way I was knew I'd been worked over, see? They had no reason not to believe me. Even the guy

who was waiting for me went for it. I told him they cleaned me
out. But things got out of hand, you know? Next thing these
guys—most of them are just dumb laborers—are forming a friggin' posse of vigilantes."

"You mean a lynch mob?" I said, feeling sick.

"Yeah, that's how it was. We piled into a couple of cars and
a guy's truck. There must have been close to twenty of us altogether. We went bustin' over to Davis Street and started breaking things up. It was a real friggin' race riot, I want to tell you."

"How did you get shot?"

"Everyone was fighting, throwing things around and holler-
ing, when some creep lets go from a window with a twelve-
gauge cannon."

"A shotgun?"

"That's right, and the son of a bitch had it loaded with
these special shells that have a big slug as well as shot in them.
That's what I got hit with. They had to take out my right kidney—lucky, I got two, right? But they also took part of my liver,
and that's a bitch." Carefully, he lifted the bed sheet and
showed me his side. Drains and stained dressings covered a
large area.

"About thirty people already gave blood for me. Would
you believe it? I got all new blood in me. I'm a new man, now,
Doc." He chuckled. "Everyone wants to visit me, too, but the
doctors don't let them. I'm a kind of hero. Even Reverend Thayer, the black preacher, came. They let him in for a few minutes.
He said I was a 'martyr, a symbol of the need for brotherhood,'
and garbage like that. You can read all about it in the back
papers. My mother is saving them for me. A new committee on
race relations was started because of what I did. How about
that? You ought to be pleased. Your old buddy Judge Farrow is
co-chairman with Reverend Thayer . . . . That Farrow is a turd,
though. He knows me because of the trouble I used to get into
and hasn't come to see me like Thayer."

"How are you feeling now, Fred? Those were serious
wounds," I said, concealing my desolation.

"I'm okay. I told you I'm a lucky cat. I've got eight more

lives, remember? They are sending me away for special treatment tomorrow morning. Didn't my mother tell you?"

"No." So that's why she wanted me to wait another couple of days. "Where are you going?"

"Down to University Hospital in the city to be under the care of some liver specialists, I think. Don't worry, I hear it's a terrific place." Fred yawned, tired from the excitement and exertion of all he had told. "Listen, Doc," he concluded, "I won't be back to see you when I return, okay? I mean, I'm somebody now, a sort of celebrity in town . . . you know how it is, I won't need a shrink anymore."

THE ALL-AMERICAN ZERO

Amy Novec

Ted Barnett called me one dank evening late in November. It was rare for him to call me at home, and when he did, it often meant something urgent. Ted is an internist, highly competent and likable.

"I'm sorry to intrude on your evening and disturb you this way," he began. Automatically I rose and carried the phone over to the window to peer outside into the murk. My brain began the process of cranking up my reluctant body, preparing for a quick change of clothes and a chilly drive back to Brentwood, probably to the hospital emergency room.

Ted seemed to anticipate my reaction. "There isn't any crisis," he hastily added, "no one for you to see tonight. I would just like to discuss a problem with you if you have some time to listen to me now."

The relief I felt not to be routed from my warm, comfortable home and compelled to desert my family was almost shameful. It pricked at my conscience and punished me with the thought I was getting older. Turning to my wife and children, who were watching and silently asking, I shook my head and smiled to signal I would not be going out. Then I went into the study to another phone. I sat down in front of a pad, opened my pen, and encouraged Ted to continue.

"I have a patient, Jerry, a lovely young woman of twenty-six who has been through an ordeal medically and now wants to see a psychiatrist. She's even mentioned your name specifically. I am, however—and I know I can be perfectly frank with you—reluctant to refer her. Can I tell you why and get your view on this?"

"Of course, Ted, please go on," I said, scribbling, "female, twenty-six, medical ordeal??" on my pad.

"Jerry, I know I'm not being as disinterested and objective about this as I probably should be. That's why I need your help. My reluctance to send this patient to a psychiatrist has nothing at all to do with her wish to see you. As unhappy as I am about this referral, I was relieved that she's chosen you. I can communicate as one physician to another with you. I don't think I'd be calling if it were someone else."

"I am pleased you feel that way, Ted," I said deliberately. I sensed that he meant what he was saying and was all the more curious to learn why he was so hesitant to refer this young woman. Was he personally involved in some way with her? I doubted that. Ted was a compassionate physician but not the sort to confuse his role with patients easily.

"You know," he continued, "there's an irony in this. The problem I usually face is how to be sensitive and tactful enough to recommend to a patient that he or she consult a psychiatrist. I worry that they'll be hurt or feel insulted or even think I am discarding them. People can be very sensitive where their feelings or their psyches are concerned, especially those who don't recognize that they need help or who look on psychological problems as some kind of weakness. Psychiatry still frightens many individuals, and they need a great deal of reassurance before they'll even consider a referral. That's why the situation I'm calling you about is so ironic. This patient brought it up herself, and I've been trying unsuccessfully so far to dissuade her."

"Why, Ted? I'm interested to know your reasons."

"Look," he said, "as an outsider I've observed many patients who've been in psychotherapy, and I know it can become pretty heavy going. Sometimes it can be such a slow, painful business that it taxes some people almost to their limits. Even a relatively normal person may have to bear a considerable strain for a long time before working things out and getting somewhere."

"Yes," I admitted, "that's true in some cases, but it is hardly typical."

"Jerry, I know this patient, and I fear it won't be easy for her. Also, she is just now getting back on her feet after being seriously ill last summer. I hate to expose her to any further stress so soon, especially if it isn't absolutely necessary." I was about to say something but thought better of it and remained silent. "I've watched her mature into a thoroughly wholesome and, in my opinion, well-balanced woman. I guess you can sense I think she's rather special, and I admit I'm very fond of her."

I thought I heard a slight tremor in Ted's voice. He seemed a little choked and picked his words carefully. "There is something rather different about Amy Novec. She's not . . . well, sophisticated like other young women today. She is so much more appealing in an old-fashioned, clean, fresh way. In fact, she's still a virgin, though she is certainly attractive and well-liked." He paused a moment then went on in a lower voice. "She and I have an unusually close relationship . . . because of her illness, I mean. . . . What I'm trying to say and getting emotional about is that I've seen her through a lot and care very much about her well-being. I'd like to spare her any additional burden and stress if I can, even if it means that she'll have to live with a few minor problems. I can't talk her out of seeing you, however, without telling her that she isn't doing as well medically as she thinks she is."

"It sounds like quite a dilemma, Ted. But apparently she doesn't share your opinion about her problems being minor ones. I wonder why, however, if she is recovering so slowly, you haven't just encouraged her to wait awhile longer until she's completely well again before consulting me. Surely, a few months more shouldn't make a great difference if she is as well-adjusted generally as you suggest."

"I only wish I could do just that," he answered. "She is an excellent, cooperative patient who would wait if I asked her, but my conscience won't let me. She's dying. Time is running against her. I'm not at all sure how long she has. It could be a matter of months or a couple of years. . . ."

"I see. . . . I am sorry. What is her diagnosis, Ted?"

"Lymphosarcoma. She has a really nasty kind. It's one of the less controllable types of cancer of the lymph glands. You know, we get excellent results with many of these lymph and related malignancies, but the particular type of tumor Amy has just hasn't proved very responsive to radiation or chemotherapy. We've had very limited success in treating her so far," he said.

"Is she in remission now?" I asked.

"Yes, she's just edging into one."

"Does she know her condition and prognosis?"

"Yes, she's insisted on knowing everything, but she believes that maybe she can beat it and outlive the statistics. I hope so, but I doubt it, although I make an effort to appear optimistic. I try to be candid with patients, but there is no point in dashing her hopes. Amy is unmarried. She lives at home with her folks. If she were married and had children, I'd probably be more frank. She would want to know in order to make plans and arrange things in that situation, and I'd tell her what she needed to know. That isn't the case, however."

I understood. "Hope is often good therapy," I commented.

"It won't cure cancer," he said bitterly.

"Maybe not, but it enhances well-being and can prolong life. Treating cancer is always a race against time in hope of some new development or breakthrough."

"Meanwhile—"

"No, wait a moment," I interrupted. "Hope isn't just some empty slogan. I'm serious about it. A number of years back Carl

Richter, a psychologist at Johns Hopkins, proved its value. He set up an experiment with a number of laboratory animals. He placed them in a situation which made death appear an absolute certainty. The animals, even the most lively ones, soon gave up the struggle to survive and seemed content to die. But when he restructured the situation to permit opportunities to live, the animals that earlier seemed resigned to their doom recovered very quickly. Hope is a potent force for survival."

"What's the relationship then between psychotherapy and hope? Don't you set about to puncture the myths and illusions people live with much of their lives?" he retorted.

"When those myths and distortions enslave and encumber people, certainly," I asserted. "It is the destructive myth of hopelessness which denies an individual incentives to strive and to improve his life that we try to demolish. Has your patient told you what it is that she wants to discuss with me?" I asked.

"Not exactly . . ." he said. "She hasn't been very forthcoming about it . . . and I find it awkward to ask. I don't want to pry."

"Come on, Ted," I coaxed.

"Maybe her illness is getting through to her, and I'm concerned that things will change if she sees a psychiatrist," he said.

"What do you mean, change?"

"Up to now, she seems to have accepted it and coped. In fact, she's been remarkable. Amy doesn't complain. She isn't morbid. To the contrary, she acts pretty cheerful considering what she has put up with, diagnostic procedures, biopsies, radiation therapy, and drugs. She is patient and pleasant, a peach, even when she's experienced some disagreeable side effects from chemotherapy. Everyone here and at the hospital who has worked with her loves her. All she wanted to do was get back to work. She's a health and physical education instructor at the Morton School, probably the best-liked member of the staff by the rest of the faculty and the students. It's easy to see why."

"You're uneasy that her attitude might change?" I echoed.

"Maybe that's all it is. . . ."

"You sound uncertain. Has she said anything else?"

"The only hint she's given me, Jerry," he said pensively, "is some comment about wanting to move out from her parents' home, where she's been living since she came back from college. Mr. and Mrs. Novec are not patients of mine, and they don't communicate with me; but I get the impression that Amy is the cog that makes them mesh. I'm not sure that they'd get along very well without her there to make things work, according to what she's said. It won't be easy for her to leave if that's the case. But I have to be honest and admit I'm also apprehensive about her leaving home."

"Why?"

"Because of her illness. I don't like to think about her being all alone. She doesn't seem to have anyone at hand to room with, and there aren't any boyfriends in the picture. The other faculty at her school are mostly older or married and living on the grounds. She doesn't want that."

"You think this is one of her problems?" I said, pumping him.

"I suspect there may be others as well, but I can't seem to get at them. She is probably aware of my attitude and telling me only what she wants me to know. I'm no psychiatrist. Maybe I've turned her off." He paused a moment. When he spoke again, his voice was stronger, sharper. "I want you to know, however, that overall I still think Amy Novec is a pretty well-balanced individual. I worry, frankly, that you might undermine her adjustment by opening some Pandora's box and stirring her up. Even if it's only on the surface, Amy has been managing all along and bearing up to her illness very well."

The challenge in Ted's voice betrayed him. He was emotionally involved with this patient. I thought of responding and decided to say nothing. A long, silent moment passed before he spoke again. Now his voice was subdued. "I don't know, Jerry. You probably think I'm making too much of this. I care about this girl. I feel bad that I can't do more for her. Am I being selfish in trying to protect her? Am I just making sure you don't change anything because Amy's attitude of acceptance and non-resistance to her illness makes it easier for me? If that's all that's bothering me, tell me so. You know, I respect your opinion; be candid with me, please," he asked wearily.

"Ted, I think you are a competent and perceptive internist. You're aware of this patient as a person, and you're conscious that your wish to safeguard her may have more than one motive. But I've learned not to disregard the intuitions of experienced clinicians. Whatever they reveal about the physician, they always contain grains of truth about the patient. I think this young woman is fortunate to have a doctor as concerned and as conscientious as you looking after her.

"You suggest that whatever problems she may be withholding from you can't be too important because she has managed well in spite of them. You may be right. Given the greater threat her illness poses to her stability, I can understand your reluctance to have me tinker with her adjustment. To risk upsetting her and altering her capacity to face her illness and cooperate as she has in her treatment is a serious responsibility. Sufficient stress and emotional turmoil could even exacerbate her disease; the mind and the body are more indivisible than most people comprehend. I regard your concern as an appropriate warning. I won't be complacent about the risks of taking this patient on.

"The crucial question is what does she want to see me about. I can't cure her lymphosarcoma or make it go away. I only hope it *is* something I can help. I understand your feelings of frustration and impotence. You're dissatisfied with what you've been able to do for her. Every one of us who fights the odds and accepts patients for treatment who have poor prognoses has tasted from that bitter cup. Tell Ms. Novec to call me. I appreciate the opportunity to see her."

"I will, Jerry. Thank you. I am sorry to involve you in such a sad case. I hope nothing I said offended you, and I'm grateful you didn't back off."

"I meant what I said, Ted, but I'm not so sure you weren't baiting me just to make certain I'd be especially careful with your patient."

He chuckled. "I'm sure you will be. I'll give her your number tomorrow. Don't keep her waiting too long, will you?"

"I'll see her this week if she calls. Count on it!"

Amy Novec looked younger than her twenty-six years. Her face was pale except for a blush of pink in her cheeks. She had delicate features, an appealing smile, and the pert, eager look one associates usually with untried youth. Her stylishly cut, curly brown hair contrasted conspicuously with the plainness of her workaday dress and shoes and otherwise simple appearance. I guessed the reason why. Chemotherapy can sometimes cause hair loss. A wigmaker had prepared Amy's coiffure. Except for tiny green posts in her earlobes, she wore neither jewelry nor makeup.

Amy settled in the chair nearer me and breathed quick, shallow breaths. We sat for a moment studying one another. "I'm sorry," she gasped, "I'm out of wind. I climbed the steps outside to get here."

I nodded. "Did you have some problem with the elevator?" I asked.

"Oh, no, I could have taken the elevator, but I'm trying to get my strength back. I need the exercise. Those X-ray treatments and drugs really socked it to me. Now I've got to build myself up again, but I guess I overdid things a little this afternoon. I'm usually more cautious than this. I hate to bite off more than I can chew." Her breathing slowed, and she sat back somewhat more at ease and sighed. I noticed now that her brown eyes were slightly sunken. There was also some concave spooning at her temples, and the muscles formed prominent cords in her neck. She'd lost a significant amount of weight.

"You're younger than I thought you'd be, Doctor. I expected a much older man somehow."

I smiled. "Tell me why. Does it disturb you that I'm not as you imagined?" I asked.

"Oh, no," she answered briskly. "It's because you once treated a friend—actually, a classmate of mine—Alice Curran. It was quite a number of years ago. We were sophomores in high school back then. The way she spoke about you being older and so patient and understanding, I guess I pictured you'd be someone more like a grandfather by now. Oh, gosh! I don't mean it that way." She grinned sheepishly. "I mean, I'm really glad you're not old. Someone older might not understand."

"I remember your friend Alice," I said, easing her embarrassment. "I hope she is well and happier now. Did you discuss your consulting me with her?" I was interested in learning what preconceptions she had about coming to see me.

"Oh, no, I don't see Alice anymore. She's married now and living in Houston, Texas, I think. Her husband is some sort of technician with NASA. I understand they're very happy and have two darling little boys. Alice and I were never really friends in a way that lasts. We were much too different." Amy was positive about that.

"You sound emphatic. In what ways were you so unlike each other?" I asked, to bring to light Amy's image of herself. She reacted with mild surprise as if the dissimilarity between her and her erstwhile acquaintance should have been immediately apparent. Her face flushed, I thought.

Amy bit her lip and frowned. However she had intended to present her problem, I had disrupted her plan. She seemed to be quickly rearranging her thoughts. "Uh, well, you must remember the troubles Alice had? Her pregnancies? It was awful back then for any single girl unlucky enough to get herself pregnant, but to have it happen twice while you were still in high school was a double disaster. Even those who were sympathetic toward her the first time turned their backs on Alice when it happened again in senior year. People were really unkind even after she cut herself. She couldn't have stood going through it a second time and giving up another baby to an agency. I know, because when all her so-called friends deserted her, Alice confided in me. You were the one who made it possible for her to have an abortion legally, in the hospital, which wasn't easy in those days. She told me about it. But you did a lot more for her, talking to her about herself and what she really wanted to do with her life. She used to tell me. You made her see what sex and real love were all about."

"I see. I wasn't aware Alice had confided in anyone else," I said.

"She wouldn't have mentioned me. As I said, we weren't regular friends. Alice and I traveled in different circles. I was too straight and square to associate with her crowd normally. It was just that I felt sorry for her and let her lean on me for a little while. She had such a horrible life, especially when her parents split up. Her mother blamed her. Both her parents drank a lot. Alice was on her own too soon, before she could handle it. She was terribly hurt and confused—but you know all this. I was really impressed by the change in her after she began seeing you."

I nodded reflectively. "But—"

"How were we so different? In almost every way. For one thing, she was gorgeous with her blond hair and her terrific figure. I don't consider myself ugly, but I was never built like Alice even at my normal weight. That's the least important difference, though, even if I wouldn't mind attracting certain men the way she could just passing by. The truth is I'm not unattractive, and I know it. I can manage to look quite good when I'm healthy and have a reason to do so. But unlike Alice, I can't seem to get a man or keep him interested long enough to make a serious pass at me.

"Alice grew up too fast, Doctor. I haven't grown up yet. Maybe she was headstrong and made mistakes, but after all, she was just a teenager and very much on her own. I'm twenty-six, still living at home, still playing it safe and getting nowhere. I often think about Alice and wish I had been more like her. In spite of her troubles, there were things I admired in her. She had a sense of humor and could laugh at herself. Did she tell you about being descended from Irish royalty? I come from a nice comfortable middle-class home with no horrendous family problems, certainly none like hers. I've had many advantages and much more education. Where has it gotten me?" She shrugged.

"I don't think I've really matured much since sixteen. I feel as if I have no more control over my life now than I had then, and time is running out. I want to grow up and make my life work. I feel I need to get out on my own, yet I'm held back. I want to be able to meet a man I like and be capable of having a meaningful relationship with him. I don't think I've ever been kissed by someone who really meant it. Either I can use some help, Doctor, or I'd better change my brand of toothpaste soon." She grinned cheerlessly.

"Apparently you feel you lack something more, Ms. Novec."

"Much more. I talk to myself at times, but I can't put my finger on what's wrong or I wouldn't be here. Ted, Dr. Barnett, didn't want me to come. He thinks I'm just fine the way I am. But he's married and has kids of his own—" She interrupted herself. "Ted thinks I'm terrific because I want him to. I never act depressed or let my illness get to me when he's around. In fact, I don't dwell on it in front of anyone. What would be the point? Let them think it doesn't bother me. They're more comfortable that way. A smile and even a little humor go a long way with people when you're really ill."

"Isn't it rather burdensome to have to act cheery all the time in front of people?" I asked.

"Not really. You get used to it, and it becomes kind of automatic. Besides, I was like this anyway, even before I got sick. I was always acting merry. I never have been relaxed with other people, especially persons my own age. In high school and college, even now, I'm sort of jolly, and people who know me expect it; but I don't truly feel that way. It's just my manner. I relate better to people much older and more mature. They don't seem to make me as tense."

"Tell me about your illness and how you really feel about it, Ms. Novec."

"All right, but I'd prefer you to call me Amy if you would."

"Fine, Amy," I agreed.

"There isn't all that much to tell. About three years ago, while I was on a trip in Europe during the summer, I started itching all over. I didn't know what it was. At first, I thought it was the linens in our hotels. Teachers' tours aren't exactly deluxe. When it finally became unbearable, I saw a doctor in Paris. He thought I had some sort of allergic condition, I guess; my French wasn't that good. He prescribed some pills, and I improved. By the time I got home again it had subsided, and I didn't think any more of it. Then, about a year and a half later, I had a routine chest X-ray for school; I teach health and physical education. The next thing I knew, Ted had me in the hospital for more X-rays and a series of tests. It seems my lymph glands here were all enlarged." She pointed to her neck and the center of her chest.

"I knew it was serious even before Ted finally told me. You can tell something like that from the way everyone goes out of his way to be nice to you. One of the technicians, though, would stare at me as if I were some special kind of creature. After they biopsied a gland in my neck, I asked, and Ted told me I had a type of lymph cancer."

"That must have been difficult to hear," I commented.

"I tried to keep up a front, but let me tell you, I was terribly shaken. I began getting tingling sensations in my hands, and I'd have horrible nightmares that I was being slowly eaten up. My nerves were really frayed, and despite myself, it must have shown because Ted put me on some tranquilizers for a while. The X-ray treatments really melt this kind of tumor dramatically, however, so I've really done quite well. I've had only some minor flare-ups. I'm just getting over the last one. They used some new drug this time. It wasn't too pleasant—ugh! My hair started coming out every time I put a comb through it. This isn't me." She patted the top of her head. "Ted thinks my hair will grow in again. He expects me to have a good remission. If I get any future recurrences, he says there are several new drugs to control them. I have a lot of confidence in him. So, that being the case, it's up to me now finally to do something about my life, which is why I came to see you."

"Your illness, then, has given you some impetus to solve some problems in the way you live and relate to people, especially men," I said.

"Exactly. You've caught on to me already. I don't want to waste the rest of my days, however long I may live. My life has been a bore, and I am dissatisfied with it. I think I always expected that sooner or later things would pick up and just fall magically into place for me. Well, something—my illness—came along and shattered that fantasy. I realize that it's all up to me now, if I am to have any kind of life before I die. I have to change somehow. I'm tired of winning all the medals for sportsmanship while everyone else goes about getting what he wants out of life. Others may think I'm courageous, but to me, I'm the all-American zero. Please help me grow up so I can taste life while there is still time. I want to be an adult, female woman."

I was moved by Amy's plea. I wanted to assure her that I would respond to it and try to assist her, but I was concerned that I would only encourage her to believe that I could change her. I thought of several things to say but rejected each of them. The appropriate way to answer her, I decided, was to proceed.

"Amy," I began, "do you have any theory as to why this illness occurred to you? Any notion or rationale, however scientific or fanciful?"

"At first, I thought it was related to my trip to Europe, especially when Ted told me that the itching had been a symptom. I thought the hectic pace of touring or the food or water. . . . I was convinced I picked it up over there somehow. It was almost like something I deserved for defying my mother in going. I had saved and talked about making the trip for years, but my mother always discouraged me. She didn't like the idea of my traveling alone as a single woman or even with another girl. It's petty of me to think this way, but my mother also may have had selfish reasons for wanting me to stay at home.

"My mother designs fabrics for a manufacturer, at home, but in the summer she has no work and is free. With me away there is no one to drive her here and there, no one to take her to the lake or shopping or to visit my sister, Irene. She managed to make me feel guilty about abandoning her when the chance to join the tour came along."

"Did you feel as if your illness were some form of retribution, a fulfillment of your mother's warnings?"

"Umm . . . well, let's put it this way. I did have the idea that if I'd stayed at home and heeded them, I would not have gotten sick. But Ted is certain my trip had nothing at all to do with it. He thinks these diseases percolate a long time quietly before they become apparent." Amy grew pensive. She grimaced as though disturbed by her thoughts.

"What is it?" I gently asked. Her shoulders drooped. She suddenly looked ill. Her eyelids appeared puffy. She moistened her lips. "Amy?" I persisted.

"Oh, God, I didn't think it would bother me again," she cried. "I'm sorry," she said, looking at me now. "I . . . I had this idea—I know you'll think it's crazy—I had this wild thought—" She broke off, breathing deeply, her eyes staring at mine.

"Go on," I gently urged. "You had a thought?"

"I believed I was being punished for something I did in school in the fourth grade." Her voice was stronger now. "I cheated. I copied on a test from the boy who sat next to me. I was a better student than he was, but I had done the wrong assignment, and I wasn't prepared for the quiz. The teacher could see from our papers that one of us had cheated. Arthur, Arthur Gretz was blamed, and he got a zero. The teacher never even gave him a chance to explain. She probably wouldn't have believed him anyway. I was her pet and above suspicion."

"You didn't confess it was you."

Amy shook her head. She was teary now. "No, I didn't have the courage, and it's bothered me ever since. I used to have bad dreams about it. I can still see Arthur's face while he waited for me to say something. I know it sounds insane, but now and then I wonder if God is punishing me. I didn't think I could even tell you about this. Am I being childish?"

"Guilt is a potent force, isn't it?" I answered.

"It must be. I think it has a lot of influence in my life. I've been such a good girl that I've never grown up. There has to be a reason for that. I'm always worrying that whatever I do will affect someone else. I try too hard to please everybody. I'd like so much just to feel free to pursue my own goals for a change. The other day, for example, I heard of an apartment that may be vacant in January. It's near my school, and I'd love to take it; but I know my parents will object and try to talk me out of it. I think they're afraid to be alone with one another. Should I sign a lease anyway and then tell them? Do you think I can handle living on my own? If you tell me to, I'll go ahead on it. I'll explain to my folks that you've recommended it."

Amy was appealing openly for my support. Her enthusiasm for this venture was apparent. But her innocent questions confronted me with a major clinical decision.

I had already made up my mind to accept Amy as a patient if she wished to continue. Now the question was to develop a therapy suited to her and appropriate to her goals. How I responded to her would commit me to a particular attitude toward her problems. I would be setting the tone to which she would tune her expectations. It is difficult to deviate from one's approach later without confusing a patient and jeopardizing the therapeutic relationship.

The issue hinged on how supportive I chose to be. If I gave her the advice she sought and encouraged her to act on her plans, I would relieve her apprehensions and provide her with the backing for which she felt a need. As a therapist I would be consenting to the role of a surrogate parent. Amy could mask her immaturity by transferring authority from her parents to me. She would be merely acting on doctor's orders. It is a common manipulation to avoid resolving neurotic dependency. When it is exposed, the patient usually affects a naïveté and protests, "But you are the doctor!" I had to decide how much I would function as Amy's advocate and help her directly and how much I would withhold support and frustrate her dependent strivings.

Years before, I had actively intervened to support her friend Alice. Amy obviously expected me to aid her in a similar way. However, not only was Amy older and more sophisticated than Alice had been, but she had more coping skills and psychological resources. I felt not only that she was more capable than Alice of working through her problems, but that the result she achieved would be meaningful and enduring if she did. There was the rub. I knew her prognosis. Could I, should I, limit my role to that merely of a catalyst and allow her to struggle longer to attain her goals? I began to formulate a plan.

No more than a minute had passed since Amy had spoken. But a minute is a very long time in a psychiatric session when questions are unanswered. Amy had become apprehensive, shifting restively in her chair. Finally, she leaned forward and spoke again. "Look, Doctor, if you think I'm acting like a child or stepping out of line asking you to help me, please say so. I really do prefer physicians to be frank with me. I think you will find I can take a lot. Maybe it is absurd for me to try to change at this late date. There are some things in my life I am thankful for, and I think I can make it as I am," she said coolly.

"You mean you're content to remain 'the all-American zero'?" I said warmly, half-smiling.

"What do you mean?" she asked, her voice rising.

"Simply that your quest for my advice and support arises from your poor opinion of yourself and of your capabilities. I've been thinking how to answer your questions without reinforcing these self-depreciatory views. Whatever gains you might make because I back you will not bring about the changes in yourself you wish to make, Amy."

"Oh . . ." she uttered soberly.

I tried to be encouraging. "Your ambitions seem reasonable and realistic. Yet you haven't been able to pursue them very successfully. Something prevents you from taking the steps required. If your hope is to grow as a person, you'll have to discover what this is and master it."

"But I've tried," she protested.

"And because you failed, you feel inadequate. It's hard to do on your own. Your psychological blind spots and defenses make it difficult. That's why, as a psychiatrist, I may be able to help you more by identifying your problem than by giving you advice about apartments. Insight should help you focus your efforts on the underlying problems that frustrate you. Whatever these are, it is likely that they've existed since your childhood. If you understand them, you can bring the knowledge and judgment you have acquired since then to bear and, I hope, to resolve them. If you wish, I'll be glad to work with you."

"Yes, I want to go ahead."

I looked at the clock. Our time was almost up. I opened my appointment book and studied my schedule. "I suggest we meet fairly frequently until we're well under way. We'll have the advantage of close continuity that way."

Amy and I discussed arrangements and agreed to a schedule of three appointments weekly. As our plans took form, she became excited and enthusiastic. "Oh, this is great," she chirped before leaving. "I thought Ted was preparing me not to be too crushed if you didn't take me on. You had me scared for a moment or two back there. I'm so happy you explained things. I was worried that I'd just have to settle for my bad karma and accept it." She laughed.

The next morning, on a break, I called Ted Barnett to report that I had seen Amy. I told him of my decision to treat her. He was already aware of her visit. From his tone he didn't sound pleased. Amy had spoken to him after seeing me, and he knew much about her session. Despite her positive reaction, it was evident that he had misgivings about the course I had prescribed. He questioned the propriety of developing an intensive, uncovering treatment with a patient who is fatally ill.

"You know," he said, "in terms of her life expectancy, Amy is nearing the end of her life. Shouldn't you be treating her more supportively and avoiding heroic procedures especially if they are likely to be painful and take a lot of time?" He repeated that in his opinion she had been managing adequately, and he urged me to reconsider my course and limit her psychotherapy to supporting her adjustment and allaying her fears. We were almost back to where we started when he first called.

I reminded Ted of our previous discussion and assured him that I remembered and had carefully weighed his reservations about Amy's consultation. I convinced him that I was well aware of her medical status and prognosis.

Any psychiatric treatment is likely to fail or to aggravate existing difficulties when the realities of a patient's life are ignored. It is also doomed from the outset, however, when it disregards the motives and goals of the individual seeking help. I had found Amy well aware of the seriousness of her illness, but she had not sought any aid concerning her fears and feelings about death. Neither was she denying her condition. What she was requesting was help so that she could experience some sense of fulfillment and could better exploit the time she had left to her. Could I deny her that?

"Ted," I said, "Amy wants desperately to 'grow up,' as she puts it, to experience her life less hindered by neurotic inhibitions and a compulsive need to please others in the time she has left."

"How do you know all this so quickly after only one session?" he asked, still dissatisfied.

"Amy was relatively open. She was quite productive, and she told me enough for me to think so," I replied, trying not to sound argumentative. "Look," I went on, "both of us have known fatally ill patients who have asked our help to maintain an appearance and a charade of well-being for the sake of others. When that is their rational choice and decision, we honor it. But Amy's pretense is not her conscious wish. Her masquerade is an involuntary burden. Even so, if she lacked the capability I think she has to overcome her psychological problems, I wouldn't begin an intensive treatment and press for insight at this stage of things. I'd opt, instead, to buttress her defenses and reassure her as best I could."

"I see . . . I wasn't aware how dissatisfied you say she really is," he murmured.

"I can readily understand why, Ted. You seem to be one of those persons she feels compelled to satisfy. She is quite fond of you and grateful to you."

"Well, you go ahead and do whatever you think best. I'll stick to treating her malignancy and will let you know if her condition changes significantly."

Amy arranged herself in the chair she had occupied before. The light-blue denim pants suit she wore seemed to hang somewhat on her spare frame. Yet her color was better, and she appeared less frail.

"There is something I must discuss with you, Doctor, before we go any further," she asserted, looking into my face and leaning forward. "Are you and Dr. Barnett very close friends?"

"Why do you ask that?"

"You did speak to him after my last visit, didn't you?" she asked.

"Yes," I admitted. "I called him to report that we had talked and that we planned to go ahead. Weren't you anticipating that Dr. Barnett and I would confer?"

"I . . . guess so," she conceded.

"It's a professional responsibility, as well as a matter of courtesy, for me to respond to a physician who refers a patient to me. While I will exercise some judgment on what I will share, I will, when it is appropriate, try to help him in a general sense to understand the patient better, especially when some degree of insight will affect and enhance his judgment of clinical issues."

Amy expressed concern that I protect her confidences. She had been disturbed by a conversation which followed my call to Ted. He had spoken to her again and reversed his position about her pursuit of psychiatric treatment. His change of attitude had alarmed her. "There are things I want to say that I don't want him to know. You see, Dr. Barnett is one of my problems in a way. . . ."

Amy revealed that Ted had long been the object of her romantic desires and that she had fantasized extensively about him. "He isn't like any other man I have ever known, not any," she insisted. "He can be so gentle and incredibly tender, yet be strong and decisive, too. He is very masculine without being arrogant about it."

"Are you saying that you're in love with Dr. Barnett, Amy?"

"Yes, I guess so. I'm not sure what being in love is. He's my doctor, and I know I'm completely stupid to care about him the way I do. I haven't really known very many men. Aside from my father and my brother, I find it hard to relate to them. Ted is the first man I have had anything to do with that I've felt this way about."

"I see," I said, encouraging her to go on.

"One night, about four months ago, I had trouble breathing. Ted was away with his family at their summer home. I hadn't felt too good even before he left but hadn't told him because I knew how much he had been looking forward to a rest. Finally, I called the doctor covering his practice, and he gave me some advice on the phone. I felt a little better, but then it got worse again. I didn't want to keep pestering the poor man; he was so busy, and he didn't really know my case well. I discussed it with the lady who runs Ted's answering service because she knows me. I guess she didn't like the way I was rattling and gasping and took it upon herself to call him at their place upstate. At two in the morning, after driving about three hours, Ted showed up at our door.

"I must have been almost blue by then because he took one look at me and literally lifted me up out of my bed and carried me out to the car. My father drove us. I kept passing out, but I remember him talking to me ever so softly, telling me I was going to be all right. When we reached the hospital, he tapped my chest with a needle and drew off some fluid that had accumulated so I could breathe again. My mother had come with us and was carrying on in her usual way. Ted sent my parents home and stayed there in my room with me the whole night.

"At first, I was quite frightened. I thought surely I was going to die. It isn't possible for me to describe all Ted did for me that night. How reassuring he was. How caringly he comforted me. I stopped being afraid and began to feel that if I did die, it would be all right. No one in my whole life had ever been so loving to me."

"Does Dr. Barnett know that you feel this way, Amy?"

"I can't be sure. I don't think he wants to know. I don't say anything, and I'm certainly not forward with him. I would never want to embarrass him or complicate matters—I'm trusting you to keep all this a secret. Lots of women probably have crushes on their doctors. I realize how ridiculous I'm being," she said with an embarrassed grin.

"Feelings aren't foolishness. They influence our lives too much to be dismissed. Even when the object of our feelings is unaware or unable to respond to them, they can profoundly affect us," I said delicately.

"You must know Ted well. Is he really happy in his marriage? I've seen a picture of his wife and children. He keeps a photograph of them on his desk—oh, don't answer, please!" she pleaded, her voice choked with emotion. She struggled for a moment in silence to maintain her control. "I wasn't ever going to ask you that. I am sorry. It just came out."

"I want you to continue letting things come out. Express your thoughts and feelings as freely as you can. We'll get further that way," I said, reassuring her.

Amy nodded, preoccupied. "It's funny," she continued, "I find I can accept something intellectually, yet in spite of what I know to be so, I go on caring anyway. Ted likes me, but I'm aware he doesn't care about me romantically. He takes a personal interest in me only because I'm his patient, and he feels responsible. If he gives me more of his time and attention, it's . . . well, because of my illness. I don't delude myself, but that doesn't seem to affect how I feel." She shrugged.

"Have you exploited your illness to attract his personal as well as his professional interest?" It was a blunt, tough question, but it was relevant to her trend, and I had to ask it if we were openly to explore her problems in relating to men.

"Oh, wow!" Amy winced. "I opened myself up for that, didn't I?" She was flustered but forced herself to continue.

"Even as I spoke a moment ago, I was wondering the same thing and hoping you wouldn't ask. Yes, definitely, if I'm going to be perfectly honest, I'm certain at times I abused my position as Ted's patient in order to get him to see me or talk to me on the telephone." Amy's cheeks glowed. "How do I get something like this out of my system?"

I was pleased by her candor. Amy demonstrated that she had the facility to observe herself introspectively and to report whatever she saw in a conscientious way. It meant that she was not too bound up in her defenses and could view herself in a relatively objective and analytic manner without feeling greatly threatened, a good prognostic sign. The revelation of her affection for Ted Barnett also provided me with the opportunity to maintain the focus of our discussion on one of her principal complaints, her inability to achieve her aims in a relationship. As much as possible, yet without appearing to be too directive, I intended to influence our course and limit the scope of psychotherapy to concentrate on her complaints. Time was such a crucial factor that to accomplish her goals, I was prepared to intervene and cause her to examine certain issues and allow others to remain blurred.

"How do you get something like this out of your system?" I repeated. "Your question sounds like, How does one cure an infection? Our first step, Amy, might be to identify more specifically what it is you seek in a relationship and how you go about it. Your history may provide us with the pattern of your behavior and clues to its cause. Certain events and circumstances can alter our expectations in relationships and affect the way we act. Like a virus that takes command of our cells to reproduce itself, these changes have a way of recurring again and again; they become habitual."

Amy dropped her eyes to the carpet before her. She sighed deeply and pushed back into her chair. "What would you like to know?" she asked quietly, not lifting her glance. Her voice was flat and toneless. She seemed suddenly deflated and resigned.

I debated whether to discuss her change in mood, decided intuitively against it, and made myself go on. "Perhaps you'd like to tell me about the other men in your life, those who preceded Dr. Barnett."

Amy drew a deep breath and slowly exhaled, a sardonic half grin on her face. She thought for a moment and then began to review the few occasions since her adolescence when particular young men had attracted her and she had hoped in vain for a relationship to develop. It was a cursory, unenlightening discussion. The therapeutic edge had been blunted. Amy was compliantly cooperating. She had little interest in what she was saying. I was disappointed and troubled by the awareness that I had erred. The session ended.

The principal drawback of directing the patient and prescribing the course of psychotherapy is that it tends to promote a shift of therapeutic responsibility from the patient to the therapist. The patient will tend to rely too much on the psychiatrist as an omniscient mentor. If one tries to confront it, the patient will take refuge in the fact that indeed he has complied. "You are the doctor," he will protest, as if he were unaware that in psychotherapy, the medical model of treatment is not entirely appropriate. For even when the psychiatrist charts the course, it is the patient's efforts that produce the "cure."

How stupid I was to have used a medical analogy to explain to Amy the compulsive tendencies we all have to repeat past patterns of behavior over again. It was particularly foolish that I chose as an example a virus taking command of our cells. It was too impersonal for one thing, and for another, it was a serious blunder to have stirred Amy's feelings about her illness unnecessarily. I berated myself for arousing her by my insensitivity and for contaminating her hopes in psychotherapy with her despair that no cure existed for her medical problem. Her feelings about her illness would have to be faced and probably discussed again but not accidentally. I would have to be more circumspect.

Amy was seven minutes late for her next session. As she entered my office, she paused, this time before the chair farther from me. "Does it matter where I sit?" she asked. "No, why should it make any difference?" she answered herself before I could react in any way. Amy seemed moody. She offered no explanation for her lateness. I decided to confront her about it. Not to do so, if I read her behavior correctly, would be tantamount to allowing an attack on her therapy to go unchallenged and would weaken her resolve still further. If she was angry, as I suspected, I wanted to face it directly. I asked her in a firm, even manner why she was tardy.

"I had to drop my mother at the chiropractor's. Her back is bothering her again. It always acts up whenever I need treatments or have to see a new doctor," she explained, scowling.

Amy was diverting her resentment onto a secondary target. I wasn't satisfied. "Amy, you seem out of sorts today. Are you angry or upset with me about something?" She dropped her eyes for a moment and then fixed her glance on mine.

"Do you really think I am going to get anything out of this therapy, or am I just wasting my time?" she asked.

"I've already said that I believe your goals are reasonable and realistic. I am quite convinced that you are capable of making significant strides and achieving them. It's clear, though, that you are feeling discouraged," I said.

Amy burst into tears. "I don't know why, but I've been so depressed. Everything seems so hopeless," she said, sobbing.

"Was it something in our last session that disturbed you?"

"No, I don't think so. It's my mother and her constant demands. It's a lot of things. I don't really know. Maybe I have been down since our last hour."

"Your mood seemed to change at a point where I likened the task before us to the treatment of a medical problem. It was an unfortunate analogy. My thoughtlessness must have upset you and taken the wind right out of your sails."

"It did bother me. I remember being jolted at the time and going on, though my heart wasn't in it." Amy wiped her face and brightened. "I guess I was counting too much on your being perfect. I thought everything you said was a message to me." She blew her nose, then smiled. "I appreciate your discussing the incident with me."

"We have a therapeutic relationship, Amy. Our willingness to expose what happens here between us is what makes it therapeutic." Amy's eyes widened; she nodded that she understood. Her mood had lifted. She was mollified and reassured. I redirected her now. "You mentioned your mother a moment ago, Amy. I'd like to learn about her and the rest of your family. Would you care to give me your personal history now?"

"Well, let's see," she began, "I was born and grew up near here in Hayesville. . . ."

Amy's parents had known each other since high school. Her father had worked for Mrs. Novec's uncle as an apprentice plumber until he was drafted during the Korean War. When he returned from the service, their relationship became more intense. After a brief courtship, and despite attempts by their respective families to discourage them, Amy's parents eloped. Mr. Novec was fired from his job and began his own contracting business in Brentwood. Within a year Amy's sister, Irene, was born.

"Irene is five years older than I am and entirely different. She is much more aggressive and hot-tempered. If something bothers Irene, she'll let you know about it. She picked on me a lot, criticizing almost everything I ever did. I always thought she was kind of disagreeable and bossy and tried to keep my distance from her. Irene and my mother used to fight and argue all the time when I was younger, but the two of them are much closer now, especially since Irene is married and has the twins. She uses my mother a great deal to help her, and Mom doesn't seem to mind for some reason. I'm always driving her over to Irene's or picking her up there.

"I feel bad about my relationship with Irene. She was born just when my parents were first getting started. It was a difficult time for them. Dad was beginning his business, taking on any job he could, working long hours for almost nothing. Builders took advantage of his situation and inexperience. Sometimes he didn't even get paid for his work. My mother had to help him. It was very trying. She's told me how she would have to call people five or ten times and beg them to pay what they owed my father so she could buy groceries. I think Irene probably suffered most. She got very little attention. By the time Dad went into construction himself and things began to improve financially, I came along to ruin it for Irene. I got all the toys and clothes she never had. Mom wasn't involved in the business anymore and stayed home with me while Irene had to go off to school.

"I also happen to look like Mom, and I was cute and athletic. Irene is sort of squat and dumpy like Dad. She even has his poor eyes and bad teeth. I'm sure Irene always envied and resented me until now. I regret that. I wish we could have been friends, but I don't think Irene ever forgave me for being born until I got sick. If you saw our family photograph album, you could see why. There are hardly any pictures of Irene in it, but there are loads of me; we even have movies of me as a toddler taking my first steps.

"I think my folks must have become much more financially secure quite suddenly, maybe when the housing boom took place back then. We moved into our present home at that time, and Anna, our housekeeper, started coming to us. It's remarkable what old pictures can tell. There I am, sitting on the hood of my father's first Cadillac, my mother posing in her new fur coat. In all of them, I'm smiling happily and often with Dad. Poor Irene always looks as if she's sulking or pulling away from someone.

"I was an easy child, they say. I was good and did whatever I was told. My father made a big fuss over me because I happened to be very well coordinated. I could catch a ball at a very early age and throw like a boy. He would play with me, and when I got a little older, Dad took me to football and basketball games with him, while my mother dragged Irene off on the train to the orthodontist. Neither she nor Irene had any interest whatever in sports. As sisters we went in entirely different directions. Irene is much more of an intellectual than I am. She's written short stories and had two of her poems published. I used to think her poetry was terribly depressing, but now, lately, I find her poems quite haunting and appreciate them more.

"I was the jock in my family for a long time. I starred on the teams in the neighborhood and at school. My grades weren't great, but they weren't so bad either. I managed a B average. Dad was really proud of me because my name was often in the local paper in connection with sports. I won some medals in track and swimming. The barber and storekeepers in town would mention me to him, and he loved it. Overall, I guess I'd have to say I had a happy life as a youngster. I used to put my parents, especially Dad, up on a pedestal and try to please them. I was very naïve. Irene knew better.

"It took me a long time—maybe I was twelve or so—before I could accept the things Irene said as being true. That's when I first seemed to realize that my parents were not very happy together. Irene told me that my parents had to get married. My mother told Irene the story, and I learned it from her. Dad is Jewish, and Mom is a Methodist. My grandparents liked my father, but they didn't want him in the family. Mom wasn't getting along well at home, and she got even with her parents by encouraging Dad to see her. Neither of my folks intended it to get too serious. Apparently, Dad's folks were also against it. But things got out of hand.

"Mom discovered that she was pregnant, or thought she was anyway. My father felt he had to marry her. They couldn't get his parents to agree, and my mother's side was against it, too, so my folks eloped. It turned out later, when she conceived Irene, that my mother had probably not been pregnant before at all. I think my dad has always resented her because of that; he felt tricked. There were times he might have walked out, but my mother is such a baby she probably couldn't have coped alone. So he's put up with her and tried to make the best of things.

"My mother, on the other hand, thinks she is a martyr. She is never happy or content. Mom would like to live in Conway, near her parents. She acts as if my father kidnapped her and keeps her away from them. Actually, he'd probably be delighted if she'd leave and go there to them, but she wouldn't go without him, and his business is here. So that's that.

"It's funny telling you all this. I'm beginning to think that maybe I always resented my mother. She constantly complains and overreacts to everything. There were always crises she couldn't handle. Whatever anyone did for her was either coming to her or wasn't quite right or sufficient to suit her. Mom is the kind of person who is thin-skinned and easily offended but is absolutely incapable of empathy for others. She's also nasty to my father in mean little ways, and she is selfish. You'd think living up here in the country, Mom would have learned to drive a car by now, but she claims it makes her too nervous. So instead, someone, usually me, has to put himself out to drive for her. When I made up my mind that I was going to Europe on that tour, she was furious because I wouldn't be around to be her chauffeur for a while. Even though she pretends everything is too much for her, she is a user and a taker.

"Mom can't face my illness. She insisted it was all a mistake for a long time. Then, when she could no longer deny it, she turned against my doctors and began giving me Christian Science pamphlets. She behaves as if my being sick is my fault somehow. No wonder I've felt guilty about it. My mother even competes with me in a peculiar way. Whenever I have to go to the hospital for tests, or today, for example, because I was coming to see you, she always has some complaint also. She won't go near doctors, however. Oh, no, it's off to her reader or the chiropractor again.

"Dad is also a little strange. For almost a year he wouldn't allow anyone outside the immediate family to know I was ill. But my father, whatever his quirks, is better with me than Mom is. When I'm really sick, I can always count on him. He'll do things for me and take off from his business at any time to help me or drive me for treatments.

"He and I were great pals once. But that was a long time ago, when I was a girl. It changed between us somewhere along the way. Maybe it was when I began to develop and mature into a woman. Maybe it was because my brother, Paul, who is twelve years younger than I am, took my place with him. I guess Dad really always wished that I had been a boy. I don't think my father has a high regard for women. Considering what he's put up with, I guess I can't blame him too much. But I do miss the closeness that we once had. It's hard to talk to him now."

Amy resumed her history in our next meeting. She began by talking about her brother.

"Paul . . . what can I tell you about Paul? He's a great kid. I love him, and I miss him now that he's off at college this year. He is a freshman at RPI. Paul has a sweet, giving nature. He doesn't brood about things the way my father does. I think his interest in engineering pleases my father a great deal. If he were huskier and more competitive, Paul would have been a terrific athlete. I think Dad put too much pressure on him. He bought Paul all kinds of nifty equipment and uniforms before he was even big enough to use them. It used to embarrass Paul among his friends. Dad was always horning into their games and interfering. He even coached Paul's Little League team. My father didn't mean to be such a heavy; he was just too overenthusiastic about everything Paul did. The sun rose and set on Paul, the future president of Novec Enterprises Incorporated."

For the first time since she had begun her story, Amy paused. She peered at me thoughtfully, drawing a deep breath and sighing wearily. I had withheld any comment thus far, satisfied to listen and pleased that she had been so productive without my prodding. Now I sensed that she was seeking some sign of my support, some indication that I understood her disappointment that Paul should have been able to usurp her place in her father's esteem. I said nothing but half smiled warmly and nodded, signaling her to continue.

"Do I sound jealous?" she asked, her voice rising, insistent that I respond.

"Is that how you feel?"

"I'm not sure. I thought I'd gotten over it. You see, I got very little attention from my mother; her own needs were too great. Dad was everything. The whole house came alive when he was home. But then, after a while, it was just between him and Paul. I envied what I thought Paul had. I know better now," she said bitterly. "It was all sports. Paul never had the relationship with Dad that Irene and I thought he did, not the kind of closeness and understanding each of us wanted. Maybe Irene didn't care as much; she seemed to be more independent and aloof. But I kept on trying like a fool to win back Dad's interest and approval. I wanted only to please him, do the things I thought he would once more be proud of and care about."

Again Amy paused. I realized that she was actively reaching out once more for contact. She wanted me to talk, to relate to her more directly, to engage in a dialogue with her. How consistent with the content and theme of her report, I thought. As she reveals the disappointment she experienced when her father withdrew his interest, she seeks assurances of mine. To interpret this transference to her would serve no useful purpose at this time, however. It would only interrupt her flow. I uttered some comment, instead, that she had apparently resorted to a futile pattern of behavior motivated by the memory of earlier successes.

"I guess so . . ." Amy answered, appearing somewhat dissatisfied that I was not more sympathetic. She bit her lip, then continued. "What I didn't know . . . or maybe couldn't accept," she said cautiously, "was that Paul wasn't pleased with all that attention and fuss Dad made over him. It was entirely my father's thing, his need. Paul was just doing what my father expected of him, but he couldn't communicate with him otherwise in any way and wasn't at all happy. The great comradeship I envied so much was really a sham, though for a long time I wouldn't believe it. We kids all used to call my father Coach because we knew he preferred it to Dad. Did you ever hear anything like that before?"

I shook my head. "Apparently you three youngsters didn't communicate with each other very effectively either."

"Well, there were fairly large age differences between us. But you're right," she conceded. "That has been the case even now that all of us are older. It amazes me as we discuss it, what a foul-up my family really is. My parents never fought the way I heard that other parents did. But they never showed much affection toward one another either. I don't think they even touched if they could avoid it. Irene was jealous of me and resentful toward them. She had her books and one or two friends. She went her own way. I was shoved aside for Paul and envied him. Paul used to try to be close, but I would reject him. It wasn't until he hurt his knees playing basketball and was finished in competitive sports that things between us began to change. Dad was terribly disappointed. He urged Paul to have an operation on his cartilages, but Paul refused. My brother was actually relieved to be out of athletics and glad to get my father off his back. That's what made me see the light.

"The joke of the matter," Amy continued, "was that outsiders thought we were a very close-knit family. Actually, when I think about it, we lived together like strangers. Every one of us was bound up in one way or another, discontented and alone." Amy shuddered and massaged her forearms.

"I hardly ever invited a friend home because of Mom," Amy said when she resumed. "My mother always made it seem like such an imposition when anyone came to the house that my friends tended to stay away. After a while I wasn't invited to their homes either because their mothers resented the one-sidedness of it. I complained about it, but my mother always denied her attitude or shrugged it off."

Long-standing conflicts with her mother continued to emerge as Amy went on. Mrs. Novec was depicted as a scared, shrill woman and a hypochondriac who exploited physical complaints to manipulate her family. "Don't you think I'd like to be able to do what other mothers can do for their children?" she would ask, silencing Amy and her brother when they expressed disappointment. Irene, however, was less easily put off. She would bark and argue back or stand before her in icy contempt, muttering hateful things through clenched teeth. But Irene left home for college, married, and never returned again except for visits. Mrs. Novec continued to use her endless ailments to bend Amy and Paul.

"I always expected my mother to come home from a visit to the doctor with the news that she had some dreadful disease. I guess it's possible I actually wished it, but if I did, it certainly wasn't a conscious wish. I was always glad to learn that there was nothing seriously wrong and puzzled that she wouldn't tell us unless we pried it out of her. I was so naïve! It should have dawned on me that she was never relieved or satisfied with a good report. Once I was with her when one of the doctors—she changed them fairly frequently—told her very tactfully at least five times that she had nothing wrong with her. As soon as we were back in the car, though, Mom burst into tears and said he had yelled and shouted at her. When I disagreed, she became upset with me. 'What do you know?' she cried. 'No one believes how I suffer. You don't really care what happens to me, whether I live or die!'

"I have never forgotten that. I was so hurt. I tried to console her but finally gave up. It was so trying and frustrating." Amy's face reddened, and her eyes became puffy and watery. She did not cry. "Before I got sick myself—Mom's quieted down about being at death's door since then—I'd get terribly churned up inside thinking about that incident whenever I had to drive her to another doctor's appointment. She would insult the doctors and tell them they didn't know their business. I was so embarrassed by her, but I couldn't say anything to her. I wouldn't risk the horrible things she could say in response."

"Doctor," Amy asked at the outset of her next visit, "did I make it clear last time, when I told you about my mother, that I really believed she was sick when I was much younger? Every night I used to ask God please to make her live and be well. You know, when I first learned about my being sick, I even had the crazy thought that I'd used up all my credit with God, praying for my mother. It used to trouble me that my father didn't seem to be concerned enough about Mom. I couldn't understand that. Much as I wanted his love and approval, it disturbed me that he seemed so unsympathetic to her.

"I couldn't fathom why he would get annoyed when we kids tried to help Mom. After our housekeeper moved to Florida to live with her sister, Irene helped out in the kitchen and did most of the shopping. I used to dust and clean. Dad grumbled about it, but he didn't interfere. Irene would say things about them, but I wouldn't listen. I thought she was just being spiteful. Irene was grumpy anyway. She was always giving me orders, and I resented it. I'd complain to Mom, who was always afraid to start up with Irene, so nothing happened. I think my mother preferred that Irene and I not get along so we wouldn't side with each other against her."

Amy went on to discuss Irene's marriage. She observed that Irene had chosen for a husband a rather passive and accommodating man. "Joel doesn't seem to mind if she rules the roost; he's a very sweet, considerate man. He would love to have had a larger family, but after the twins, Irene said that was enough and made him have that operation. A vase—" Amy looked to me for the correct term.

"Vasectomy," I supplied.

"That's it. I heard Irene tell Mom about it. My mother liked to hear all the gory, medical details in those days. It made me sick, literally." At that moment Amy's voice weakened. She looked pale and swallowed repeatedly. She shook slightly and hunched her shoulders together. Her eyes widened, then narrowed.

"Are you all right?" I asked, concerned.

"I . . . feel sort of woozy," she gasped. "I hope I'm not going to be ill."

"Put your head down . . . that's it, on your knees. I'll get you some water." Quickly I rose and brought her a cup of cool water from the lavatory. Amy swallowed a sip. She began to choke and cough. Her breath came in staccato snorts and wheezes. Her neck reddened. She pushed the cup at me and opened the button of her collar. I put the cup on my desk and gently seized her shoulders from behind, pulling them up and backward. She panted for a moment, then began to breathe more easily. I released her and sat down again.

"I'm sorry," she finally managed to say. "I don't know why that happened. Suddenly I felt very light-headed and faint. I started to see black spots and thought I was going to pass out. Then the water seemed to go down the wrong way."

"Do you feel better now?"

"Yes, thank you, but I don't understand why that happened."

"It hasn't occurred before?"

"No," she answered. "Something really must have gotten to me. I don't understand," she repeated, slightly bewildered.

I suggested that she had experienced an anxiety reaction in response to some intolerable idea stirred by what she was saying.

"But," Amy protested, "I don't remember any such thought."

"The mind functions simultaneously at more than one level," I explained. "It is possible for a threat to be perceived and to initiate a reaction before awareness of the danger is conscious."

"Wouldn't I know what bothered me now if that were the case?" she argued.

I sensed that she was stalling, asking questions to give herself time to regain control. "No, Amy," I answered, "not necessarily. Your reaction not only serves as an alarm to alert you, but also functions as a decoy, diverting you so the disturbing thoughts can be obscured. You were talking about your sister's domination of Joel, your brother-in-law, about your feelings with regard to—"

"His vasectomy. Did I say it correctly?"

I nodded and observed her carefully. She has courage plunging back into it, I thought. "Yes, Amy, what about his vasectomy?"

"Nothing, it's none of my business really. It's just that"—her voice faltered—"Irene doesn't let him function as a—"

"As what, Amy?"

"She won't let him be a—" Again she was unable to say the next word. Her voice was hoarse and strained. She broke off and stared at me amazed and uncomprehending.

I waited, silent.

Amy took a deep breath, her young face fierce with determination. "She . . . doesn't . . . let . . . him . . . " Every word she rasped took great effort. Her breath came in short, anxious gasps. Finally, she gave up and shook her head, defeated. Wearily she sprawled back in her chair and began to cry soft, mewing, almost timid sobs.

We sat there quietly for some time. I watched the tears trickle down from her closed lids. Occasionally she would wipe them and open her eyes to look over at me, and I would nod reassuringly. Something important was pushing up from the depths of her unconscious, something terrifying to her perhaps, and I could not aid her. For if I tried, the balance could have tipped in favor of her defenses and the menacing thought would descend once more to a point beyond our reach. I chose instead to say nothing. Our time ran out.

Finally, Amy rose to leave. She rose slowly, heavily, and walked to the door. "I'm beat," she murmured.

"You'll work it out," I assured her, smiling confidently.

I scribbled a note about the session, reminding myself that Amy had stumbled in describing her sister's relationship to her husband. The key to her upset was something to do with his vasectomy. If she did not get back to it spontaneously, I would bring it up again. We were moving along, but somehow there was little satisfaction in our progress.

I left my desk and walked over to the window. In the early twilight, bright Christmas lights gleamed from the lampposts they adorned. I watched pedestrians carrying packages bend against the wind as they hurried along Main Street. But Amy, choking, each breath an anguished gasp, kept returning to my mind. A sombrous weight lay upon my chest, and I felt chilled. I returned to my desk to write a summary of Amy's history and to organize my thoughts.

Although aspects of every case tend to suggest certain well-established formulations, I try to avoid strict axiomatic prescriptions and rely, instead, on more general schemata. One of these involves four fundamental issues that help shape the development and quality of the personality. By relating what I learn about a patient's life and my own direct observations to this schema, I can conceptualize the patient's problem in a therapeutically useful way.

The first of the four issues is the wish to be loved. The success of loving, caring parents in stimulating a baby and gratifying it will have a profound effect on personality development. The intrusion of a parent into the little universe of the infant's awareness diverts it from its visceral concerns and fascination with its inanimate environment. The baby accepts stroking and gratifying human contact. It does so even when it is hungry or uncomfortable and, in this way, acquires an ability to postpone satisfaction and tolerate discomfort. The infant learns to want the love and affectionate attention the parents provide and actively seeks a relationship with them.

The quality and intensity of this experience have enduring effects. If the baby is understimulated, neglected, or, because of illness, unable to find sufficient gratification in parental contact, there will be untoward effects. Such experiences will tend to produce individuals who relate ineffectively and have little tolerance or perseverance. The infant who is greatly overstimulated, on the other hand, will also relate poorly. Such a baby, constantly toyed with, will become so addicted to this excessive attention that it is diverted from adequate self-cognitive experience. The result may be an individual relatively unable to find gratification except from the interest of others.

The second basic issue concerns the fear of losing love once it has been acquired. The forming personality, having learned to associate gratification with the parental objects, seeks to secure its relationship to them. The outcome of these efforts imparts further characteristics to the individual. The relationship between demanding child and overly compliant parent may produce arrogance and future frustrations for the child when others do not conform and obey commands as his parents did. At the opposite extreme, the needful child, unable to feel sufficiently confident of continued parental affection and interest, will be inhibited and unadventuresome. He may be fated to become a fawning pleaser or a compulsive, destined to go through life working to prove he is worthy of love.

Fear of bodily harm is the third fundamental concern. Unhappily, every growing child discovers sooner or later that he is subject to harm and injury. How he or she integrates and assimilates this knowledge is significant. Will the child view himself as fit and capable or as fragile and puny? How will he view his body and its natural functions—as complete and normal, with pride and acceptance, or as defective and malformed, a cause for disappointment, a source of disgust? One's physical being and habitus can provide satisfaction and promote confidence, or they can be a burdensome prison.

Finally, there is the issue of conscience. How matters of right, wrong, approval, and discipline are presented and structured and how parental models function contribute to the development of one's personal morality and ethical self-concept. A conscience can be rigid and punitive or resilient and adaptable. It can be a positive force providing internal incentives and satisfactions or a relentless critic that is never appeased. The conscience can prod one to act or can paralyze one's initiative.

I ruminated about Amy and looked through my notes. I thought about the ambivalent feelings of relief and anger her mother's hypochondriasis elicited. Her fear that she had used up God's favors and her persistent guilt at having cheated and provoked His wrath came to mind. I pondered what impact her father's wish for a son had on her self-image and what effect the quality of relationships between the members of her family had on her own impaired capacity to relate to men. Does she unknowingly discourage suitors and misperceive the result as evidence she is unlovable?

"I don't know whether dreams interest you, Doctor," Amy began when she had settled in the chair near me, "but I'd like to tell you about this one I had after our last session."

"Please do," I encouraged her.

"Well, maybe first I ought to explain that when I was a

child, I had a collection of puppets, the kind you slip over your hand and work with your fingers." Amy demonstrated. "I used to play with them for hours on end whenever it rained or I was sick and couldn't go out. Each of my puppets had its own special personality, but my very favorite was Pinocchio because he was always getting into mischief and having adventures.

"In my dream, I was alone in my house; only it was strange and I was scared. I'm not sure why. I remember looking in all the rooms downstairs and finding no one there. Finally, I climbed the steps and went into my room. There, on the dresser, were all my puppets as if I were little again and about to play. There was Pluto, the dog, Bozo, the clown, Raggedy Ann, and the rest. I picked up each one and tried it on, but Pinocchio was missing. I remember thinking in fun that it was just like him to be off somewhere when I wanted him." She grinned.

Amy paused and drew a deep breath. "Then, suddenly," she continued, "I realized that someone else was in the room with me, lying in my bed." Her voice tensed. "I went over to yank the covers off him, thinking it was my brother. I . . . I'm not sure who it was. It was a man, or a boy anyway, except that he was horrible!" she gasped. "In the center of his face where his nose should have been was an ugly gaping hole." Amy shuddered. "I dropped the covers and jumped back, shrieking and screaming in my sleep. I was absolutely terrified and woke up shaking." Amy caught her breath.

"You had quite a nightmare," I observed, giving her a moment to recover. "You say the figure in the bed might have been Paul, your brother?" I prompted.

"I don't know," she repeated in a small, hesitant voice. "The hair and clothes were peculiar; it was more like a life-size real Pinocchio. It was confusing." Amy shook her head uncertainly. Mindful of her anxiety attack in our last session and suspicious that the cause of her unease would soon surface again, I gingerly began to explore Amy's associations to the nightmare.

Dreams have long been held to be highly significant and revealing. In recent years there has been considerable scientific research into their physiological basis and controversy over what function they serve. We have more reliable data on the effects of dream disruption and deprivation than on their meaning. Psychiatrists differ on their clinical significance and interpretation. I prefer to regard dreams as complex codes, each containing more than one message. While reminding myself of the dangers of reading too much meaning into them, I feel I do gain further insight into the patient's psyche when I think I am able to decipher all or parts of his dreams. To accomplish this and to promote the active participation of the patient in his treatment, I enlist his help in the decoding process.

I elicited information from Amy that in her play fantasies as a child, Pinocchio seemed clearly to have represented herself, not as the obedient conforming youngster she was, but as she wished she were. In this role, Amy could escape from her overbearing sister and the routine life at home into one exciting adventure after another. I asked her about Pinocchio's hopes and ambition to become a real boy. Did his wish represent her yearning?

"No," she said. "No, I don't think so. The fact that in the original story Pinocchio wanted to become a real boy didn't matter much to me. As far as I know, I was perfectly happy to be a girl. Remember, as a girl who was athletic I was already kind of special. I could do most things any boy could. I wasn't jealous of them. I think it was more that Pinocchio played hooky and got into such exciting situations that interested me."

"You mean, he was always putting his nose into things he shouldn't have?"

"I guess so," Amy replied, looking into my eyes for some message. "You're trying to tell me something."

"I'm just wondering how the Pinocchio in your nightmare might have come to lose his nose."

"Oh, it was grotesque!" She shuddered. "But I don't know. . . . What does that mean?"

"I'm not certain . . ." I said, retreating. For a long time neither one of us spoke. The atmosphere in the room changed; it now seemed tense. Finally Amy broke the silence.

"I guess I'm supposed to figure things out," she said, clenching her hands anxiously, her jaw set and determined. "I've had enough psychology in college to know that a nose is supposed to be a phallic symbol, but . . ." Amy paled. Her face took on the same sickly greenish look I had seen in the previous session. She moistened her lips. "Why am I reacting like this? I feel queasy and light-headed again, the way I did the other day."

I realized the futility of beating around the bush to protect her. "You were talking about your brother-in-law's vasectomy at that time," I reminded her, determined to confront the issue.

"I thought it was terribly unfair to make him—" Amy sat up, erect and rigid. Her face registered amazement. She tried again. "It was horrible to force Joel to submit to that operation. . . ." Amy struggled to get the words out. "To let them cut—" She gasped. Amy stood up and paced behind her chair. Words now tumbled out rapidly in profusion and relief. She described Irene proudly, almost boastfully telling her mother how she had coerced her reluctant husband into allowing himself to be sterilized. "I couldn't stand to listen to her. But the worst thing was that my mother agreed with what she had done. Mom saw nothing wrong with forcing Joel to do it. She even joked about it," Amy said, sitting down once more, incredulous and appalled.

I waited, weighing how to bring matters to a head. Then I spoke. "In your dream, Amy, it seems that your brother, or Pinocchio, or whoever the figure in your bed represented had also been cut, in fact, mutilated. His nose was missing."

At first, Amy just stared at me, waiting for me to continue. She did not appear to understand the significance of the association between her remarks, her anxiety reaction, and the dream. She appeared surprised that I saw some connection. Then the implications began to sink in. She didn't speak, but I thought her lips formed the word "penis." Amy colored furiously. "Oh, my God," she murmured. "Oh, my God," she repeated softly and began to cry.

"I haven't thought about this in years. It used to bother me a lot, but I hoped I'd gotten over it." There was pain in her voice, as well as an edge of bitterness. "Doctor, I left out something when I told you my history, something important that didn't occur to me at the time."

"Go on," I urged.

"You probably noticed that there is a long gap in age between my brother and me, twelve years. I don't think my mother ever wanted a third child. She's hinted as much. But my father insisted. He apparently wanted a son, and he had his way; he got one."

Amy's voice grew sharper. "I told you, my parents have a mixed marriage. As a result, religion wasn't something we discussed in our home. My sister and I went to the Methodist Sunday school when we were little; we got presents at Christmas, and that was that as far as religion went. Mom might have wanted to attend church with us, but she never pushed Dad to drive us. We just slept late on Sundays.

"When Paul was born, however, things changed. My father decided that if my sister and I were Gentiles, his only son would be Jewish like him and would have a ritual circumcision. Maybe he had to prove something to his side of the family or maybe to Mom's. All I know is that my mother didn't object so long as Dad arranged matters and took care of everything. He did and made a big fuss. They set up a special room at the hospital, and we had to take Paul back there for the occasion.

"Three carloads of relatives, most of whom I'd never met before, came up from the city for the ceremony. It was unbelievable! They even brought an old man with an enormous beard to perform the actual circumcision. I thought it was scary and horrible."

"Did you understand exactly what was to be done?" I asked.

"My father tried to explain it to me, but he was embarrassed and not too clear about it. My sister, of course, acted as if she knew all about it and teased me when she saw I was upset and confused. She told me—" Amy realized what she was about to say and stopped abruptly.

"She told you they would cut his penis off."

Amy clenched her teeth and nodded briskly. "Irene said they cut it off," she repeated. The words came out with such bitterness that I knew Amy had believed them. "I was so shocked and horrified that they could do such a thing to a baby"—she grimaced—"and make a celebration out of it, too." She shook her head slowly as if still uncomprehending. "I became very frightened. My mother tried to reassure me, but I don't think I really believed her. I was quite shaken. When the time actually came for it to be done, I remember everyone in the room seemed to be pushing and crowding around to watch. I felt as if I were suffocating. I must have been in a panic. I couldn't seem to catch my breath. Of course, I never saw the circumcision. I couldn't look. But I have a memory of Paul suddenly screaming and all the grownups bursting into laughter. They even told jokes and had whiskey and cake. It seemed so bizarre. I think I was sick; someone took me home."

Amy slumped back in her chair, drained. I noted that our time was spent. After a moment I indicated we would stop, and she rose heavily and followed me to the door. I said good-bye, and Amy nodded and managed a weak smile. Wearily I returned to my desk to write up our session.

Psychiatrists are peculiar when it comes to their own emotions during psychotherapy. Their eccentricity is the butt of much humorous ridicule. They are the hapless victims of an occupational irony: Much as they promote the value to the people of expressing their emotions and encourage their patients to vent their feelings in therapy, they strive to keep their own feelings and emotions under firm control lest they intrude and contaminate the treatment process. The result is that they often succeed too well and appear unfeeling and wooden.

The psychiatrist's feelings, however, do enter into therapy, enhancing his understanding of the patient. The therapist's reactions and attitudes toward the patient constitute what is called the countertransference, and he regards it warily. It is not entirely conscious by any means, so the therapist is burdened continually to observe and analyze himself in order to recognize and to neutralize the countertransference. Thus, caricatures of the stiff, preoccupied, and emotionally fettered analyst and the freely emoting patient on the couch abound.

There are, however, many less orthodox therapies in which the therapist freely expresses his feelings and attitudes. Leaders of encounter and consciousness-raising groups, as well as other practitioners, actively take part in exercises with their clients, which are designed to mobilize feelings considered stuck or frozen. The client, eager to be liberated emotionally or unaware that he harbors certain feelings, is exhorted to overcome his inhibitions and to emulate the therapist, who may demonstrate his own emotional freedom by expressing himself openly. "You make me feel very sad when you look that way," or, "I feel tense because of the way you are sitting there," may be said by the leader. As the client is drawn out to communicate his feelings, he and the therapist tend to form a *real* relationship and become friends. The unconscious needs of the client, as well as those of the therapist, may in this way be gratified. These strivings, however, usually remain uninterpreted.

By contrast, the psychiatrist, disciplined in the constraints of traditional, conservative psychotherapeutic procedure, wrestles continually with the countertransference and the question of how *real* he should permit the therapeutic relationship to be. The late Dr. Sidney Tarachow, a noted psychoanalyst, would create various scenarios to illustrate this problem for his residents. He would say something like this: "It is raining heavily outside. Your patient looks ill and is coughing and sneezing. He has noticed that you have two umbrellas in your stand. Would you offer him one of them?"

The answer, of course, depends on many variables. The therapist might gratify his own humane impulse and promote one kind of relationship with a suicidally depressed patient. He might stifle the same impulse with another patient who might view it as a manipulative or seductive gesture. The therapist who is not sufficiently circumspect about his own feelings will mismanage the therapeutic relationship and be unable to effect significant insights and growth in his patients.

Amy was not an ordinary patient. Because of her illness and prognosis, there was a large reservoir of compassion within me that had to be contained if she were to mature by achieving her goals herself.

Amy led off our next session with an insightful query. "Doctor, do I have some sort of castration complex?"

"I'm not exactly sure what you mean by those terms, Amy," I answered, pleased, nevertheless, by her grasp. She frowned, put off that I had not answered her directly.

"Well,"—she pouted— "I've decided that I do."

"You certainly seemed to think the circumcision was cruel and mutilating," I offered.

"Uh-huh," she said, unmollified. "I guess I did."

"What are you thinking now?" I finally asked.

"I am thinking that it really did affect me. I—"

"You what?"

"It's not important."

"Please say whatever is on your mind, Amy," I demanded.

Amy made a face. She seemed to be quickly thinking of something to answer, to substitute for her real thoughts. "I've had lots of bad dreams since then . . ." she began, then gave up the pretense. "I was scared afterward. I could never touch myself down there." Her voice was low, almost timid. "Not even," she continued, "when I washed. Once I remember developing a painful irritation there and being afraid to tell my mother about it. Finally, however, Mom must have suspected something, and she forced me to show her. She dragged me, I mean literally, over to Dr. Ratner's, though I begged her not to and cried. I was absolutely frightened to death. I fought and struggled with her not to undress and let him examine me. That poor doctor. What he put up with that morning. You don't have to contend with that kind of problem as a psychiatrist, do you?" she asked a little testily.

"On the contrary, Amy. I find people are quite modest about revealing themselves here. I sympathize with their difficulties and with yours," I said, looking into her eyes. "But tell me what happened."

"Oh," she said in a softer voice, "he promised not to touch me, and I finally gave in. It turned out to be a big fuss over almost nothing. I was given some salve which cleared the condition up, and that was that, except that dear, old Dr. Ratner and I became good pals. I never carried on about seeing him again. In fact, I looked forward to it. We had a really great friendship. I used to write to him from college. When he died, it was like losing a grandfather," she said sadly.

I felt a slight jolt at this reference to death. Amy's prognosis intruded once more into my thoughts. Automatically I glanced at my desk clock, which is turned so that I alone can see how late it is, relieving the patient of the pressure of time. Amy had stopped talking. A lull ensued. I decided to direct her back to her dream once more in order to explore further her male-female identification. "Amy, I've been wondering again about your nightmare in light of all you've been saying. I still find it interesting that as a little girl you identified so with Pinocchio, a male puppet who longed to be a real boy."

"But I told you," she protested, "the part about his wanting to be a boy never interested me. I am glad I'm a woman, and I don't feel inferior about it." She went on to repeat that it was only Pinocchio's adventurous life that had once appealed to her. We then had a lengthy discussion during which I pointed out that a parallelism seemed to exist between the circumstances of Amy's childhood and those of her puppet, Pinocchio. Even though the celebrated marionette was not a real boy, he had filled the void in the lonely life of the old man who created him just as, perhaps, Amy had in many ways relieved her father's longing for a son until the birth of her brother. She conceded the similarities.

We reviewed highlights of her childhood, bearing this in mind. Amy revealed that up until Paul's birth, which happened also to coincide with her puberty, she had taken no particular interest in her femaleness and found little in common with other girls her age. "Even afterward," she asserted, "I couldn't be catty like other girls I knew or be coy around the boys at school, if that's what you mean." The influence of her femininity on her self-esteem and the development of a social role seemed negligible. "Perhaps," she speculated at the end of the hour, "I never worked out how I felt about being a woman. Maybe I ended up in physical education because it seemed neutral to me and I was still interested in sports because they were important to Dad."

Early in the next session I made a mild quip about puppets who pull strings to manipulate their masters and brought Amy back to her nightmare. I recapitulated it to her again. She was impressed that I remembered it accurately. I asked her what her feelings had been as she had proceeded through the empty house. "I remember being afraid and lonely," she said, "as if I had been abandoned. But I didn't know why." Amy shivered and began to massage her forearms, briskly trying to warm herself. She grew tense and described her response in the dream as a terribly painful feeling that no one loved her anymore; she felt as if she had been rejected, cast off.

Amy spoke now in a small, strained voice. "It was like some kind of hell or confinement. I was being punished . . . I knew, in a way, that I deserved it somehow, but I didn't know why. It isn't too different from a feeling I often have, a vague sense that I'm wrong or a bad person. I can't explain it any better than that." Amy's voice had begun to tremble. I saw her lips were quivering. Suddenly her self-control was slipping. "Oh, God!" she cried, closing her eyes tightly. "I don't want to fall apart!" Desperately Amy blinked and fought back the tears. "Why? . . . Why do I feel so rotten? So guilty?" she begged. Then, wearily, her shoulders drooped, and she slumped far back in her chair and wept.

I waited. When Amy looked up again, her eyes were red and bleak. On her face was a plea for help. I spoke softly to her. "Perhaps, Amy, the clue is in your dream." Her eyes widened with interest. "Your terror reached its peak when you discovered the mutilated figure in your bed. That figure could have represented you since we know you identified with Pinocchio, or it could have been Paul, the real boy who had displaced you." I paused to be certain Amy understood. She nodded and edged forward again, curious. I went on. "We know from what you've said that with the fulfillment of your father's hopes for a son, and the excitement Paul's birth generated, you were replaced as his favorite. I suspect that you were very hurt and resentful to be neglected for your new rival."

Slowly, pensively, Amy nodded again. "Go on, please," she said tonelessly, her face looking determined.

"Is it possible, Amy, that the circumcision you found so barbaric and disturbing also gratified your own jealous and malevolent wishes for revenge? Have you felt guilty about that since then?"

Amy's eyes betrayed her comprehension. "Was your aversion to your own sexual parts a sign of your guilt, as well as a fear of retribution? I wonder if your difficulties in adjusting to a mature social-sexual role are not some late outcome of your fears and your guilt, perhaps a self-punishment because you feel unworthy of love."

Amy listened wide-eyed until I had finished. "I see," she finally breathed after a pause. She rose from her chair now and went over to the window, her back toward me. "It's snowing," she quietly announced, and began to cry again softly. Nothing more was said. In a few minutes I showed her out.

At the outset of our next session Amy announced that she would be away for two weeks over the approaching Christmas-New Year's period. This would be her first Christmas away from home. A group of friends from her college days had invited Amy to spend the vacation with them. Despite some misgivings about deserting her family, she had accepted. To Amy's surprise, Mr. and Mrs. Novec were not the least perturbed by the prospect of her absence. Her mother immediately called Irene to urge her older daughter to visit her in-laws on Christmas. "My mother was so pleased not to have to cook Christmas dinner for everyone that she couldn't even pretend to be let down. Dad seemed relieved that he could watch his football and other games without interference," Amy said tartly.

I commented on Amy's chagrin and her ambivalence to find that she could leave so easily. She said nothing. I pressed further, wondering aloud about the appropriateness of the concerns which bound her to living at home. Had she invented her fear that moving away would disrupt her parents' marriage? Was it a device to pretend they needed her more than they actually did? Amy scoffed. I went on. Could she have cultivated her mother's dependence for the same reason? I asked. Amy shrugged angrily and shifted in her chair. She looked away.

"My mother does as she pleases," she growled, still avoiding me. We sat awhile in silence. Finally, Amy sighed loudly. The anger seemed to drain out of her. The ideas I had suggested were beginning to sink in. She turned and looked at me, expecting the worst.

"It is possible that by staying at home with your parents, you are helping hold their marriage together, Amy, but it is a costly sacrifice, isn't it?"

"Yes," she conceded quietly.

"It is also just as likely, however, that by stabilizing their relationship as it is, if that's what you're doing, you are making it possible for them to coexist together with little incentive to resolve their marital problems."

The full implications of what I proposed slowly began to penetrate. Irene had told Amy something similar. We reexamined relationships in her household for the rest of the hour and also the next session. Gradually Amy began to see how she functioned at home in a new light. She admitted that unawares, she had manipulated her mother and had contrived obstacles which made leaving difficult. She disclosed that Irene had repeatedly urged her to go and had even observed to Amy that

Mr. and Mrs. Novec had managed and communicated better when Amy had been away at college.

I saw Amy twice more before we broke for Christmas. During these sessions we went back over the same themes, developing and refining them further. It went more easily. Amy probed her own past and present attitudes and behavior, testing the insights she had gained. She was troubled by doubts about the sincerity of her affection for her brother, but ultimately she satisfied herself that she was genuinely fond of Paul. She also reported that Irene and she had recently developed a closer rapport.

These positive developments were reassuring to Amy, but she remained self-reproachful and bitter about other matters. "I've been such a self-righteous sap!" she hissed scornfully. Considering all she had been through in therapy so far, I was surprised by her vehemence. "I've been so prissy and straight because of my own neurotic guilts . . . a goody-two-shoes!"

We were at the end of our final session before the holidays, and I wished I could send her off on a somewhat happier note. "I think you're being hard on yourself, Amy," I said, hoping to ease her. "You've shown a lot of pluck in facing some knotty problems. I—"

"I know, I know," she said impatiently, shrugging my compliment off. "Oh, don't think I'm not grateful to you for your help. I understand myself a lot better now." Her voice grew sharper. "But I am exactly what I said I was when we first started. Only now I know why. I'm still the all-American zero. I wish a little of Alice Curran had rubbed off on me. I'd have traded some insight for some experience," she said, coloring, a brittle grin on her lips.

"The real challenge, Amy, is to develop now into the kind of person you wish to become, not someone else," I said, hoping my words didn't sound preachy.

Amy tilted her chin up. "Don't worry, Doctor. I don't intend to waste my opportunities anymore." The intensity in her voice unsettled me. Amy noticed my unease and rose to offer me her hand. "Enjoy the holidays, Doctor. Don't be concerned about me. I've got a lot of catching up to do, and I intend to have a good time down in Washington."

I had an impulse to caution her but restrained it and wished her well.

I also took a brief vacation, and though I found Amy and other patients intruding on my thoughts from time to time, I devoted mysef largely to relaxing with my family. Psychiatry is a uniquely isolating and exacting profession because there is little of one's work that can be shared with others. Often I have felt drained and exhausted at the end of a day spent merely sitting behind my desk. It is at such times that I am concerned lest I deprive my own family of my interest and energies. I worry that when I am so spent, I may be dull company at home or, occasionally, guilty of an impatience that would never occur in my professional role. It cannot be easy to be married to a psychiatrist or to have one for a parent. The discordant lives of too many in my profession testify to that. For these reasons I try to take full advantage of holidays to join my wife and children in some recreational activity.

I noticed the change in Amy the moment she strode into my office. It wasn't the bizarre outfit she wore, a fitted, double-breasted coral coat over a white blouse and blue shorts—she had resumed working in the gymnasium, I surmised—nor was it the fact that her hair was different. It was something more subtle. She smiled in a friendly way and seemed pleased to see me, but she seemed more confident of herself, more poised and demure.

After a moment's pleasantries to reestablish rapport, Amy indicated that much had happened since our last meeting which she wished to discuss. "My Washington trip was a huge success." She beamed. "I had a really good time, and I learned a lot," she added with a coyness that was meant to communicate something more.

I stared at her thoughtfully for a moment. She sobered. "There's no point in my being cute about it, is there? I am sorry. I've had an affair." Amy colored. "I didn't mean that quite the way it came out," she tried to explain, flustered. "I am not sorry I have had an affair, I am glad about it."

Amy went on to describe a young attorney, an acquaintance of her friends, whom she had seen a great deal of during her vacation. "Ralph is a really neat fellow, Southern . . . but well educated and very bright," she hastened to add. "Oh, there I go again." She frowned. "Ralph told me I was a Yankee chauvinist, and I am, darn it! Anyway, we met the first night I was there at a small party in the apartment where I was supposed to stay." She grinned. "We liked each other immediately. Well, one thing led to another and we ended up spending almost the whole time together." A sheepish smile crossed Amy's face. "I sort of moved in with him the last week."

Amy looked over at me, searching my face for some sign of a reaction. I smiled warmly, deciding to give her the reassurance she sought, and said, "You seem to have enjoyed your time in Washington."

"Oh, yes." She sighed and closed her eyes to emphasize her satisfaction. "I learned so much about life, about men, and about myself. It was really good." She smiled. Amy went on to relate the events and experiences of her trip. I made no attempt to interrupt her. I did not question her behavior. I made myself listen, instead. She was filled with the joy of living and bursting to tell about it.

I realized that a turning point had been reached in Amy's therapy. Our relationship would shift, if I encouraged it, to another level. Amy was no longer telling me things she wanted to analyze and understand. She was sharing experiences she wanted me to know about and accept. She was seeking my support once more, as she had at the outset, but this time I decided not to withhold it.

"I've decided to take that apartment I mentioned to you weeks ago, Doctor," she announced near the end of the hour. "Ralph has promised to come up for some weekends, and I don't want to see him in some motel. I've already told my folks I'm moving, and Dad said he'd help me. I think they sense I intend to go anyway."

I commented that paying rent would strain her income and suggested that perhaps the time had come when we could reduce the frequency of her visits. Amy's eyes and the grin on her lips told me that she had intended to ask about that next. We agreed to meet thereafter at weekly intervals.

That afternoon Amy left my office euphoric. I felt gratified but hoped she would not become overconfident.

Amy moved into a small apartment with a separate entrance in a house near her school. Her affair with Ralph lasted about six weeks. Just before Valentine's Day she learned that he'd met someone else. I feared Amy might react badly to this turn, but to my surprise, she was hardly touched at all.

"Ralph is a marvelous fellow, Doctor," she explained. "I owe him a lot, but I knew, and so did he, that we weren't right for each other. There were too many differences, things that made us interesting to one another but couldn't really be shared. I wish him well, and if we ever see each other again, I'm sure we'll be friends."

Amy had acquired sophistication. In a brief period she'd transformed herself into a much more worldly and knowing woman. She was participating in the social milieu of the unmarried singles, meeting many new people. Her evenings were busy and full.

Two men, one a teacher from a nearby district, the other an accountant, were frequently mentioned in her sessions. She was seeing both of them frequently. Each had taken her away for a weekend, and each had stayed with her in her apartment on occasion. The weeks sped by.

"I've got to make up my mind," Amy finally complained early in April. "Howard and Jon know about each other. I couldn't keep telling one I was busy while I saw the other. They know me too well." She frowned. "I wish that they both weren't so bent on getting serious. It worries me that Jon introduces me to his married friends now, and Howard wants to take me to Pennsylvania to meet his folks."

"Why does that distress you?" I asked.

"I can see that each of them wants to have an exclusive relationship with me. But even though I've come a long way, I don't feel comfortable about living with someone, and I have no intention of getting married." Amy stared at me expectantly, waiting for me to comment.

I made myself ask, "Why do you feel that way?"

"Because of my illness," she answered bleakly. "It wouldn't be fair."

Amy hadn't mentioned her condition for months. She looked well and was working full time without difficulty. "Does either of them know you've been ill?" I asked quietly.

She shook her head. "No, I never told them. Maybe I should have and been honest from the start. But how do you tell someone that you've only recently met that you've got a possibly fatal disease without its changing things between you?" The words "possibly fatal" struck me, but I did not react. It represented a change in Amy's attitude, a shift to a more equivocal and hopeful outlook. "I hadn't dreamed of getting this deeply involved. Now I'm in a quandary." She didn't speak for a while but sat there thinking. "Well"—she sighed—"I've got to tell them, don't I? I'll do it this week."

At the door, as she was leaving, Amy paused and grinned. "Don't be surprised if I call you before our next appointment. I may be a basket case by then."

During the week Amy kept returning to my mind. Several times my phone buzzed, and I anticipated her voice, almost hoping it was she. Something significant was taking place that would shape the rest of her life, yet she didn't call. Amy didn't need me.

When she appeared for her next visit, I was eager to learn what had occurred. I had to wait, however, while Amy complained that she'd been feeling tense all week. She'd had headaches. Her appetite had vanished, and she was sleeping poorly. I was surprised when she disclosed that she had gone to see Dr. Barnett. He'd expressed some concern that she seemed strained and run-down. He'd taken some blood for tests and sent her for a precautionary X-ray.

"I told him it was my hectic love life." She grinned. "He seemed pleased by that and by all I told him. But he also took me to task for not getting enough rest. He wants me to get to bed early and take it easy until next week when I am off for spring recess."

"I see," I said, trying not to show my concern.

"Well, don't you want to hear my latest saga?" she said teasingly.

"Of course." I laughed.

"They both want to marry me!" Amy exclaimed. She moved forward and sat at the edge of her seat, flushed with excitement now. "I've had two proposals!" Her eyes teared, and she smiled broadly.

"Tell me about them."

"I will! It's perfectly unbelievable! These two dear, sweet men want me to marry them. I'm all confused. I thought I had everything in my life finally under control. Now this! You know I thought all along that by alternating between them—I realize how awful that must sound—I could keep things from getting too involved. I never considered marriage. I told myself that was definitely out. But now they tell me I'm being selfish, that I am arbitrarily deciding their futures, as well as my own, quite unfairly." Amy stopped abruptly. "Oh"—she blinked—"did I tell you the three of us got together to talk?"

I shook my head, smiling. "No."

"Oh, Jon suggested it. We met at Guido's for dinner and talked. Jon and Howard liked each other right away. It was uncanny, as if they were old shipmates or buddies. I was a little put off by the way they got on together. I wondered whether they regarded me as their team mascot or something after a while. I told them so." She laughed.

"What did you three decide?" I asked.

"Jon and I are going away together for the vacation."

"Is he the one you prefer then?"

"God!" Amy exclaimed with mock impatience. "Listen, any

girl would be lucky to have either one of these fellows. When I told them I was sick, separately, before we met, I could see they both were shocked. Howard said I was full of you-know-what. He couldn't believe it. But when he realized I meant it, he said it made absolutely no difference except that we wouldn't tell his folks. We would just elope."

"And how did Jon react?" I asked.

"Jon couldn't say a thing. He choked up and just held me and stroked my back."

"It's Jon you chose," I repeated.

"It wasn't easy. Yes, Jon's the one. I know it now. Maybe I did all along and was afraid to face it." Amy began to cry.

I got up to offer her a box of tissues. Amy rose to her feet and threw her arms around me. She wept on my shoulder. "I'm so lucky," she cried.

I held the shaking girl a moment. Then we sat again. Amy planned to be married in June at the end of the school year. We decided that this would be our final session, and she told me she was deeply grateful for my help. It was left that Amy would call and return for a consultation should some problem arise that she might wish to discuss.

"It will be strange not coming here every week," Amy remarked before leaving. "I won't forget the things I've learned." She quickly leaned forward and kissed my cheek, then turned and was gone.

No other patient followed Amy that afternoon, and I was glad to be able to sit awhile alone with my thoughts. After a time I picked up the telephone and called Ted Barnett to tell him I had discharged Amy.

"It's funny," he said. "I was waiting until ten of the hour to call you." I told him the purpose of my call.

Ted listened in silence as I gave him a brief synopsis of Amy's therapy and its outcome. When I had finished and he remained quiet, I crowed, "Barnett, are you still there?"

"Yes, I'm here," he rasped dryly. I knew something was very wrong from his tone.

"What is it, Ted?" I asked soberly.

"That poor kid" was all he muttered.

"Amy?"

"Her mediastinum and hilar areas are loaded with tumor again."

"Oh, no . . ." I moaned, a sudden sinking sensation in my gut.

The mediastinum is the space behind the breastbone running down the center of the chest between the lungs. Through it pass the forking windpipe, the esophagus, and a number of vital vessels and nerves. The hilar areas of the lungs adjacent to the mediastinum on either side receive the parting airways, or bronchi. In these areas the main bronchi divide and give rise, like the trunks of trees, to their principal branches. In malignancies of a lymphatic nature these are frequent sites of involvement.

"Are you going to give her more radiation?" I asked.

"I don't think we should. There is extensive scarring already, and this tumor was pretty refractory to X-ray the last time we used it."

"What about chemotherapy then, Ted?"

"Amy's had everything available already. I'm going in to the city to see George Kravitz on Thursday," he said. "He is chief of oncology at University and an expert on these unusual types. I consulted him about Amy once before, and he was helpful."

"Is he working on anything new?" I asked hopefully.

"I don't know, but he's the outstanding man in lymphatic malignancies. If anyone knows what's new and effective, he should. In fact, he is authorized by the National Institutes of Health to field-test new agents. He may be running trials on one or more drugs now."

"You don't sound too optimistic, Ted."

"I can't expect too much. Amy may not be a suitable candidate, or it may be too late to get into their study. It all depends on the criteria for admittance to the program. I've had other patients rejected in the past. I can't get my hopes too high," he explained.

I said nothing. I always find my head and my heart in confrontation when medical research requires this type of selection process. It troubles me now as it did when I was a callow adolescent sympathizing with the agonies of Martin Arrowsmith. "Did Kravitz give you any hint of interest in Amy's case when you called him for an appointment?" I asked desperately.

"Well, to my surprise, he really impressed me by remembering her from my presentation to him last September. He's a very bright and retentive fellow and, like so many other really top-notch people, very decent, too. He invited me down to review her course with him again, but I noticed he carefully avoided saying anything encouraging."

"I see. . . . I realize you haven't discussed her status with Amy yet. What are you planning to do about informing her?" I asked.

"That's why I was going to call you," he replied. "Amy always insisted she wanted to know everything. Except for hedging a bit here and there, I've been generally open and honest with her all along, as you know. I tend to tell my patients when they're sick and not likely to recover. I think they are entitled to know, and it does away with a lot of subterfuge and deception that can tie you up and backfire. It's better for the patient usually, and for me also. But do you think there is any reason to handle it differently with Amy at this point, now that you know her pretty well?"

"Ted, let me ask you first, did you tell Amy her illness was incurable or fatal or did you hedge on that?"

"No, I told her quite frankly that the disease she has is fatal. I promised her we would do everything possible to retard and control it, but I offered her no false hopes or illusions about it."

"I see. Then there has been a shift in her attitudes. She recently referred to her illness as 'possibly fatal.' Ted, Amy may not be in the same frame of mind to accept the truth now as she was when you originally discussed her prognosis with her."

"Go on," he urged.

"Well, I understand your attitude and approach to these problems, and in general, I agree with you. The confidence and trust of the patient that his doctor is competent, truly concerned, and doing all that is possible for him are the key to managing these dreadful situations. The truth can support that faith even as lies can undermine and destroy it. Complete honesty, however, is not the primary issue; it may even be untherapeutic and contraindicated at times. There's at least one authoritative study which seems to indicate that at least some patients who do not accept the idea that they are dying and deny it have outlived others with the same disease at similar stages who accepted their prognosis. We need to study this kind of finding more and be better able to discriminate and identify these individuals. All people, however, seem to vary during the course of their illness as to their capacity to cope successfully with the facts of their condition and status. I suspect that for each one of us there is a time that is optimal for us to face up to things, and it must differ to some extent according to our personalities and circumstances."

"We talked about hope and its importance to survival once before in connection with Amy," he reminded me.

"That's right. I recall our conversation," I said. "That's why I don't consider complete candor the critical issue. Our forebears were not scientists; they were healers who tended to the ill and the dying, even when they had no effective medicines to cure them. Our responsibility lies more in the realm of being sufficiently close to our patients to understand when and how much of the truth to tell them. We must know the patient well and grasp his capacity to cope successfully with it. Otherwise, we rely on formulas and sometimes act arbitrarily, either withholding information the patient desires and is ready to face or confronting him with more than he can handle. Perhaps we do this because we feel an inappropriate guilt that we cannot cure him."

"You're telling me that you don't think Amy can cope with the truth at this time?" he asked pointedly.

"Right. Before, when she was so dissatisfied with herself and her life, perhaps living didn't have great value to her. But I'm afraid that now, when she is suddenly finding life so exciting and rewarding, she is much more vulnerable. Can we wait until after you have seen Kravitz again and then decide what to tell her?"

"I'll call you Friday," he said.

For the next few days I heard nothing more about Amy. I busied myself almost gratefully with the problems of other patients. On Friday, just as I was breaking for lunch, however, Ted called, as he had promised.

"Jerry, on Kravitz's advice we're going to try a different combination of drugs this time. In fact, they've been selected by a computer. Unfortunately, none of them is new, but the dosages and schedule are. Amy is coming in this afternoon, and I've got to tell her something. She'll need to go into the hospital again. This is just too dangerous to do on an outpatient basis."

I wanted to ask what Amy's chances were, but something in Ted's voice told me not to ask. Instead, we discussed what to tell her. In view of her deteriorating status, I thought it likely, and so did Ted, that questioning would elicit from her some further physical complaints. It was planned that he would suggest further tests and treatment in light of these complaints and that he would not be more explicit about her condition unless she asked.

I had lunch at the hospital. I heard Ted paged on the public address system, which was unusual because all of us carried beepers. "Barnett's got an emergency," I was told. "I saw him running into the building five minutes ago." My phone was buzzing when I got back to my office. There was a message to call Ted. I reached him at the hospital.

"Jerry, right after we got off the phone earlier I was notified that Amy had collapsed at school and was on her way in by ambulance. She's here now in Room five-seventeen. I just left her. She has a high fever, and I don't like her condition. I thought you'd like to know."

"Thanks, Ted, I'll come over as soon as I'm free."

At three o'clock I took advantage of a canceled appointment to meet Ted at Amy's room.

"She's a very sick girl," he said gravely. "I'm sure she has a pulmonary empyema on the left side. It doesn't look too good."

Pulmonary empyema is a collection of pus in a lung which has been at least partially collapsed by accumulated fluid.

"Isn't that rather sudden?" I asked, perplexed.

"Amy's obviously been holding back and keeping quiet about her condition. She's probably had a pneumonia for days and been dosing herself with antibiotics she had from before, as well as aspirin. She admitted as much to me when I saw her in the emergency room and put her in. She's sleeping now." Ted left, and I opened her door and stepped quietly inside.

Amy looked pale, drawn, and painfully thin, lying there with an intravenous drip running into her outstretched arm. Her eyes were closed; the lids seemed unusually dark and dusky. She stirred uneasily. Her parched lips seemed pasted. She tried to moisten them. I took some gauze sponges, wet them, and gently dampened her mouth. Amy opened her eyes and blinked to bring me into focus.

"Hello, Amy."

"Hi, Doctor J." She smiled weakly.

"Are you comfortable?"

"Yes, I guess so. But my mind keeps drifting and fading. I guess my temperature must be pretty high."

"You do have a fever, Amy. But what have you been thinking about?"

Amy lifted her head and grinned. "I knew you'd ask me that!" She chuckled and lay down again, coughing and hiccuping.

I helped her up into a semisitting position and patted her back lightly until she subsided. Then I held a cup for her, and she sipped some water.

"I've been dreaming off and on," she whispered, "good dreams about my cozy little apartment. I've fixed it up so it's really darling. Jon loves it. I dreamed we were already married— but sometimes I get confused, and it's Ted. Please don't say anything. I know you wouldn't. I'm just a little mixed up . . . it must be the fever." She smiled and dozed off again.

Amy Novec died that evening. Ted Barnett called to tell me as I was changing into casual clothes for dinner. "Her family and her fiancé were there," he said, sounding weary and depressed.

"You did everything any physician could—and more, Ted. Amy felt very secure because of your efforts and your interest. You meant a great deal to her, and she was more grateful than you know. She told me." Ted thanked me.

I finished dressing and pulled on my worn, old cardigan. My wife would make a face seeing it on me again, and the children would tease me, but I felt cold and a little sick.

I drove to my office the next morning. Lacy fronds dangled from the budding branches of some of the trees that lined the road. I parked behind my building and walked slowly toward the door, thinking of Amy. Mayflies were swarming. I watched their lively movements. How mysterious the ways of nature are. The fragile mayfly waits until conditions are just right to mature. Then it eases forth from its pupal case, briefly flies and dances on the breeze, mating and dying all within a summer's day.

ABOUT THE AUTHOR

JEROME L. JACOBS is a graduate of Cornell University College of Medicine. He took his residency training in Psychiatry at the New York Hospital–Westchester Division and at Hillside Hospital. He is a Diplomate of the American Board of Psychiatry and Neurology (P) and is a Fellow of the American Psychiatric Association. Dr. Jacobs developed the in-patient psychiatric treatment service at Grasslands Hospital in Westchester County and was its first director. He was later Director of Psychiatry at Northern Westchester Hospital and has been in private practice for many years in Westchester County. Dr. Jacobs is married and has a daughter and a son.